WORK AND ITS INHIBITIONS

Psychoanalytic Essays

WORK AND ITS INHIBITIONS

Psychoanalytic Essays

Edited by

CHARLES W. SOCARIDES, M.D.

and

SELMA KRAMER, M.D.

INTERNATIONAL UNIVERSITIES PRESS, INC.

MADISON   CONNECTICUT

Library of Congress Cataloging-in-Publication Data

Work and its inhibitions : psychoanalytic essays / edited by Charles
W. Socarides and Selma Kramer.
    p.   cm.
Includes bibliographical references and index.
ISBN 0-8236-6866-5
    1. Work—Psychological aspects. 2. Psychoanalysis. 3. Pleasure
principle. I. Socarides, Charles W., 1922—   II. Kramer, Selma.
BF175.5.W67W67 1995
158.7—dc20
                                          96-9688
                                          CIP

Manufactured in the United States of America

For Jacqueline Nicole Socarides

CONTENTS

Contributors   ix
Acknowledgements   xi
Editors' Introduction and Overview   xiii

I. Theoretical Considerations

1 Child's Work: Developmental Aspects of the Capacity to
  Work and Enjoy It   3
  ERNA FURMAN

2 Psychoanalysis and Playful Work   19
  HAROLD P. BLUM, M.D.

3 The Self and the Principle of Work   35
  W. W. MEISSNER, S.J., M.D.

4 Infancy and the Essential Nature of Work   61
  ANNIE REINER, L.C.S.W., and BERNARD W. BAIL, M.D.

5 Freud: Man at Work   79
  PATRICK J. MAHONY, PH.D.

6 A Self Psychological Perspective of Work and Its
  Inhibitions   99
  ERNEST S. WOLF, M.D.

7 *A Room of One's Own* Revisited   115
  LUCY DANIELS INMAN, PH.D.

8 In Praise of Leisure   133
  JOHN E. GEDO, M.D.

9 Men at Work: Work, Ego and Identity in the Analysis of
  Adult Men   143
  HOWARD B. LEVINE, M.D.

10 Work and Its Inhibitions as Seen in Children and
  Adolescents   159
  SELMA KRAMER, M.D.

II. Clinical Considerations

11 On Writer's Block: For Whom Does One Write or Not
Write? 183
STANLEY L. OLINICK, M.D.

12 Creative Work, Work Inhibitions and Their Relation to
Internal Objects 191
MARIA V. BERGMANN

13 The Vicissitudes of Shame in Stage Fright 209
GLEN O. GABBARD, M.D.

14 Aggression, Body Image, and Work Inhibition 221
STAVROULA BERATIS, M.D.

15 Genital Self-examination: The Precursor of Examination
Anxiety in Women 229
ELEANOR GALENSON, M.D.

16 Ambition: Normal and Pathological Aspects 241
ADRIENNE APPLEGARTH, M.D.

17 On the Sense of Being "Incomplete": Fragments from the
Analysis of a Narcissistic Personality Disorder 253
CHARLES W. SOCARIDES, M.D.

Author Index 265
Subject Index 269

CONTRIBUTORS

ADRIENNE APPLEGARTH, M.D., Training and Supervising Analyst, San Francisco Psychoanalytic Institute; Clinical Professor of Psychiatry, University of California Medical School, San Francisco.

STAVROULA BERATIS, M.D., Clinical Professor of Psychiatry, Department of Psychiatry, University of Patras Medical School, Patras, Greece.

BERNARD BAIL, M.D., Training and Supervising Analyst, Los Angeles Psychoanalytic Institute; Assistant Clinical Professor, University of California, Los Angeles.

MARIA V. BERGMANN, Training and Supervising Analyst, New York Freudian Society.

HAROLD P. BLUM, M.D., Clinical Professor of Psychiatry, The College of Medicine, New York University. Psychoanalytic author and editor.

ERNA FURMAN, Cleveland Center for Research in Child Development, The Hanna Perkins Therapeutic Nursery School.

GLEN O. GABBARD, M.D., Bessie Callaway Distinguished Professor of Psychoanalysis and Education, Karl Menninger School of Psychiatry and Mental Sciences; Training and Supervising Analyst, Topeka Institute for Psychoanalysis; Clinical Professor of Psychiatry, University of Kansas School of Medicine.

ELEANOR GALENSON, M.D., Clinical Professor of Psychiatry, Mt. Sinai School of Medicine, New York; Faculty, Columbia Psychoanalytic Institute and New York Psychoanalytic Institute.

JOHN E. GEDO, M.D., Training and Supervising Analyst (retired), Chicago Institute for Psychoanalysis; author of numerous psychoanalytic publications.

LUCY DANIELS INMAN, PH.D., Clinical Psychologist in private practice; Founder and Executive Director, the Lucy Daniels Foundation dedicated to the study of psychoanalysis and creativity.

SELMA KRAMER, M.D., Professor of Clinical Child Psychiatry, Thomas Jefferson University Medical School; Training and Supervising Analyst, Philadelphia Psychoanalytic Institute.

HOWARD B. LEVINE, M.D., Faculty, Boston Psychoanalytic Institute, and Massachusetts Institute for Psychoanalysis.

PATRICK J. MAHONY, PH.D., Training and Supervising Analyst, Canadian Society for Psychoanalysis; Professor of English Literature, Université de Montréal.

W. W. MEISSNER, S.J., M.D., Training and Supervising Analyst, Boston Psychoanalytic Institute; University Professor of Psychoanalysis, Boston College.

STANLEY L. OLINICK, M.D., Clinical Professor of Psychiatry, Georgetown University School of Medicine; Training and Supervising Analyst, New York Freudian Society, Washington Chapter.

ANNIE REINER, L.C.S.W., Private practice, Beverly Hills, California; Lecturer and Psychotherapist.

CHARLES W. SOCARIDES, M.D., Clinical Professor of Psychiatry, Albert Einstein College of Medicine, Montefiore Medical Center, New York City; President, National Association for Research and Therapy of Homosexuality.

ERNEST S. WOLF, M.D., Faculty member and Training and Supervising Analyst, Chicago Institute for Psychoanalysis; Assistant Professor of Psychiatry, Northwestern University Medical School.

ACKNOWLEDGEMENTS

We owe a special debt of gratitude to Margaret Emery, editor-in-chief of International Universities Press, for her support and encouragement for the project *Work and its Inhibitions*, as well as to Irene Guttman for her keen editorial skills.

Our thanks and gratitude go to Claire Alford Socarides who first suggested the project and assisted in the compilation and editing of the work during the initial and middle phases of the project.

Charles W. Socarides, M.D.
Selma Kramer, M.D.

EDITORS' INTRODUCTION AND OVERVIEW

Work and its Inhibitions: Psychoanalytic Essays is an initial effort at penetrating the problems and manifestations of the inability of people to integrate libidinal and aggressive drives so that they can function successfully in the work area. In this book we examine profound work inhibitions that revolve around (1) problems of entitlement, (2) narcissistic conflicts, (3) the relationship to external objects, (4) fears of examinations, fears of performance, deeply held yet vulnerable self-doubt and anxieties. The inability to perform may be due to resisting the remembering of events and early traumas related to incest, false identifications, introjective and projective anxieties. In these pages we explore the dynamics, unconscious meanings, and content of profound inhibitions and disturbances in individuals whose personalities and psychic structure appear to be, on the whole, relatively free of overt psychosis. We provide definitive conceptualizations of many aspects of this subject which has received so little systematic study compared to sexual disorders, the narcissistic neuroses, psychoses, and neuroses.

The contributors to this volume touch on many aspects of our concern: work as a psychological phenomenon, the metapsychology of work, work as sublimation, work inhibition in both men and women and their differences, work and the pleasure principle, choice, decision-making within the structural metapsychological psychoanalytic theory, the relationship among joy, play, and work.

We do not pretend that the answers to all these problems will be offered within the pages of this book. At the present time there still remains no consistent and comprehensive theoretical formulation of how work comes about. We know that an integration of instinctual drives, superego, and autonomous ego functions can produce successful work performance, but the details remain a mystery. The mechanisms of aim inhibition and sublimation, neutralization, and identification are all important and have yet to be defined in the evolution of successful work adaptation. Such definitive studies remain for the future and are tantalizingly explored in the pages that follow. The reader is exposed to psychoanalytic theories of work derived from

A significant portion of the proceeds from the sale of this book is being donated to the Margaret Mahler Psychiatric Research Foundation, Philadelphia, PA.

classical, developmental, self psychology, and object-relations theories. We leave to others the psychoanalytic theory of learning itself as it pertains to work, action theory, and decision-making.

As noted by Lantos (1952), "The question about what 'work is' is not treated as a problem. We look upon work as an obvious necessity, the mastery of which is proof of good adaptation to reality, whereas neurotic disturbances indicate failure in this adaptation" (p. 439). Work itself has been accepted by analysts as an essential function which is restored when a neurosis is successfully treated, rather than being a subject for intensive psychoanalytic study itself. We have readily accepted the notion that when fear, rage, and guilt intrude, successful functioning, including successful work performance, is automatically derailed, and have not concerned ourselves with delving into the intricate psychodynamics that have brought this about. Furthermore, we remind our readers that the psychoanalytic literature on work is quite meager. As background for our studies we reach back to the work of Karl Menninger (1942), Ives Hendrick (1943), Barbara Lantos (1952), and, above all, Elliott Jaques (1960) to illuminate our research path. Following their exciting contributions there was a dearth of psychoanalytic contributions on this important subject, dating approximately from 1960 until 1965.

In 1965 Douglas Holmes published a paper entitled "A Contribution to a Psychoanalytic Theory of Work," followed by "The Psychoanalytic Work Ego," by Olinick et al. (1973). An interesting clinical paper on work compulsion was supplied by Paul Kramer (1977). In addition, Lawrence Kubie had by then produced his important monograph *Neurotic Distortion of the Creative Process* (1958). Adrienne Applegarth (1976) wrote on work inhibitions in women. Of major importance were contributions on the problem of work inhibitions made by Leo Rangell (1969, 1971, 1986). His 1986 paper, "The Executive Functions of the Ego: An Extension of the Concept of Ego-Autonomy," was the Heinz Hartmann Award Lecture of the New York Psychoanalytic Institute for 1985. It has become increasingly clear that Rangell's comments on the process of decision-making are central to the whole area of disturbances in work.

The book is divided into two main sections. The first pertains to theory and consists of essays on the work principle, ambition and its relation to work, the analytic work, self psychology, leisure, child development and its pertinence to work, the development of the capacity for work, creative work and inhibitions and their relation to internal objects, and, of course, Freud: the man and his work.

Selma Kramer, in "Work and Its Inhibitions as Seen in Children and Adolescents," reminds us that the "work" of children is to *learn*. Conflicts about "knowing," especially family secrets, give rise to intrapsychic conflicts within the child. Severe problems in learning occur from childhood sexual abuse, especially from maternal and paternal incest. "Somatic memories" of incest may not only produce bodily hypersensitivities and depression, but result in difficulties in retaining what was learned and in "showing what one knows." Unique clinical examples document these findings.

Howard Levine, in "Men at Work: Work, Ego, and Identity in the Analysis of Adult Males," opines that the relative lack of analytic descriptions of work symptoms may well lie in the fact that work-related issues have often been considered as defenses or screens against the underlying "core conflictual issues." Building his theory upon the theoretical contributions of Erikson (1959) who described work as offering the "ego a vital setting for the exercise of its activity in regard to the definition of a sense of self and the regulation of self-esteem" (ego identity), he postulates the concept of "work identity." Several clinical illustrations exemplify the continuity of unconscious factors leading to a disturbance in such "work identity."

Clinical papers encompass the psychopathology of work, with essays on stage fright, writers' block, castration anxiety, narcissistic disturbances, and a compelling and absorbing autobiographical study of work inhibition in a psychoanalyst author.

In "Child's Work: Developmental Aspects of the Capacity to Work and Enjoy It," Erna Furman highlights the basic characteristics of work and the capacity to work and enjoy it. This study is derived from the Cleveland Center for Research in Child Development of the Hanna Perkins School in Cleveland, Ohio. It describes many years of careful study of children, the young child's personality, and his interaction with parents and teachers which contribute to his capacity to work. It provides insights into the ways in which parents are "unhelpful" in promoting the ability to work. The author states, "work, like play, has its roots in the good enough earliest mother-infant unit at the point when the child begins to differentiate himself from it. Whereas play initially fills and bridges the gap of separateness and creates imaginary interactions, the beginnings of work are linked in identification with mother, becoming like her by doing what she does, i.e., taking care of his bodily needs, 'all by myself.' Being able to play improves the quality of our lives, getting satisfaction from work makes us feel that we are quality people. Those of us who, as adults, enjoy working, appreciate that it does more for us than earn a living, though this alone is no minor accomplishment." In this study lasting years, the earliest developments contributing to the capacity and pleasure of working are described—"the role of bodily self-care, the role of the drives, and the role of relationships and identifications, starting with the earliest developments."

In "Psychoanalysis and Playful Work" Harold P. Blum provides a brilliant exposition of the psychoanalytic process as both work and play or, as he puts it, "playful work." He reviews some of the many additions to the analytic literature pertaining to work such as holiday neurosis, the working alliance, the therapeutic alliance, the analytic pact, and Freud's (1930) comment that "no other technique for the conduct of life attaches the individual so firmly to reality as laying emphasis on work" (p. 80). He touches on Holmes's (1965) theoretical construct of the function of work as adaptive or reality-oriented behavior, and work as a form of drive discharge or gratification and comments on the multiple functions and meaning related to the individual's entire developmental history as regards work: "Patients who have not been able to play, to tolerate fantasy, to enjoy wit and humor, may acquire or regain such pleasurable sublimations after successful analysis." He reminds us of Freud's (1920) early theoretical formulation regarding the play of a child who is attempting to master separation anxiety and object loss. He asserts that there may be a playful character to the psychoanalytic work, but neither the analyst nor the patient actually role-plays, nor does the analyst attempt artificially to direct or construct the patient's fantasy life. "Analytic work is not free play and the patient can not be analyzed by the analyst's self-analysis and narcissistic self-regard of the patient's unique individuality. . . . Analytic work, however playful, departs from serious play to scientific reflection. Analysis is therefore serious play and playful work; it is serious work and highly organized play. . . . Analytic work is then organically related as exploration and play in the service of mastery." Blum furthermore supplies an analysis of a college student's inability to do work brought to a successful conclusion through psychoanalytic work and play.

W. W. Meissner asserts in "The Self and the Principle of Work" that the usual claim in psychoanalytic parlance for the role of work focuses on the maintenance of self-esteem. This is partial and fragmentary and is, unfortunately, couched only in narcissistic terms. It leaves aside the place of work and the organization and functioning "of the person's self as defined in structural and supraordinate terms" (Meissner, 1986). The meaning of the work principle in human affairs must be more broadly and meaningfully conceived than simply as a function of narcissistic dynamics. Meissner addresses the problem in terms of the concept of the self as a supraordinate, structural, and hierarchically organized system. He defines the work principle as the psychological component in terms of effort directed toward the achievement of a goal that serves some purpose or has a measure of utility within some frame of personally meaningful reference. He proposes that " . . . the work principle is neither an instinctual drive nor a form of ego energy, but a more complex expression of matters pertaining to efficacy and agency in the psychic economy. . . . The capacity for work and related motivation for goal direction and achievements are basic to the work principle." Meissner examines "the meaning of work," and "work and the false self." He notes that individuals with a "false self" (Winnicott, 1960) are convinced that they can never make things happen. He illustrates his hypothesis by the examination of two individuals, one, a patient who had a false-self organization and could only emerge as a functioning individual through the "emergence of his more authentic and true self." The other is a study of the life of Vincent Van Gogh, whose artistic work led to a sense of self-esteem and a justification for his existence despite his ultimate breakdown. Only when Van Gogh broke through "the ring of parental demand—a task he must have accomplished during the period of isolation and depressive retreat . . . and embraced the artistic vocation, did he find the medium of self-expression and self-discovery that made his work commitment meaningful and fulfilling."

Reiner and Bail, in "Infancy and the Essential Nature of Work," address the earliest precursors of the capacity to work. They believe that the capacity to do any work is, first of all, dependent on the development of a "true self." The authors note that every healthy infant has a *potential* for an integrated self, a potential that must be realized through interaction with the parents. Strongly influenced by Bion, they assert that an integrated conscious/unconscious can only be realized by the infant with the parents' help, for the infant exists solely within the unconscious at the beginning. We must therefore provide the function of consciousness to the infant's unconscious state, thereby giving him an experience of mental unity. This mental unity *is the self* which is an extension of the mother's and a shared energy. The capacity for any kind of work is based on the true mind or self, for one " . . . cannot work if one does not mentally exist and therefore does not advance the 'individual's' mental growth." In several clinical examples, the authors clearly show that the unconscious parental projections may cause a lack of mental integration in the child. In earliest infancy the child becomes a "ready receptacle" for all of the mother's repressed unconscious thoughts and feelings, e.g., unconscious feelings of envy, jealousy, etc. In the authors' view, "all mental illness is an outgrowth of these conditions, as the infant is filled with mental debris that divert him from his true work—the natural development of his own mind." In this important paper, work inhibitions can be seen to begin in the earliest weeks or months of life.

Patrick J. Mahony begins his essay "Freud: Man at Work" by stating, "Given the immensity of my task and the limitation of my essay . . . I shall touch on Freud's 'theory of work' but focus on the 'practical place of work' in Freud's life." At the outset he makes the point that play was part of Freud's work and could not be separated from it. He lived in creative enjoyment, but for optimum achievement, Freud needed "disgruntlement, whether it be from physical fatigue or psychic misery." Mahony's immersion in Freud as a writer clarified two misconceptions about Freud's creativity. The first was a popular belief or assumption that intellectual geniuses are blessed with continuous inspiration and create works that spring ready-made from the brain. The second was the idea that Freud engaged in dualistic thinking rather than pluralistic reflections. In fact, Freud's initial analytic moves are dualistic, and then he typically proceeds to undercut them. It is of interest to note that Freud's means of attempting to control anxiety when writing on an idea was to think of something as an "electrical grounder which would distract him from the task at hand." In presentations before an audience, Freud controlled anxiety by forming a reassuring closeness with one or two other individuals in the audience. Mahony describes Freud's courage and a kind of talent, "a dauntless love of truth, . . . a rightful sense of the values of life, and the gift of working hard and finding pleasure in doing so." We are exposed to the idea that Freud's work capacity sprang from his "character" and, according to Freud, "from the absence of outstanding intellectual weaknesses." We are made aware of Freud's working thesis: "Sincerity is the source of all genius, and man would be more intelligent were he only better." These and many other fascinating insights into Freud the man and Freud the man-at-work are offered in this engaging paper. It is startling to note that if all of Freud's letters, papers, manuscripts—all handwritten—were put end to end, they would consist of 150 volumes.

Ernest S. Wolf, in "A Self Psychologist Looks at Work and Its Inhibitions," brilliantly and succinctly develops self psychology concepts in their relation to work and its inhibitions. He carefully reviews Freud's views on work, as they developed over the years and summarizes seminal papers by other analysts, as well as philosophers over the centuries. He arrives at the conclusion that a "serious interference with the capacity to work may well be the result of a disturbance in self function that may be related to the structure of the self. These disturbances are (1) fragmentation of the self, (2) an imbalance among the constituents (e.g., a hypertrophic overidealization of work), and (3) a lack of energic vigor due to a weakened tension arc due to insufficient idealization of the polar values and ideals of the self. He illustrates with several clinical vignettes.

In "A Room of One's Own Revisited" by Lucy Daniels Inman, we are presented with an enormously rich and inspiring account of the author's psychoanalysis, her severe struggle with work inhibition, and an account of the creative activities that have brought such pleasure to the nation's readers. The essay is both personal and clinical, as well as highly informative, by a woman who experienced it all—feelings of success as well as despair and failure, writing inhibition and freedom—attained both in writing and in her life. She states that psychoanalysis allows the patient to work at the inhibited endeavors, while providing substantive relief, for his or her innermost problems. She warns that there must be a capacity to tolerate symbolic expression of one's own material to be successful as a writer, and proceeds to give a condensed history of her own writing activities and the problems that beset it. The material is rich in dreams, and the analysis of conflicts and their resolution. She concludes that the writer must be able to put the "innermost self out before the world" and not be "compromised by despised characteristics clung to unconsciously."

John E. Gedo, in "In Praise of Leisure," suggests that "psychoanalysts should not speak *ex cathedra* about work constituting a requirement of mental health." In a lively and provocative essay, he explains his feeling that the motto that "mental health involves a capacity to love and work" should read that mental health involves a *freedom from any incapacity* in these spheres. "The name of the game is to pick a challenge that one has a reasonable chance to overcome." He posits that an excellent adaptation to life "does not require any record of work accomplishment." In lively and witty style, he presents two case histories of patients who did not have to work for financial reasons but who ultimately found salvation when the principal motivations for their activities were the private satisfactions to be derived from them. Reading and rereading this essay provides us with Gedo's vision and wisdom.

Section two of this book is generously sprinkled with gems of clinical and theoretical value. In an elegant piece of writing entitled "Writer's Block: For Whom Does One Write or Not Write?" Stanley L. Olinick probes the origins of writer's block, examining the successes and failures of professional writers and sculptors such as Henry Roth, Jacob Epstein, and Lionel Trilling, among others. He strikes to the heart of the matter when he states that stories are devised for and told to an "imagined and projected transference imago." "Fantasy figures" must be kept quite satisfied "with the quality and nature of one's output." The writer's transference imago is a "ubiquitous phenomenon." With exquisite sensitivity, Olinick succinctly describes the causes leading to Roth's severe writer's block after the publication of his brilliant novel *Call It Sleep*. Olinick calls his essay "a meditative one," but it is one with obvious clinical value.

Maria V. Bergmann, in "Creative Work, Work Inhibitions, and Their Relation to Internal Objects," presents, in three highly dramatic and illustrative case histories of creative women, how (1) a therapeutic alliance plays a crucial role in helping the patient to form a communication with the creative aspects of the self, thus liberating the forces of creative self-expression; (2) work inhibitions protect against destructive impulses toward internalized objects; and (3) intrapsychic conflict may become fixed in an interaction between ego and superego with resultant permanent inhibition. She tellingly demonstrates that creative work represents an unconscious communication addressed to an internal object which must be brought into consciousness, assimilated, and brought to free expression.

In "The Vicissitudes of Shame in Stage Fright" by Glen O. Gabbard, stage fright is examined as a form of work inhibition. It is a highly overdetermined symptom that relates to a variety of intrapsychic conflicts that stem from various developmental levels. He notes several prominent themes in the stage-fright experiences of performers he has treated: (1) shame related to the experience of genital inadequacy or loss of bowel or bladder control, (2) impulses that produce feelings of guilt in the unconscious in triumphing over oedipal and sibling rivals, (3) the phenomenon of separation anxiety, (4) narcissistic issues, (5) the affect of greed inherent in attempted successful performances, (6) fears of envy that will be stirred up in the audience, and (7) general fears of failure as well as of success. Inherent in all these phenomena, he states, is the common thread of shame.

Essentially, failure is the origin of a negative self-evaluation by the infant. Shame is what happens when an affirmation by the parent is not forthcoming, and the action component of shame is the wish to hide.

In "Aggression, Body Image, and Work Inhibition," Stavroula Beratis describes her psychoanalytic findings in the case of a medical student who suddenly developed a severe work inhibition and could not continue in medical school. This proved to be due to a defective, castrated, body image as the patient experienced himself as missing parts of his body, especially his brain. His non-neutralized aggressive energies had been turned inward and had a crucial impact on various developmental tasks and processes including the patient's formation of psychic structure, and also the body image. The work inhibition functioned to protect the paternal mental representation from being destroyed and, at the same time, produced a severe masochistic picture.

In "Genital Self-examination: The Precursor of Genital Anxiety in Women," Eleanor Galenson reports on a specific group of symptoms in connection with university examinations of Ph.D. candidates. These symptom patterns were similar to an entirely different age group in a different setting, namely, in the nineteen-to-twenty-four-month-old infant girls whom Roiphe and Galenson had studied in the course of their research on the emergence of early genitality. The symptoms of the doctoral candidates were similar. They represented three major anxieties—fear of object loss, fear of anal loss, and castration anxiety. This cluster represented preoedipal castration reactions related to the awareness of genital differences. These three anxieties are a normal developmental feature in girls at the end of the second year and are revived by intellectual competition with men, particularly when examinations leading to success in a career are involved.

In "Ambition: Normal and Pathological Aspects," Adrienne Applegarth notes that ambition "is the guiding star for the course of action." She notes how remarkable it is that numbers of people are unable to register possibilities for life because of the mobilization of the ego's defenses. She examines ambition from the point of view of ego defenses, superego conflicts, and the ego ideal, putting all of this against the backdrop of the evolving role of women in current society. She describes disturbances of ambition as well as some special features of ambition in women. Having ambitions themselves may be so invested with aggressive, libidinal, or narcissistic meaning that severe conflicts may prevent expression of these in consciousness or in action. Ambitionlessness may be caused by the sense that one is worthless or defective, the internalization of parental attitudes in one's own self-representations, fantasies of parental envy, a self-representation of worthlessness or defectiveness beneath a narcissistic character disorder, as well as an unconscious sense of guilt. Excessive ambition may also be present in some patients, and it is difficult to distinguish an inhibition of ambition from a disturbance in the work function itself. In several clinical examples, she describes some special features of ambition in women. Charles W. Socarides, in "On the Sense of Being 'Incomplete': Fragments from the Analysis of a Man with a Narcissistic Personality Disorder," describes the severe work inhibition of a forty-five-year-old man who never actually worked for any sustained period of time. He desperately complained that he needed someone or something to "complete" himself in order to help him achieve a structuralization of the self, without which he could not function. His varied and desperate efforts to achieve this, through both conscious and unconscious means, are described. Fragments from the analysis of this extremely intelligent patient offer important insights into the nature of his condition.

Finally, the essays that appear in this volume are illustrative of the multiple theoretical and clinical aspects of disturbances in work and the myriad forms of expression of work disturbances. We trust that this volume has brought together for the first time a number of contributions in a format designed for study and enjoyment. Disturbances in the work area should no longer be consigned to the realm of "stepchildren" of psychoanalysis (acknowledged, but not cultivated), playing a minor role to studies of other forms of distorted behavior. It is our hope that this collection of essays will prove to be an enticing invitation to others to further probe the psychoanalytic mysteries surrounding disturbances in work, and begin to provide a systematized theoretical, clinical, and therapeutic schema for the alleviation of the many afflicted by the "terror of nonperformance," thereby improving the quality of life and the potential for its enjoyment.

Charles W. Socarides, M.D.
Selma Kramer, M.D.

xxii   WORK AND ITS INHIBITIONS

xxii   WORK AND ITS INHIBITIONS

xxii   WORK AND ITS INHIBITIONS

REFERENCES

Applegarth, A. (1976), Some observations on work inhibitions in women. *J. Amer. Psychoanal. Assn.*, 24:251–268.
Erikson, E. H. (1959), *Identity and the Life Cycle. Psychological Issues,* Monogr. 1. New York: International Universities Press.
Freud, S. (1920), Beyond the pleasure principle. *Standard Edition,* 18:4–64. London: Hogarth Press, 1955.
———— (1930), Civilization and its discontents. *Standard Edition,* 21:59–145. London: Hogarth Press, 1961.
Hendrick, I. (1943), Work: Thoughts on the pleasure principle. *Psychoanal. Q.,* 12:311–329.
Holmes, D. (1965), A contribution to a psychoanalytic theory of work. *The Psychoanalytic Study of the Child,* 20:384–393. New York: International Universities Press.
Jaques, E. (1960), Disturbances in the capacity to work. *Internat. J. Psycho-Anal.,* 41:357–367.
Kramer, P. (1977), Work compulsion: A psychoanalytic study. *Psychoanal. Q.,* 46:361–385.
Kubie, L. (1958), *Neurotic Distortion of the Creative Process.* Lawrence, KS: University of Kansas Press.
Lantos, B. (1952), Metapsychological considerations on the concept of work. *Internat. J. Psycho-Anal.,* 33:439–443.
Meissner, W. W. (1986), Can psychoanalysis find its self? *J. Amer. Psychoanal. Assn.,* 34:379–400.
Menninger, K. (1942), Work as sublimation. *Bull. Menninger Clin.,* 6:170–182.
Olinick, S. L.; Poland, W. S.; Grigg, K. A. & Granatir, W. L. (1973), The psychoanalytic work ego: Process and interpretation. *Internat. J. Psycho-Anal.,* 54:143–151.
Rangell, L. (1969), Choice conflict and the decision-making function of the ego. *Internat. J. Psycho-Anal.,* 50:599–602.
———— (1971), The decision-making process: A contribution from psychoanalysis. *The Psychoanalytic Study of the Child,* 26:425–452. New York: Quadrangle.
———— (1986), The executive functions of the ego: An extension of the concept of ego autonomy. *The Psychoanalytic Study of the Child,* 41:1–37. New Haven, CT: Yale University Press.
Winnicott, D. W. (1960), Ego distortion in terms of true and false self. In: *The Maturational Processes and the Facilitating Environment.* New York: International Universities Press, 1965, pp. 140–152.

I. THEORETICAL CONSIDERATIONS

1

CHILD'S WORK: DEVELOPMENTAL ASPECTS OF THE CAPACITY TO WORK AND ENJOY IT

ERNA FURMAN

Being able to work and being able to derive satisfaction from the process and achievement of working represent the mature level of a highly complex developmental line. It encompasses the harmonious integration of most aspects of the fully structured personality and, in its turn, affects many aspects of personality functioning. My interest in the beginning phases of this developmental line goes back many years and has been an ongoing focus of study (E. Furman, 1969, 1985a, 1987, 1992). Increasing data from the analyses of children and from psychoanalytic observation and work with the youngest ones and their families in the setting of the Hanna Perkins Therapeutic School, especially its Mother-Toddler Group, have led to ever better and deeper understanding. Follow up of cases indicates that the early steps described below form the crucial foundation for the later developments (R. A. Furman and A. Katan, 1969; E. Furman, 1992). The present attempt at summarizing these findings is nevertheless a mere milestone along the path of inquiry. All aspects are not fully or equally explored, nor are their connections as yet sufficiently integrated and related to later phases of growth.

First, I shall highlight the basic characteristics of work, and of the capacity to work and enjoy it, by comparing work with play and by delineating the relationship between work and learning, and work and mastery. Next I shall describe the earliest developments within the young child's personality and in his interactions with parents and teachers which contribute to his capacity and pleasure of working.

3

WORK AND PLAY

Work and play are often linked, and just as often differentiated, in ways that are unhelpful to our understanding of each and, hence, to our ways of supporting children's development in both these areas.

Many parents and educators take the attitude that "Play is the child's work." This sometimes leads them to assume that children are working when they are really playing, or that their play will turn into the ability to work in the course of time, or that play can be a substitute for work. Many a schoolchild, teacher, and parent discover their mistake too late, perhaps after years of games with words and numbers have not brought about the desired knowledge of spelling and multiplication tables, or when extensive opportunities for fantasy play during the early school years have failed to motivate children to work on assignments. Analysts too have endorsed the idea that play forms the basis for progression to work, following A. Freud's outline of the developmental line from play to work (A. Freud, 1965). It is true that the more sophisticated forms of work require personality attributes that mature slowly (such as a considerable degree of frustration tolerance and secondary-process thinking), but this is equally true for the more sophisticated forms of play. Observation of toddlers and preschoolers indicates that play and work coexist from early on and proceed along different developmental paths (E. Furman, 1992). Moreover, "Play is the child's work," with its assumption of play forming the basis for progression to work, implies that children play and adults work, a division that would impoverish the lives of both age groups. The child's play and work may be simpler, the adult's more sophisticated, but all of us need to play and work and are enriched by doing so (E. Furman, 1985a).

Another widely accepted, but misleading, attitude is conveyed by the statements, "Play is fun; work is a chore," "This work is just child's play," and "This is child's work, not man's work." They suggest that work only qualifies as such when it is difficult, frustrating, and joyless, and that it turns into childish, undignified play when it is easy and pleasurable.

Work and play are not really distinguished by criteria of relative ease or difficulty. Work may be easy or difficult, and so may play. Both may provide special pleasures and satisfactions, regardless of how easy or hard they are. Moreover, whereas some people believe that only easy work can be enjoyed, others think that only hard work can bring satisfaction, or can bring satisfaction only when it is linked with sublimations and/or social status. Actually, not only children, but many adults too find simple, repetitive, and rhythmic work pleasurable in itself—from spelling drills to knitting, dishwashing, chopping wood, or even piecework in the factory. They may even prefer such work for its calm security and opportunity for motoric discharge. Others find their greatest pleasure in sophisticated professional work or craftsmanship, the skills for which took years of training to acquire, and which continue to challenge their mental and/or bodily resources. And many people like some of each kind of work, varying the satisfactions to be derived from them. Likewise, the pleasures in playing vary from person to person rather than from ease to difficulty, or even from young to old. The difference between play and work lies neither in their developmental sequence nor in the ease or difficulty of the activity.

Play always deals in symbols, that is, in things and activities we endow with meaning, so that they stand for something other than what they are. With the help of these symbols—be they a blankie, toy, utilitarian object, artistic medium, gesture, or words—play creates an imaginary world, a world of illusion that mediates between ourselves and others. Through the use of pretend, playing increasingly satisfies many impulses and wishes indirectly, soothes frustrations and disappointments temporarily, gives meaning to the puzzles of life, and, through mutually accepted symbols, enables us to share ideas, feelings, and experiences with others. Although the very beginnings of play, even the transitional object, and its development during the early years depend very closely on the phase-appropriate participation of and communication with the mother, play draws on many inner and outer experiences, selects elements from them, blends them in new combinations, and brings them to new resolutions. This provides at least a respite, more often an imagined gratification, which help to come to terms with reality, and there is also the special satisfaction that comes with creating something and achieving a measure of intrapsychic mastery. But play never really changes the child or his world. The pilot's seat is still a chair, and the pilot is still the same little boy when it is time to have lunch (E. Furman, 1985a, 1992).

In contrast to play, work always deals with reality and effects real results. Something, however humble, really gets done, something that contributes to becoming a self-sustaining individual and participating member of one's community or society. It enables one to take care of oneself and to play a part in the functioning of the larger group. This applies as much to the toddler who masters his bodily self-care and no longer relies on mother's ministrations, or to the older child who takes on some of the family chores, as it does to the adult who earns his living and, through his work, provides a product or service for his society. The sense of mastery and of achievement that accompany the completion of work, of something externally real and useful, are some of its special pleasures and satisfactions. Another may derive from the process of working, which may be enjoyable in itself, and may be linked to the anticipation of achievement or to the outer and inner valuing of expending effort and coping with frustration. The baby who tries and tries to handle his cup or to reach and hold on to his teething ring, experiences the first beginnings of the process of working. When he succeeds, his beaming face tells us in no uncertain terms that he senses the glow of accomplishment. This good feeling can only be acquired through working, through devoting effort to achieve results, for one of the great advantages of the pleasure in working and achieving is that it adds in a lasting way to our self-esteem, to our confidence in "I am somebody because I can do." Even for the young child it can far surpass the gratification of being catered to but remaining helpless and dependent. As will be described later, the self-motivation for and pleasure in working and achieving are particularly marked during the toddler time when they contribute so much to the growth and positive self-investment of the personality. Yet work and self-esteem are in a reciprocal relationship. Work enhances self-esteem and self-esteem, in turn, enables us to like our work. As already mentioned, pleasure in working depends in large measure not on the type of work, but on the person doing it. Some can find satisfaction in the most menial routine tasks; others can never like their work, whatever it may be. This has a lot to do with the way we extend our liking, or not liking, of ourselves to our work and whether we can use our work to make us feel good—all related to how we were helped to develop our attitudes to work early on.

Work, like play, has its roots in the good-enough earliest mother-infant unit at the point when the child begins to differentiate himself. Whereas play initially fills and bridges the gap of separateness and creates imaginary interactions, the beginnings of work are linked to identification with mother, becoming like her by doing what she does, i.e., taking care of his bodily needs, "all by myself" (E. Furman, 1992). Being able to play improves the quality of our lives; getting satisfaction from work makes us feel that we are quality people. Those of us who, as adults, enjoy working appreciate that it does more for us than earn a living, though this alone is no minor accomplishment.

The pleasures and satisfactions derived from work and play do differ, but they also share an important characteristic. They never provide direct gratification of bodily needs, such as hunger or elimination, or of impulses, sexual or aggressive. The pleasures of work and play are neither bodily nor instinctual. As such they are acquired tastes, acquired in the course of development and, like most other ego activities, acquired with the help of the relationship with the parents at first.

Work and play also often overlap, affect, and complement one another. A skill that was work to acquire may come to be used in the service of play. For example, learning to throw and catch a ball is work, but having achieved a sufficient level of skill, it may be used to play ball on one's own or in games with others, and it may even become work again for the professional ballplayer. With some kinds of work, play is an essential preliminary. For example, playing with ideas, objects, or materials usually constitutes one stage in the work of the creative artist, scientist, and writer. In yet other instances, play may turn into work (as when someone who likes playing with puppets becomes a professional puppeteer), or work may turn into play (as when a retired railway engineer likes to set up miniature railroads). However, these interactions or overlaps between play and work do not imply a shared or identical maturational progression, and the individual concerned usually senses some of the differences between working and playing in his or her own attitude, even when he or she enjoys both.

WORK AND LEARNING

Young schoolchildren are often told that learning is their job, just as Dad's job is, say, fixing cars, the school and garage being their respective places of work. Yet when these youngsters go through high school, perhaps even college and graduate school, they are told (and usually also tell themselves) that it is time for them to get a job, to start real work. For many this is not an easy step, internally as well as externally, and some never make it. Obviously, learning and working share some characteristics, but they are not the same. They share the goal-directed process of expending effort toward the achievement of specific masteries. They share the neutral pleasure and satisfaction inherent in the process and achievement. Unlike play, the contents and products of their activities are not imaginary. They also overlap a great deal in that learning often entails work and work often requires learning. For example, learning to write and spell usually includes much practicing and demonstration of progress through ''worksheets.'' Likewise, working as a, say, dishwasher, requires learning several skills, be it rinsing and drying or operating a dishwasher, not to mention the skills of getting to work on time and fitting in with the people and rules of the workplace. Some types of work, such as being an analyst, require ongoing learning. However, although many believe that a good education leads to a good job and to the ability to hold it, this is not necessarily so, not least for intrapsychic reasons. There is no direct maturational progression from learning to working. Some excellent students do not become good workers, and vice versa.

The difference between learning and work lies in the nature and use of the achievement. The end result of learning something, be it a skill or a piece of knowledge, may remain a purely private mental accomplishment. It may be used to satisfy one's curiosity, to enhance one's self-regard, perhaps to impress others, but only when it is put in the service of effecting something in the external world, which contributes to one's self-reliant and useful functioning as a member of the community, does it lead to achievements that characterize work. This applies as much to the toddler who dresses himself and thereby becomes a more independently functioning member of his family (how often we hear "He knows how to put on his jacket but he won't do it") as to the scientist who shares his new knowledge with others (teaches them) or applies it to further his work (thereby perhaps earning his living), as opposed to merely knowing but not using what he has learned. When learning is put to effective use it has contributed to and turned into work. There are many similar inner rewards to be gained from learning and working, but the satisfaction of actually doing in the service of self-maintenance as an active member of one's group adds a pleasure that mere knowing does not afford—a dignity in one's own and others' eyes. Society recognizes this difference by remunerating work. Except for parents who mistakenly pay their offspring for good report cards, financial support of learning is generally given only with a view to it leading to its effective use in the form of work. Learning alone keeps us dependent; working makes us independent and even useful. Toddlers and preschoolers are keenly aware of this. No putting together a big jigsaw puzzle makes them as proud as using the toilet on their own, no amount of well cut out playdough shapes compares to baking real cookies. The later difficulties in going from learning to working do not usually relate to insufficient learning but are, in large measure, caused by earlier interferences in the developmental line from dependence to independence.

WORK AND MASTERY

The term mastery has already been used in several contexts—the gratifying sense of inner mastery related to creative play, mastery accomplished through learning, the pleasure of working derived from the mastery of achievement. Mastery is a concept unto itself and plays a part in many areas of personality functioning. It is not limited to work and cannot be equated with it, but it is an essential part of it, in the sense of inner mastery (understanding) and outer mastery (accomplishment) of a task. Even the simplest work involves both these aspects of mastery, and it is the sense of mastery that brings so much pleasure, perhaps the greatest pleasure, in working. There is little doubt that the relationship and identification with the parent, at least initially, contribute to this experience of pleasure, but we observe it frequently as a spontaneous manifestation in young toddlers as they succeed in getting off a boot or in completing a simple inset puzzle on their own, without encouragement or praise from mother or teacher. This great pleasure in mastery does not happen when the toddler's achievement is the result of lucky chance, nor is it related to the extent of effort he has devoted to the task. It comes from a feeling of "So that's how it works! That's how it all fits together! Now it makes sense!" It is an experience of integration.

I have similarly described how the pleasure in learning derives not from acquiring isolated bits of knowledge but from the thrill of "It makes sense!" when a total process is understood; for example, when, in our Toddler Group, the youngsters share in the whole cycle from planting peas to harvesting and eating them (E. Furman, 1992). This mastery too implies integration. In "Fusion, Integration, and Feeling Good" (E. Furman, 1985b), I attempted to show how drive fusion, neutralization, and the developing integrative function enhance one another in a reciprocal process that promotes a modulated experience of feeling good. Suffice it to say here that the pleasure that accompanies the mastery of these intrapsychic processes, particularly the ability to integrate (synthesize), is always a more or less neutral pleasure in the service of the ego.

I think that the pleasure in mastery represents primarily the pleasure of integration. Observation of young children as well as analytic material gained from their treatments indicate that this pleasure is not only a powerful motivation for learning and working, but that a developmentally adequate integrative function is an important prerequisite for the capacity and pleasure of working as well as of learning. At the same time, the experience of pleasurable working and learning supports the growth of the integrative function—another reciprocal, mutually dependent process. It begins with the integration of the body-ego through the mastery of self-care. Hence the importance of this early development for the capacity and pleasure of working as well as for many other aspects of personality functioning.

SELF-CARE: THE CHILD'S FIRST WORK

Self-care means being able to gauge and meet one's basic bodily needs—knowing when one is hungry and feeding oneself, when one is cold or warm and dressing/undressing oneself, when tired helping oneself to fall asleep, when needing to eliminate taking care of one's toileting and keeping clean, recognizing pain and seeking and accepting comfort, avoiding common dangers to keep safe. Achieving these goals to a sufficient extent is the crucial developmental task of the toddler phase, the process by which the very young child comes to own his body, integrates the basic concept of his body-ego, and invests his developing functions. The process and step-by-step mastery of self-care build tolerance for frustration, pleasure and confidence in achievement through effort, positive self-regard and self-esteem, and further personality integration—all of which underlie the later ability to learn and work.

The impetus for and progression toward self-care are intimately linked with developmental changes in the mother-child relationship. Relative success or failure therefore depend largely on the way mother and child respond to each other's feelings about these changes, and how these feelings color their interactions (E. Furman, 1982, 1992, 1993, 1994). The zest for "me do" starts when the infant's experiences within the earliest mother-child unit have been good enough to enable him to begin differentiating himself from her, to love her as an at least partially separate person, and to admire and want to own what she can do, especially her care of him. The wish to feed himself is usually the first manifestation of the intense desire to become like her, to mother himself. This admiring wish for identification with her caring activities leads him to prefer doing to being done for and to persevere with trying despite frustrating failures. Usually, the more positive the relationship and the more consistent and enjoyable the mother's care has been, the sooner and more insistently does the child want to become like her and to do for himself.

For the mother this involves a difficult change in her investment of her child. In supporting his efforts, she needs to surrender her ownership of his body and related narcissistic gratification of caring for it, in exchange for the different pleasure of loving and admiring him as a separately functioning person with his own body—a love object who no longer needs her in the same way. Unless the mother can effect this change in herself and adapt to her older infant's and toddler's characteristically back-and-forth path toward self-care, his achievement in this vital area will be flawed or jeopardized. His persistent, even angry, demand for "me do" is the surest sign of his trust in her ability to help him grow up and away.

I have described the mother-child progress toward self-care as proceeding through four overlapping steps, "doing for," "doing with," "standing by to admire," "doing on one's own" (E. Furman, 1992). During the first step of "doing for," the mother conveys her enjoyment of caring for his bodily needs. During the second step of "doing with" she supports his bit-by-bit expanding efforts at mastering the various caretaking skills. It is an often painstaking process for both, as she values and "libidinizes" his trying, his enduring and overcoming the frustration of mistakes and failures, shows confidence in his ability to master, and lets him own his ultimate success with an appreciative "Good for you." However, where the first two steps may entail their own individual difficulties and the fourth step largely extends into the preschool years, the third one of "standing by to admire" is usually the hardest for the mother and the most crucial for the child. It is the time when he has mastered the specific skill enough to minister to himself, but needs the mother's bodily and emotional presence to value and admire his independent achievement, i.e., to transfer to his ownership not only his body, but her pleasure and gratification in caring for it. When the impetus for self-care springs from motives other than the wish to acquire mother's enjoyable caring activities, efforts at self-care will not persist and will not become autonomous, pleasurable, or self-enhancing. This may happen when self-care is prompted by mother's demand or lack of pleasure in caretaking, or when it serves as a defense against the stress of separation from her. Whereas the skills of self-care are readily learned from others, such as father, sitter, sibling, or in daycare, they will remain labile, object-dependent, and will not contribute to self-esteem. For self-care skills to be integrated as lasting secondary narcissistic investments they have to be acquired through help from and identification with the mother, i.e., the primary caregiver with whom the initial unit experience led to beginning self-differentiation. Similarly, it is only when frustration tolerance and trust in achieving are developed with mother's help around mastery of self-care, that they will readily transfer to other activities, to the neutral pursuits of learning and working. And it takes *her* "standing by to admire" to acquire regard for one's body and trust in one's ability to care for it, which later extend to liking one's work and feeling good about working. We have seen this amply illustrated by observing and following up the toddlers in our Mother-Toddler group as well as others who attended daycare centers (E. Furman, 1984, 1992).

Toileting and keeping clean are particularly illustrative of the connection between bodily self-care and working. The phrase "doing one's job" refers to both. R. A. Furman (1984) has helpfully contrasted toilet training with toilet mastery. The former is characterized by mother remaining in charge of the child's body, from gauging his need to eliminate to owning the successful achievement when the child has surrendered his bodily products to her. The latter consists of the mother engaging her toddler's active participation in all aspects of the process (from recognizing his inner signals to flushing the toilet), fostering his identification with her reaction formation (from love of dirt to liking oneself clean), and supporting and valuing his efforts and achievement of independent mastery. Accordingly, "doing one's job" may become an unwelcome chore, perhaps a self-sacrificing duty of surrender to the authority (boss or superego), or it may become a proud, gratifying activity in the service of self-supporting independence. This same developmental matrix may either lead to learning as a perpetual but unproductive preoccupation, or may pave the way for learning to be applied to self-reliant, useful work.

THE ROLE OF THE DRIVES

Toilet mastery also involves mastery of the anal and urethral drives—their ego regulation in terms of recognition and time and place of discharge, their "turn around" in terms of the developmentally adaptive defense of a reaction formation, their at least partial neutralization and channeling into activities. In all these areas they contribute to personality growth and functioning, and facilitate work. This shows not only in the already mentioned transfer of the acquired frustration tolerance and self-motivated pleasure in mastery to neutral pursuits, but in the new interest in a large variety of goal-directed activities (painting, pouring, cleaning, etc.), in the ability to execute these activities in an organized, neat manner, and, not least, to pursue them without interference from excretory impulses. How often the young toddler's painting turns into messing or is interrupted by his wiggling-withholding, wetting, or last-minute dash to the toilet! and how often we say, "It'll feel so good when you'll be the boss of your pee and BMs, and will be able to enjoy and finish your good work!" But toilet mastery also contributes to the self-concept of the body-ego which is newly and much more clearly delineated by integrating the excretory organs and being in charge of their sensations and functions. This brings about a confident sense of identity which is at once reflected in the toddler's purposeful approach to activities. It contrasts sharply with the bumbling, tentative or impulsively ill-directed approach of the youngster who is still at the mercy of his drives or dependent on the adult's care of them (E. Furman, 1992).

We have found that toddlers' toilet mastery, body-ego integration, and related attitude to learning and working with neutral activities are adversely affected when their phallic sexual impulses are stimulated prematurely. This happens through exposure to the sight of sexual differences in peers or adults, through excited interactions, such as tickling or roughhousing, or through direct stimulation of their genitals, as happens with excessive handling, medical-surgical procedures, or abuse. Often the toddler's avoidance of neutral activities, diffidence in working at them, or dissatisfaction with his accomplishment are the first indication of such an interference. When we alert mothers to the child's behavior and they then explore it further with the analyst in their treatment via the parent, they invariably trace and link it to such stimulating experiences and can then address them with their child (E. Furman, 1992).

With the older toddler and preschooler, phallic impulses are, of course, phase-appropriately manifest and play their part in his learning and working. In 1969, I described ways in which the partial drives of curiosity and showing off, concerns over bodily differences and adequacy, as well as unrealistic self-expectations derived from the envy of parental performance affect the preschooler's attitude to activities. Many a good nursery school teacher can spot the boy or girl who withdraws into fantasy play to avoid "hard" or "boring" projects, or who rushes to get praise for his work to hide his own disappointment and deprecating opinion of it, or who can at best copy or denigrate others' achievements but dares not, or cannot, come up with his own ideas, much less devote sustained effort to their execution. Yet on the positive side the phallic sexual impulses contribute so much to self-motivated enjoyable learning and working, especially in the context of a relationship with parents and teachers who help to channel them from bodily to neutral interests.

Aggression plays a particularly important part in the development of the capacity for and pleasure of working. As already mentioned, the favorable drive balance within the mother-child relationship is crucial to the impetus for and successful process toward the achievement of self-care. At best, however, this process is frought with much anger, often for both partners. The task of drive fusion, i.e., of taming anger for the sake of love, is as crucial a developmental task of toddlerhood as self-care and is closely linked with it.

For example, John's mother insisted on dressing her struggling and kicking two-year-old in her lap but could not get on his outdoor clothes despite her stranglehold and pleas for his help. Finally she would put him down with an angry, "Well, you can just do it yourself. I am through!" John would then yank at his jacket with equal fury, give up in frustration, and have a tantrum, or run around teasingly, or helplessly surrender to mother's renewed dressing efforts. When he did manage to get on his garment, he looked defiant and sheepish rather than proud (E. Furman, 1992). Sometimes such excessive mutual anger focuses only on some aspect of bodily care and reflects a mere temporary out-of-tuneness in the mother-child relationship. Sometimes it invades all areas, indicative of the mother's difficulty in relinquishing her narcissistic investment of his body, and results either in ongoing overt strife in their relationship and/or the child's "giving up," remaining dependent, failing to channel aggressive energy into functions and activities, and becoming diffident about his capabilities. In extreme cases there is such a dearth of mutual pleasurable narcissistic *and* object investment that mother and child can at best muster sadomasochistic interactions, i.e., sexualizing rather than binding the aggression between them—an insufficient minimum of drive fusion. For the most part, however, the very young struggle with phase-appropriate ambivalence and their mothers maintain sufficient love for their children to be in charge of their own anger, despite provocations and difficulty with catching up with his changing needs. This enables them to convey that anger can be tamed and to help them with it.

Taming anger does not mean merely learning to verbalize it, nor does it mean stopping aggressive behavior just to please mother or to avoid her punitive retaliation. Taming anger in the sense of effecting drive fusion involves drawing on one's love for another to put one's anger into proportion, bind it, and restrain its potentially hurtful discharge to protect both the external loved one and his or her intrapsychic representation. This is no easy task, given the young child's intense raw aggression, with its omnipotent pressure to destroy everything. The toddler justly dreads the force of his own anger and cannot believe that his own or others' loving feelings can survive it. It therefore takes much motherly help to remind him of his love, to assure him that he can and will use it to subdue his anger, just as the adults have learned to do, and to value and praise his efforts toward that goal. When we observe children in the midst of this inner struggle, we appreciate how tempting it is to "justify" their aggression by letting it erase all love, and how hard to renounce anger's omnipotent sway. But when the toddler succeeds in using his love to bind his aggression, there is enormous relief and good feeling. The inner mastery thus achieved in an ongoing bit-by-bit process has a marked, clearly observable effect on personality functioning. The child is more at peace with himself and more cooperative and considerate in his relationships with others; there is an increase in pleasure in all areas of functioning; he has much more available energy for neutral interests and pursuits as well as more confidence in his abilities. When mothers comment, "He's got it all together now" or "Isn't it great to see her so 'with it.' " they sense that a big step in personality integration has taken place. Drive fusion has facilitated this integration, generated pleasure in living and relating, and freed aggressive energy for neutralized ego use. All these developmental personality achievements are most important for working. Observation and followup of the toddlers in the Hanna Perkins Group has shown that these masteries not only pave the way for successful later steps in drive fusion, but are essential to the subsequent growth in the capacity and pleasure of learning and working (E. Furman, 1992).

RELATIONSHIPS AND IDENTIFICATIONS

In tracing the earliest personality developments that form the basis of the capacity and pleasure in working and underlie its progressive maturation, I have repeatedly emphasized the unique role of the relationship with the mother and of identification with her. Just as the impetus for self-care and its achievement through the four progressive steps are intimately linked with the good-enough mother-child relationship and, without it, fail to contribute to personality growth, the same applies to the beginnings of working at other tasks and the pleasures derived from it. Beyond self-care, the initial focus of "me do" in relation to work are the mother's caretaking activities in the home, all she does for the house and family. These daily tasks are part of the toddler's ongoing experience and, for the most part, lie within his limits of comprehension. With mother's patient help they also often lie within the limits of his capabilities, at least at the level of the "doing with" stage. When the mother enjoys these activities and is willing to share them with her youngster, even hand some over for his mastery and satisfaction, he will, as with self-care, integrate them as an autonomous self-enhancing part of himself. The older child's willingness, or unwillingness, to do "chores" in the home is largely related to these early identifications. The basic daily caretaking work is always more desirable and more satisfying when mother likes it enough to be just a little reluctant to give it up. When she cannot enjoy this work or encourages the child to do some of it to rid herself of a burden, her attitude will become part of his identification, albeit in a negative way. And when mother relegates all home caretaking to others, be they father, family members, or employees, their pleasure in working (if any) will serve as a positive impetus for identification only insofar as she values and appreciates their work, enjoys working with them at times, or substituting for them at other times. Without her pleasurable investment, early caretaking identifications with loved ones other than mother are labile at best, conflictual at worst. In either case, they do not serve as a self-motivating springboard for other neutral interests and activities. The adults' belief that young children only want to play, rather than work, and that it is therefore necessary to entertain them with toys or programs, stems largely from their own dislike of working at tasks the child can understand and participate in, i.e., the tasks so often regarded as menial.

Throughout the toddler period, learning to work from and with others depends on mother's participation and attitude. It proceeds best when linked to the caretaking activities that are part of the mother-child relationship and only gradually encompasses other areas of neutral activity. Thus, the most enthusiastically welcome projects in the Mother-Toddler Group include baking cookies, serving snack, washing dishes, even cleaning the tables. Other activities, from doing puzzles to gardening, all draw the toddler's interest and engage his wish to work at and master the skill only to the extent that they are just as interesting and pleasurable for his mother. Sometimes a teacher-initiated activity taps into something mother and child have previously enjoyed together (and the helpful teacher makes it a point to find out about such shared interests and to expand them in the group setting). Sometimes the teacher has to first engage the mother's interest and enjoyment so that the toddler can follow her lead in what can then become a threesome project. Regardless how invested and skilled the teacher may be, without mother's eager and pleasurable participation, the child's interest and achievement will, at best, remain limited to the class period. It will fail to carry over to other activities, and fail to contribute to self-esteem. We found that whenever we could not engage the mother's pleasure and support in our Mother-Toddler Group, the children still learned and worked, but with much less pleasure, and their abilities remained dependent on the relationship with the teacher. They never became self-motivated and autonomous (E. Furman, 1992).

The toddler's need of his mother and of identification with her in regard to working relates to the immaturity of his personality and nature of his relationships. The mother (a term here always used to designate the primary mothering person with whom the unit of earliest experience led to self-differentiation) remains in large measure a functioning part of the toddler's personality, a part he gradually makes his own by identification with her and with her help. What was self outside becomes self inside. Such narcissistic identifications differ from the later identification with love objects who were invested as separate people from the start. These latter relationships, mainly with father and other family members, begin very early and, during mother's presence and availability, serve as important additional relationships. She supports and enjoys them and they are loved and enjoyed in that context—just as mother's availability and her support of the toddler teacher helps the child to like and interact with that additional person, but these relationships do not yet contribute to self-investment.

At the same time, another development takes place. The more the toddler becomes his own person, the more he invests mother as a person in her own right. But this relationship is easily threatened by his as yet untamed aggression. Relationships with others tempt him to be disloyal when he is angry at mother. He may ward this off by avoiding others or not allowing himself to like them (lest he like them too much and burn his bridges), or he may give way to temptation and "prefer" them while rejecting mother (which later usually causes him much anguish and fear of retaliation by her). Either way, the unresolved ambivalence in the mother-child relationship is an ever-present interference in the toddler's ability to benefit from the relationships with others, unless mother remains supportively available. Toddlers with double parenting or in daycare often struggle with exaggerated loyalty conflicts. Some cope by isolating their experiences with the nonmother from those with the mother, and hence cannot integrate them.

The young child can begin to use relationships with others and identifications with them only when self-investment is sufficiently advanced and aggression has been sufficiently tamed to provide a considerable degree of self- and object constancy. This usually takes place in the older toddler and preschooler, and is helpfully reenforced and stabilized by the identifications of the oedipal period and the emergence of the superego as a functioning structure. The true teacher-pupil relationship is a part of these developments and plays its most important role from early latency on in contributing to the child's increasing capacity for and pleasure in working (E. Furman, 1987). However, even during these later phases, helpful identifications with teachers, just as with parents and others, always depend on the good-enough relationship, the loved one's real enjoyment of his work as well as readiness to value the child's efforts and to appreciate *his* owning of his success.

REFERENCES

Freud, A. (1965), *Normality and Pathology in Childhood. The Writings of Anna Freud*, Vol. 6. New York: International Universities Press.
Furman, E. (1969), Some thoughts on the pleasure in working. *Bull. Phila. Assn. Psychoanal.*, 19:197–212.
———— (1982), Mothers have to be there to be left. *The Psychoanalytic Study of the Child*, 37:15–28. New Haven, CT: Yale University Press.
———— (1984), Mothers, toddlers and care. In: *Preschoolers: Questions and Answers*. Madison, CT: International Universities Press, 1995, pp. 85–105.
———— (1985a), Play and work in early childhood. In: *Child Analysis*, 1:60–76, 1990.
———— (1985b), On fusion, integration, and feeling good. *The Psychoanalytic Study of the Child*, 40:81–110. New Haven, CT, Yale University Press.
———— (1987), *Helping Young Children Grow*. Madison, CT: International Universities Press.
———— (1992), *Toddlers and Their Mothers*. Madison, CT: International Universities Press.
———— (1993), *Toddlers and Their Mothers: Abridged Version for Parents and Educators*. Madison, CT: International Universities Press.
———— (1994), Early aspects of mothering: what makes it so hard to be there to be left. *J. Child Psychotherapy*, 20:2:149–164.
Furman, R. A. (1984), On toilet mastery. *Child Analysis*, 2:98–110, 1991.
———— & Katan, A. (1969), *The Therapeutic Nursery School*. New York: International Universities Press.

2

PSYCHOANALYSIS AND PLAYFUL WORK

HAROLD P. BLUM, M.D.

There has been no consensual definition of "work" within or outside of psychoanalysis. The dictionary definition of work emphasizes a general term for purposeful effort. Work is defined as exertion of strength or faculties to accomplish something; or that which is produced or accomplished by exertion or toil; or that which is produced by mental labor, such as a painting or poetry or needlework. Labor commonly implies more strenuous exertion than work; toil is painful or fatiguing labor; and drudgery is defined as especially irksome and distasteful work. Work is also denoted by its opposite—by antonyms of play, diversion, recreation, and relaxation. Work, which here includes aspects of psychoanalytic work, is goal-directed, and aims to achieve real change with a capacity to alter reality. Analytic work also aims at changing psychic reality and the representational world. Work is not necessarily immediately pleasurable and may be associated with highly sublimated aims and goals or with infantile drive gratifications. Work, like play, implies activity. This can be ego activity or physical activity, and the distinction is significant. The activity is designed to have a desired effect or influence in the inner or outer world, whether to solve a problem of architectural design or to find the precipitating cause of an anxiety attack. Work also has peripheral meaning such as to provoke or incite, as to work the crowd or to work oneself to exhaustion or to rage, etc.

Psychoanalysis is replete with work metaphors, many of which were introduced by Freud. Freud spoke of analytic work, dream work, mourning work, joke work, working through, and he commented on the meaning and value of work as well as work inhibition. One notion of a psychoanalytic norm for normality or adult maturity, following Freud (1916–1917), was the ability to work, love, and play.

There are many additions to the analytic literature pertaining to work. Weekend, Sunday, or holiday neurosis was related to the absence of work and to familial conflicts activated when returning from work to the home situation. To the time-honored importance of the transference in the analysis of resistance, concepts of a working alliance were formulated as part of the psychoanalytic process. The working alliance (Greenson, 1965) was essentially congruent with the therapeutic alliance (Zetzel, 1956) and closely related to Freud's (1939) analytic pact. It was noted that analytic work could proceed in the face of negative transference; it no longer required the maintenance of a positive transference for successful interpretation. Anna Freud (1963) noted that there is a developmental line from play to work, and that play helps to advance ego development and controls which are necessary precursors of the capacity of the older child and adult to work. The capacity to work consolidates during latency. Latency children are able to do schoolwork and homework with increasing levels of competence and the acquisition and refinement of skills. Work is thus related to mastery and adaptation, and self regard.

Work is much more directly connected with reality than play, although play may be a preparation for reality, provisionally connecting needs and goals with possible ways of realizing them (Hartmann, 1939). Work has many social and cultural functions, and it is usually an activity that is both socializing and demanded by society. Freud (1930) commented on the profound psychological and social dimensions of work:

> No other technique for the conduct of life attaches the individual so firmly to reality as laying emphasis on work; for his work at least gives him a secure place in a portion of reality, in the human community. The possibility it offers of displacing a large amount of libidinal components, whether narcissistic, aggressive or even erotic, on to professional work and on to the human relations connected with it lends it a value by no means second to what it enjoys as something indispensable to the preservation and justification of existence in society. . . . The great majority of people only work under the stress of necessity, and this natural human aversion to work raises the most difficult social problems. [p. 80n]

Holmes (1965) observed that a theoretical dichotomization between the function of work, adaptive or reality-oriented behavior, and work as a form of drive discharge or gratification, is artificial and neither necessary nor fruitful. Work has multiple functions and meanings related to the individual's entire developmental history and to his society and culture. Work is certainly related to self-regard in the fulfillment of ideals and in the realization of fantasy identifications, e.g., in the case of an individual who works as an attorney or analyst in identification with a parent. To be deprived of work often means loss of dignity and status, a narcissistic injury and blow to self-esteem; it may also represent castration, punishment, or masochistic gratification. However, while there may be a sense of work as driven play, e.g., being a workaholic or compulsive gambler, there are many intermediate and overlapping realms of work and play. Work and play are thus not only opposites, but may also be mutually facilitating and synergistic. There are activities intermediate between work and play such as forms of recreational interest and hobbies which have serious intent, require considerable skill and knowledge, and involve work that is very playful.

Maturity involves the capacity to work, love, and play, often the ingredients are part of the psychoanalytic process. Psychoanalysis is, indeed, very serious work, with a major goal of self-understanding, insight, and attenuation of the unconscious conflicts and traumas underlying symptoms and character disturbance. It is generally expected that this will lead to improvement in many areas of work and love-life, and the capacities for flexible control of regression, and for achieving satisfactions and pleasures consistent with mature ideals and values. Patients who are not able to play, to tolerate fantasy, to enjoy wit and humor, may acquire or regain such pleasurable sublimations after successful analysis. However, analysis requires some initial capacity for commitment to the work and goals, and for reversible playful regression.

Play is an activity in the adult that is related to freedom for amusement and diversion, to fantasy activity, to role play and performance, and it is associated with pleasure and fun. It is often regarded as the antithesis of work or being serious or having overt reality-oriented goals. Play has the connotation of something unreal as distinguished from activity designed to conform to reality, to alter reality, or that is based on adherence to the reality principle (Weinshel, 1988). Play is a fundamental phenomenon that is actually found only in higher-level mammals, and the more intelligent the mammal, the longer the period of play, the more extensive and intensive the play. It appears throughout the life cycle as noted by Erikson (1966). He observed that adults tend to judge play as neither serious nor useful, unrelated to central human tasks and motives. For Erikson, the latency period is associated specifically with industry and the ability to work. Although the adult is not comparable to a playing child, the adult may engage in a maturing playfulness endowed with adult competence which heightens the sense of reality. Freud (1908) stated that the opposite of play is what is real, and suggested that as people grow up they cease to play, substituting fantasy for actual play. After infancy, childrens' play involves the enactment of fantasy. Adults may fantasize without the readiness for enactment characteristic of small children or traumatized individuals. Games involve organized play in which there are rules, regulations, and roles. For Freud, playing games was a manifestation of the child's imaginative activity and capacity to create a world of his own and to rearrange his world in pleasing new ways. Children's play is spontaneous; they tend to play with much less self-consciousness, shame, and performance anxiety than adults. In an early reference to the reconstruction of childhood fantasy from adult fantasy, Freud (1908, p. 147) refers to fantasies that are played out, changed, during development. Freud would later give an elaborate example of the development of fantasy through childhood and into adolescence, with a range of enactment from perversion to socially derivative play (Freud, 1919).

Freud (1920) also formulated important further functions of play in his study of his grandson's *Fort-Da* play with a reel on a string. Freud related the play to the child's attempts to master separation anxiety and object loss. The play was related to the child's "great cultural achievement—the incendiary enunciation . . . which he made in allowing his mother to go away without protesting" (p. 15). Play was thus related to processes of ego development and socialization. It helped the growing child to deal with anxiety and the fear of helplessness or traumatic anxiety. It provided a safe form of satisfaction of otherwise forbidden gratifications, a source of consolation for insult and injury, and compensation for loss, disappointment, and deflation. Infant play emerges very early with the development of primary object relation, imitation, and increasingly higher levels of identification. Since fantasy always includes objects and identifications, it may be questioned whether there is "solitary play" or whether solitary play represents play with internalized objects, fantasy objects, as occurs in masturbatory play. Of course, both work and play and working recreation can be more or less narcissistic versus object-related.

As play becomes increasingly complex and socialized, the child gradually learns rules of the game, so important to adaptation in a given society and culture. According to Waelder (1932) play has a very important role in the mastery of trauma and in the growth of ego competence. The ego actively assimilates and masters where it was formerly passive and relatively helpless. Play involves piecemeal assimilation, as in the analytic process, and experiences that are too large to be quickly assimilated are constantly worked over in play. Waelder remarked that play was a leave of absence from reality and from the superego, a point of view that could be compared to free association and transference dramatization within the analytic process. Peller (1954) further analyzed the formal elements in style and social aspects of play, the organization, rules, and developmental levels of play, and proposed secondary gains achieved in the play. She notes that there is an oscillation between regression and progression in development, for example, the cognitive and affective processes. Peller describes how more sophisticated developmental levels of play overlie more archaic forms, which may reappear regressively. Winnicott's (1971) work on the capacity to play and the pathogenic incapacity to play is of great importance to the understanding of the analytic situation as an experimental as-if seen in relationships. Winnicott (1971) repeatedly observed that play belonged to an intermediate space to that which is subjective and that which is objectively perceived in shared reality. Winnicott's proposal that psychoanalysis develop into a special form of playing tends to neglect the working, reflecting, and reintegrating aspects of analysis while stressing the capacity to play as fundamental to the analytic process.

Weinshel (1988) refers to the role of imagination both as fantasy and as a mode of problem-solving and planning ahead. His elaboration of the necessity of imagination for both analyst and analysand, crucial to analytic progress, drew attention to Rosen. Rosen (1960) observed how the impairment of imagination presented resistance to the analytic process. This might appear as an incapacity for controlled delusion or make-believe, with difficulties in coping with perceptual ambiguity—and one might add with other forms of ambiguity. Fantasy might be excessive or impoverished, and there might be impairment of the observing ego; the capacity for playful, imaginative participation; or any variation of the disturbances of fantasy or reality.

Before proceeding to some later contributions to the playful character of psychoanalytic work, it is pertinent here to note the fantasy character of the psychoanalytic situation. Loewald (1975) remarked on this dimension of analytic work:

> This fantasy character is apparent to the patient and between his own inner experience of the moment and the over-all context of his life in which the analysis takes place. These two distinctions are intimately related, but I shall concentrate now on the latter. There are again parallels between the analytic situation and the situation of the various participants (including the spectator) in the performance of a play. The deeper the spectator gets absorbed in the action of the play, for instance, the more does he lose his over-all perspective on himself as a person who has gone to the theater for a certain purpose and in a certain frame of mind or mood. The actors become even more identified with the play's action and personages. So do the author and the director during certain phases of their work [p. 361].

This notion of psychoanalysis indicates the closeness of the science and art of analysis as well as the difference between the scientific claims of psychoanalysis and the art of clinical analysis. Analysis requires the capacity for illusion and fantasy, the capacity to distinguish between fantasy and reality, and neither being addicted to nor overwhelmed by fantasy. Analysis attempts to differentiate between subjectivity and objectivity while recognizing that absolute truth, total objectivity, and the analytic method can never be entirely free of subjectivity. The playful, creative imagination enriches both science and art (Greenacre, 1959), although there are many remaining crucial differences between science and art in method, goals, and values. Freud (1914, p. 154) refers to the transference neurosis as an artificial illness, a transition between illness and real life. He also refers to the analytic process, in which the compulsion to repeat is admitted "into the transference as a playground in which it is allowed to expand in almost complete freedom." Thus the transitional zone of transference is linked to play. Winnicott (1971) refers to the patient and analyst as playing together, although neither Freud nor Winnicott overlooked, of course, the serious analytic work in dealing with the conflicts and resistances encountered in clinical analysis. Some patients are more playful than others, and this may promote or impede analytic work.

In the promotion of regression and in the development of the transference relationship, the analytic partners cooperate in the creation of the "as-if" nature of the transference experience so similar to drama and to a play. Loewald (1975) notes that the impact of the transference depends on its Januslike quality, and the patient experiencing it as both a fantasy creation and a reality. Both analytic partners are participant observers, but the patient is the primary author who must be able to recognize his own and the analyst's contribution to the unfolding process. It should be kept in mind that the analyst is never really a playmate, and that the art of fine analytic work consists in being able to identify with and empathize with the patient, understand the patient's fantasies and other communications, and with appropriate tolerance and patience, tact and timing, be able to explain to the patient what is transpiring in his communications. Eventually, the analyst will leave the scene of analysis in his interpretations and indicate to the patient the source of his conflicts and fantasies in his life outside analysis, particularly in his pre-adult life and unconscious infantile (intrapsychic) conflicts and traumas. Neither the analyst nor the patient actually role-plays, nor does the analyst attempt artificially to direct or construct the patient's fantasy life. There are irreducible elements of subjectivity and suggestion, but the analyst attempts primarily to convey impartial clarification, understanding, and insight into the patient's unconscious mental life. This requires joint work on the part of the analyst and the patient, with a willingness to listen and learn, to engage in controlled regression, as well as to oscillate from and to a more detached point of observation and contemplation.

As the patient associates and communicates verbally and nonverbally, the communications are processed by the analyst with as little subjective distortion as possible. Furthermore, the analyst attends to the influence of his own communications and tries to be aware of the impingement of his own conflicts and resistances. The analyst makes use of the emotions activated in him by the patient and as in the theatre, the roles the patient wishes to assign to him (Sandler, 1976) and the fantasies stimulated within and related to that particular analytic situation.

The working analyst has his own fantasy play and play with fantasy. If the countertransference is used constructively and creatively and does not lead to miscommunications and misunderstandings; it may be a valuable source of information about the entire analytic situation. At the same time, analytic work is not free play, and the patient cannot be analyzed by the analyst's self-analysis and narcissistic disregard of the patient's unique individuality. The analyst is able to listen to the patient with the "third ear," with a capacity for attunement, emotional resonance, and with a regard for omissions, distortions, and inconsistencies in the patient's reports. Here analytic work, however playful, departs from serious play to scientific reflection. The patient not only gives a history and factual data about his life beyond any dramatization, but also reports observations, memories, characterological attitudes and dispositions, thoughts and feelings about the responses and behavior of his love objects. The construction of the analytic autobiography and the elaboration of the patient's familial and childhood object world is a slow process, requiring the analytic work as well as the playful imagination of both participants, both observers, and sometimes both interpreters. What is presented and sometimes dramatized in the transference in nonverbal enactments as well as verbal associations is never a mere repetition of the past. It is the past that is transformed and edited.

The patient may represent a parent with whom he is identified, and the analyst may be assigned the role of patient in the patient's fantasy. Where the patient was passive in a childhood traumatic experience, the patient may fantasize or dream of driving a vehicle with the analyst in the back seat. The patient may actually have been traumatized and hospitalized in a childhood automobile accident, and separated from his parents. Tragedy may be dramatized and reexperienced in a setting of safety. The transference is the new edition, influenced but not created under the present life and life circumstances and in the particular analytic situation. The "interplay" between patient and analyst may represent a series of transference-countertransference reactions. The transference will display accretions, phase overlap, and developmental transformations from infancy through adolescence and within the analytic process. The transference, therefore, has to be reconstructed and is a prime source and target of reconstruction. Reconstruction is childhood revisited and recreated, the infantile and childhood past uncovered, discovered, and constructed anew (Blum, 1994). The analyst has to be able to work at and play with alternative hypotheses in the process of reconstruction as part of analytic work. The past will appear differently in different phases of analysis, under different transference conditions, and after new material has come to light which alters personal and familial myths. Reconstructive work will involve integration of the past and present, modified in the analytic process.

In all this, there is a child at play in the patient, the patient and analyst as adults observing the patient as a child, and what is childish in the patient, and the constant correction of fantasied distortions because of defense and wish fulfillment. Analysis is, therefore, serious play and playful work; it is serious work with elements of highly organized play. This is not to minimize the shameful, painful, embarrassing, and sometimes mortifying experiences in the course of analysis. The patient's pain and suffering are not the same as in real life because of the analyst's availability, tolerance, and helpfulness, and the supporting and understanding aspects of the analytic situation. Traumas are reexperienced in fantasy and illusion, and the patient's worst fears and expectations do not materialize. Furthermore, the patient's regressive reactions, defenses, identification with the aggressor and victim, are being clarified and analyzed so that panic and tendencies toward flight or fight can be reintegrated in the personality and brought under ever greater ego regulation. In this process, the pathogenic past and the unconscious conflicts and fantasies underlying symptom and character disturbance are brought into the arena of analytic work.

It is of interest here that what was formerly avoided by the patient, over time, may be approached by the patient with less resistance and greater willingness to participate in the immediacy of the transference experience and to observe his or her own irrational reactions. Patients who could not entertain fantasies of incest or murder, infantile spite or bisexual illusion, may gradually entertain and tolerate previously repressed fantasies. The patient may begin to play with frightening fantasies that previously promised only danger and punishment. What was perilous may become playful and patients may, in the long run, be amused by childish fantasies that previously had a terrifying character. To be able to play with such fantasies as, for example, eliminating a sibling, having sexual relations with a parent, or reducing others to fecal objects that can be magically flushed down the toilet, may be explored in the fantasy play. Analytic work is then organically related to play as exploration and play in the service of mastery. These intervening dimensions of analysis may be critical to the analytic resolution of a work inhibition or compulsion, or avoidance of play or addictive play.

This aspect of analysis is also related to what has been called "working through." Working through may be defined as the application of psychoanalytic insight to derivatives of conflict and trauma as they appear in analysis and in the patient's life situation. Patients will gradually acquire the ability to interpret the thoughts and feelings, attitudes, and actions of themselves and others with connections and coherence that was not possible before analysis. The patient's capacity for self-scrutiny, self-searching, and some self-analytic understanding will usually have grown *parri passu* with the progressive depth of analytic work, the serious play with fantasy, and the continuous interplay of fantasy and reality. The transference experience is real, but not realistic; the transference is differentiated from reality only with the help of interpretation, because the transference is unconscious and is initially experienced by the patient as if it were realistically determined. In both the daydream and play there is some conscious awareness of reality, similar to the "as-if" quality of analytic transference.

Much was learned from pioneer studies of daydreams and children's play. Play on words, play associations, verbal bridges, infantile sexual theories, and infantile scenes reappeared in the disguised visual imagery and associations to the dream. Freud studied his own oscillating considerations of fantasy and reality as well as infantile and adult modes of thought and action. The discovery of the primary process, its unique characteristics, and its differentiation from secondary-process thinking was closely associated with the interpretation of dreams, parapraxes, neologisms, and some of the mechanisms of wit. The dream could be compared to a rebus, and visual imagery could be understood again as a pictorial language. The creative imagination, playing with words and images, working and playing with concepts while discarding erroneous or irrelevant ideas, were all involved in the development of psychoanalysis. Freud was able to link the interpretation of dreams and daydreams to the understanding of drama, exemplified in his analysis of the quintessential play by Sophocles, *Oedipus Rex*. Psychoanalysis unified the play enactment of children's fantasy, adult fantasy as a substitute for play, and the myths and legends of nations. Analytic work illuminated, interpreted, and transformed the fantasy play of children, the central technical dimension of child analysis.

For Freud, the dream work and work with dreams were particularly instructive. I shall cite a relevant dream in which work is manifest, to be followed by a clinical vignette. I refer to the "Riding on a Horse" dream of Freud (1900):

> *I was riding on a grey horse, timidly and awkwardly to begin with, as though I were only reclining upon it. I met one of my colleagues, P., who was sitting high on a horse, dressed in a tweed suit, and who drew my attention to something (probably to my bad seat). I now began to find myself sitting more and more firmly and comfortably on my highly intelligent horse, and noticed that I was feeling quite at home up there.*

My saddle was a kind of bolster, which completely filled the space between its neck and crupper. In this way I rode straight in between two vans. After riding some distance up the street, I turned round and tried to dismount, first in front of a small open chapel that stood in the street frontage. Then I actually did dismount in front of another chapel that stood near it. My hotel was in the same street; I might have let the horse go to it on its own, but I preferred to lead it there. It was as though I should have felt ashamed to arrive at it on horseback. A hotel 'boots' was standing in front of the hotel; he showed me a note of mine that had been found, and laughed at me over it. In the note was written, doubly underlined: 'No food' and then another remark (indistinct) *such as 'No work,' together with a vague idea that I was in a strange town in which I was doing no work* [pp. 229–230].

From this complex dream and associations, I have selected the issue of work. The explicit reference to work occurs at the end of the dream in the manifest content of ''no food . . . no work.'' I will not attempt an extensive review and interpretation of the dream, but rather will deal only with those elements specifically involved with Freud's serious psychoanalytic work, his horseplay, and the playful work and play with words and ideas that proceed from the dream imagery to the associations. Freud was suffering from a boil on the scrotum following an attack of influenza in October 1898. It was actually hard for Freud to work, and he had lost his appetite as well as any inclination to exercise, such as riding horseback. The dream was used to demonstrate the somatic sources of dreams and may have indicated the wish to preserve sleep, denying the infection, pain, and anxiety. Although he ascribed the infection to possibly having eaten spicy food, there is manifest reference to his earlier and continuing social and economic insecurity. He might be deprived of both work and food. References do not include his own concerns about being in debt; nor does Freud reveal the hidden identification with his father who was so often out of work and seemed to be waiting for a turn of fortune. The Freud family had to be supported by subsidies from relatives. P. would like to ride the high horse over Freud, a condition of belittled inferiority which Freud reverses by being high in the saddle on his own highly intelligent horse. Freud had cited the Jewish wit, ''Itzik,'' in describing his writing as following the dictates of the unconscious, ''Itzik, where are you going? Do I know? Ask the horse!'' (Letter to Fliess, July 7, 1898; in Masson, 1985, p. 319).

Regression in the service of the ego and analysis appears in the dream, the associations, and the humor. The horse is not only the id, but is Freud's playful infantile self. His rational adult personality is firmly in the saddle, holding the reigns. The oedipal-sexual interpretation of the mounting and riding and dismounting, returning to the chapel in the strange town, may be readily inferred from the dream imagery and symbolism. In the association, the horse is a female patient whom P. had taken over. Freud had performed remarkable feats with her, but she had taken him where she felt inclined. The analytic work, like the dream imagery, has alternated between activity and passivity. Oedipal ambition and narcissistic wishes are also clear, and the threat of castration implicit in the very source of pain, in the scrotum. Freud's interpretation leads to his travels in Italy and references to Italy in the dreams of a woman patient, *Gen-Italien* (to Italy—genitals). The sexual dream thoughts were acknowledged but not further elaborated. Freud's vacation travels away from work seem to have taken him to fantasies of sexual play. The horse play is typical of infantile masturbation, and it is not surprising that an interpretive path leads from the wishful situation of riding a horse to preoedipal scenes of playing with his one-year-old nephew.

Freud (1900) states, "But I knew I could not go on long with my peculiarly difficult work unless I was in completely sound physical health" (p. 231). He reassures himself in the dream that he is firmly in the saddle at work, on vacation (at play), and in sexual activity. The shame at arriving at his hotel on horseback suggests the shame associated with infantile masturbation and forbidden oedipal fantasy. Playing with one's self and with another reader-rider may be unconsciously identified with playing with concepts.

What is also of importance here is the shame associated with first going to the small chapel. Being Jewish hindered Freud's professional advancement. He does not wish to feel inferior, servile, and is ashamed of a lowly position like the hotel "boots." It was also humiliating to be faced with a lack of work and money. Freud was certainly aware of the plight of the unemployed and the hungry. Work is associated with social position and economic power; it is a major determinant of social status and real achievement. Furthermore, riding high or feeling ashamed and humiliated confirmed the important connection of work with self-esteem. The ability to work and play is also here interrelated since work is associated with social and cultural recognition and reward. Highly paid work also permits more refined forms of recreation and play. The opportunity for vacation travel, for example, may depend on career advancement; the struggle for survival may not allow much room for play or the playful work of hobbies and pastimes. One should be able to enjoy the fruits of one's labor and hard-earned attainments. Freud will surpass Fliess and his father with his bold strides.

The relation among health, age, and vigor on the one side, and the capacity to work and to play may be quite complex. Remarkably, Freud was able to carry on analytic work for fifteen years after the development of his oral cancer. Despite multiple operations and procedures, severe pain, and some impairment of speech and hearing, his powers of sublimation were untouched and he made continuing fertile contributions to psychoanalysis. Sublimated forms of play and playful work were not visibly altered, nor were the signs of change in his enjoyment of wit and humor. However, vacations that required physical effort and extended travel were curtailed. Freud no longer attended international congresses and symposia. Freud's creative work continued in clinical analysis and analytic publications. The processes of inspiration, preparation, management, and regulation are all part of creative work, but none of the components of the work accounts for innovation. The clash and compromise between conservation of the old and introduction of the new made for some involved shifts between work and play in the intermediate areas of playful work and serious play. This is analogous to the flexible interweaving of primary- and secondary-process modes of thought in work and play, regression and reorganization, activity and passivity.

Complex relationships between work and play may be clinically observed in the following vignette: The patient, a male college student, was unable to apply himself to goal-directed work, especially homework. He felt unable to concentrate in class, found himself daydreaming about movies and books, and did not complete his assignments. He thought of taking a job and switching to a part-time study program, but felt that he could not work with any more stability than he could study. The situation deteriorated in a circular process; he was poorly prepared for exams, received low or failing grades, which left him further disinclined to attend class and attend to his studies. He then began to "truant," cut class, and virtually gave up his former pleasure in reading both fiction and nonfiction. At the time he started treatment, he had turned ever more away from work to pastimes and play. He would spend consecutive nights going to movies, and when not watching movies or television, would be glad to partake of board games with his fellow students. In fleeing the reality of his studies, the patient was reminiscent of Freud's (1900, p. 233) sleepy student who lazily stayed in bed, dreaming he was in bed at the hospital.

He was utterly bewildered by his behavior. He felt powerless to stop it and, although he wanted to succeed in college, he found himself drifting toward failure. Placed on probation and in danger of being dismissed from the college, he seemed only mildly anxious. He was able to defend against an inner sense of panic, manifesting a good deal of denial and avoidance, and frenzied efforts at escape. Superficially, he seemed addicted to recreation. There was actually a rather compulsive, frenetic quality to his immersion in movies and television. Feeble attempts to return to his books and his class assignments were unsuccessful and soon gave way to escapist activity. He tried to console himself that many of the films that he saw were of artistic calibre, that he was, therefore, receiving an education outside the classroom. Initially he had no idea of different types of treatment, but he wondered if psychoanalytic insight would not provide a form of education. He wanted to learn about himself and his problem and seemed sincerely to claim that he wanted to understand himself. Confused and perplexed, he became visibly anxious when confronted with the pattern of his avoidance of schoolwork and his escapist activity. He had been an excellent student throughout his school experience from first grade to the first half of college.

His initial therapeutic alliance was in the form of a learning alliance, as if he were in school with a private tutor. His claim that he was ready for analytic work would prove to be correct, despite his resistance to reflection and tendencies toward escapist enactment. He did not miss sessions, but could be variably late. Struggles over the timing, schedule, sequence, and payment for sessions proved to be related to his obsessions and ritual counting of minutes and intervals. He was intrigued by various forms of periodicity, both astronomical and biological, for example, the moon and tides, the menstrual cycle, and the gestation periods of different species. He enlarged on the initial depiction of his closeness to his parents who were in biomedical professions. His mother was once a midwife. The patient had read freely and extensively in medical books on obstetrics and gynecology. His mother brought her obstetrical and biomedical experience home in the rearing of her child. She was strict about labor to be done about the house; all had to be accomplished on time, according to completion or delivery schedule. There was strict attention to bodily change and functions, and his mother was particularly intolerant of the patient's boyhood tendency to constipation. Giving enemas as part once of routine obstetrics and presurgical care was repeated at home with her son as part of routine treatment of his constipation. Since the enema induced a powerful urge to defecate, his mother instructed him to count in order to retain the enema. These "anal rapes" were a phase-specific traumatic disruption of latency, a time when industry and work skills develop.

Further investigation of his fantasies and symptoms led to the discovery of the patient's counting during sexual activity. When masturbating or having intercourse, he would count in order to prolong the activity prior to orgasm. Before treatment he had never connected his tendency toward premature ejaculation and his compulsive counting with his childhood enema experience. Behind his feminine identification and passive homosexual submission to this phallic, intrusive mother/father, the patient was gradually able to become aware of his underlying anxiety and anger. Frightened of castration and narcissistic humiliation, he had developed a masochistic façade of "grin and bear it," and an appearance of calm and "everything under control."

Overstimulated and underprotected by his parents, he was frightened of both the homosexual transference and oedipal rivalry. He had fantasies of dangerous doctors and nurses who were intrusive, seductive, and coercive. Hearing some noises in the building, he localized the sounds to the air-conditioning ducts in the office. Something foreign and frightening might come through the ducts and invade the office. This led to associations to the medical texts in which he had seen anatomical diagrams and plates of the female reproductive tract. The ducts were associated primarily with the fallopian tubes, but also with the birth canal. Males had ducts in which sperm was transported. He recalled the textbook pictures of childbirth he had seen, of the baby's passage through the birth canal during vaginal delivery. He could then discuss his forbidden excitement and adolescent masturbation with the medical drawings and photographs. For him, the movies had the unconscious meaning of forbidden play, looking at photographs and movies of the reproductive and birth processes.

In this period, the patient then made a crucial connection from his childhood back to his adult disturbance. The onset of his disturbance had occurred when he was taking a course in comparative anatomy. The patient had just begun to study the comparative anatomy of the genitourinary system. He had also begun to read about the physiology of human reproduction. It was then that he ceased doing "homework" and work assignments. What had seemed to be an unknown, insidious onset of his inability to study and to work steadily toward the fulfillment of his scholarly aspirations was actually a set of rationalizations and avoidance that disguised his flight from comparative anatomy. He was fleeing from the revival of the conflicts and fantasies that aroused so much anxiety and guilt. These persisting oedipal and narcissistic conflicts were also activated by the many temptations of college life and particularly by the patient's romantic interest in a girl. He wanted to marry her but was afraid of marriage and "reproduction." His unconscious anticipation of fatherhood and identification with motherhood and with the infant all contributed to and reinforced his defensive regression.

The patient made rapid progress and regained his capacity for work and schoolwork, with concentrated diligent application. He gave up the escape, attended class regularly, and regained a sense of stability and self-confidence while becoming more aware of the power of unconscious fantasy and childish defensive reactions. He was able to complete college with "flying colors," to pursue his graduate studies and work interests, and to establish an apparently successful marriage relationship. In the process of regaining the capacity for work, he also regained a capacity for imaginative play, and a lively sense of humor emerged. He was now able to love, to work, and to play, the major attainments traditionally linked to the successful outcome of analytic work. The renewed capacity to work and play emerged clinically prior to termination. His therapeutic progress potentiated his falling in love and remaining in love, though ambivalent. He and his girl friend could work and play together and apart. Work represented his love object and his potent self, their shared ideals. He also worked for her and his own goals and satisfactions. It was my impression that his capacity for persistent, hard mental work was supported by his alternate playful work, by his enjoyment of work and achievement, by his improved self-esteem, and his working alliance with his analyst, and with his mate and playmate.

REFERENCES

Blum, H. P. (1994), *Reconstruction in Psychoanalysis: Childhood Revisited and Recreated.* New York: International Universities Press.

Erikson, E. H. (1966), Ontogeny of ritualization. In: *Psychoanalysis: A General Psychology*, ed. R. M. Loewenstein et al. New York: International Universities Press, pp. 601–621.

Freud, A. (1963), The concept of developmental lines. *The Psychoanalytic Study of the Child*, 18:245–265. New York: International Universities Press.

Freud, S. (1900), The Interpretation of Dreams. *Standard Edition*, 4 & 5. London: Hogarth Press, 1953.

——— (1908), Creative writers and day-dreaming. *Standard Edition*, 9:141–153. London: Hogarth Press, 1959.

——— (1914), Remembering, repeating, and working through. *Standard Edition*, 12:145–156. London: Hogarth Press, 1958.

——— (1916-1917), Introductory Lectures on Psycho-Analysis. *Standard Edition*, 15 & 16. London: Hogarth Press, 1963.

——— (1919), A child is being beaten. *Standard Edition*, 17:175–204. London: Hogarth Press, 1955.

——— (1920), Beyond the pleasure principle. *Standard Edition*, 18. London: Hogarth Press, 1955.

——— (1930), Civilization and its discontents. *Standard Edition*, 21:59–145. London: Hogarth Press, 1961.

——— (1939), An outline of psychoanalysis. *Standard Edition*, 23:141–207. London: Hogarth Press, 1964.

Greenacre, P. (1959), Play in relation to creative imagination. *The Psychoanalytic Study of the Child*, 14:61–80. New York: International Universities Press.

Greenson, R. R. (1965), The working alliance and the transference neurosis. *Psychoanal. Q.*, 34:155–181.

Hartmann, H. (1939), Psychoanalysis and the concept of health. *Internat. J. Psycho-Anal.*, 20:308–321.

Holmes, D. (1965), A contribution to a psychoanalytic theory of work. *The Psychoanalytic Study of the Child*, 20:384–393. New York: International Universities Press.

Loewald, H. (1975), Psychoanalysis as an art and the fantasy character of the psychoanalytic situation. *J. Amer. Psychoanal. Assn.*, 23:277–299.

Masson, J. M., Ed. (1985), *The Complete Letters of Sigmund Freud to Wilhelm Fliess 1887–1904*. Cambridge, MA: Harvard University Press.

Peller, L. (1954), Libidinal phases, ego development, and play. *The Psychoanalytic Study of the Child*, 9:178–198. New York: International Universities Press.

Rosen, V. H. (1960), Some aspects of the role of imagination in the analytic process. *J. Amer. Psychoanal. Assn.*, 8:229–251.

Sandler, J. (1976), Countertransference and role-responsiveness. *Internat. Rev. Psychoanal.*, 3:43–48.

Waelder, R. (1932), The psychoanalytic theory of play. In: *Psychoanalysis: Observation, Theory, Application*, ed. S. A. Guttman. New York: International Universities Press, 1976.

Weinshel, E. (1988), Play and playing in adults and in adult psychoanalysis. *Bull. A. Freud Centre*, 11:108–127.

Winnicott, D. W. (1971), *Playing and Reality*. New York: Basic Books.

Zetzel, E. (1956), Current concepts of transference. *Internat. J. Psycho-Anal.*, 37:369–376.

THE SELF AND THE PRINCIPLE OF WORK

W. W. MEISSNER, S.J., M.D.

An old cook, who has spent half a century preparing meals in someone else's kitchen, commented to me once that "Work is a wicked word!" No scripture scholar he, but the authors of the book of Genesis would have agreed with him—in the expulsion from the garden of Eden, Yahweh said to Adam, "Because you have listened to the voice of your wife, and have eaten of the tree of which I commanded you, 'You shall not eat of it,' cursed is the ground because of you; in toil you shall eat of it all the days of your life; thorns and thistles it shall bring forth to you; and you shall eat the plants of the field. In the sweat of your face you shall eat bread till you return to the ground, for out of it you were taken; you are dust and to dust you shall return" (Gen. 3:17–19). The forbidden tree was the tree of the knowledge of good and evil, and work was the primal punishment for violating God's command. Even then, work was a wicked word!

What has happened in the course of the intervening millennia to make this primal curse a staple of man's existence and a primary necessity both socioeconomically and psychologically? We are accustomed in our contemporary culture to regard work as a necessity for both economic survival and psychic well-being. We tend to make work and productivity a measure of psychic health—as analysts we never seem to stray very far from Freud's criteria of *lieben und arbeiten*. Society tends to cast a jaundiced eye on anyone who does not earn his keep—whether in the form of the wealthy playboy or social gadfly, who seems to do little else than seek self-gratification and self-amusement, or in the form of a welfare recipient, who spends too much time accepting government checks and too little time seeking gainful employment. As analysts, we can wonder first of all about the sources

35

of this social and cultural mandate, and second, about the role of the
work principle, as I would call it, in the intrapsychic economy.

I shall stake out an immediate objection that may serve as an
archimedean point on which the rest of my argument rests. The usual
claim in psychoanalytic parlance for the role of work focuses on the
maintenance of self-esteem. I regard this, as a context for consideration
of the meaning of work, as partial and fragmentary. Connection with
self-esteem ties the work principle into issues of narcissism, whether
in terms of satisfaction of a work-oriented ego ideal or as contributing
to the stability of narcissistic equilibrium and self-enhancement. The
classic portrait of the hard-working and dedicated corporate employee
of fifty years, who retires and then retreats into isolation and depression, is typically cast in narcissistic terms—retirement involves loss of
something that has served to sustain narcissistic investments in the
course of a lifetime of productive work, and the resulting disequilib-
rium has devastating effects on the individual's self-esteem. No longer
is he sustained by the work commitments, the personal involvements
and gratifications that provided the functional matrix of his life and
gave it meaning and purpose.

All this, I would argue, is fair enough as far as it goes, but it is
only a partial picture. The focus on self-esteem is not wrong, but it
leaves aside the place of work in the organization and functioning
of the person's self as defined in structural and supraordinate terms
(Meissner, 1986a). In other words, the meaning of the work principle
in human affairs can be more broadly and meaningfully conceived
than simply as a function of narcissistic dynamics. One reason for the
failure to address work issues in a broader context may be the uncertainty and ambiguity of our theories about the self. I shall try to address
the problem in terms of a concept of the self as a supraordinate, structural, and hierarchically organized system (Meissner, 1986a, 1993).
But first some comments on the work principle.

THE WORK PRINCIPLE

Work is an essential element in the economy of human psychological
functioning. It is important to be clear about what work is not—it is
not holding down a job, having a career, or making money. Work may
be involved with all of these, but it is not synonymous with any. I
would rather define the work principle as a psychological component
in terms of effort directed toward achievement of a goal that serves
some purpose or has a measure of utility within some personally meaningful frame of reference. Work in this sense has nothing to do with
recognition or reward—the unknown artist working in his garret or the
writer in the obscurity of his library are both hard at work without any

acknowledgment or reward. If the gods smile on them, recognition and rewards may come their way, but not necessarily and not in the moment of work. By the same token, holding down a job or pursuing a career will not meet with much success without work, but many a job is held with little more than token work of lesser meaning, and many a career is followed with minimal or modest work effort. And conversely, many a hard worker receives little thanks and appreciation for his efforts.

Analytic efforts to define a principle of work—presumably following the inspiration of Freud's *arbeiten*—have met with middling success. Most of these have arisen out of the ego psychology matrix and have focused on the role of the ego in purposeful achievement and mastery. Hendrik (1942, 1943a, 1943b) tried to suggest an "instinct to master, . . . an inborn drive to do and to learn how to do" (1942, p. 40). He viewed the ego as integrated developmentally out of early functions of learning to suck, walk, manipulate objects, speak, understand, and reason—all functions related to mastery of the environment. The instinctual emphasis was modified by White (1963) who spoke of "competence" and "effectance" as forms of independent ego energies undergirding the ego's capacities for effective action and accomplishment and viewed in terms of incentive motivation rather than drive reduction. Effectance connoted learning, mastery or accomplishment through action—quite similar to Piaget's notion of sensorimotor intelligence. Playful exploration, curiosity, and manipulation of the environment are pleasurable in themselves, not because of some connection to drive reduction. Competence was meant to describe an individual's capacity to interact effectively with his environment; correspondingly, the sense of competence expressed the subjective experience of actual competence. We could also count Erikson's (1959, 1963) descriptions of the developmental crises of autonomy, initiative, and industry as direct contributions to the formation and growth of the work principle. Frustration of these developmental initiatives lays the groundwork for depression (Markson, 1993).

I would propose that the work principle is neither an instinctual drive nor a form of ego energy, but a more complex expression of matters pertaining to efficacy and agency in the psychic economy. I take the view here that, on a microanalytic level, every psychic function has an inherent potential for activation and effective operation. If the term "psychic energy" has any meaning, it simply refers to that potential for activation and by implication to the capacity for accomplishing goal-oriented work (Meissner, 1995b). Raising our sights to a macroanalytic level, the same principle finds application in the inherent capacity for the integration of functions—psychic and organismic—to undertake specific tasks and direct effort to the accomplishment of specific goals. The capacity for work and the related motivation for goal direction and achievement are basic to the work principle.

While the work principle is not itself a direct expression of instinctual drives, it is related to and makes use of elements of wish and desire from the libidinal side and effort, striving, and mastery from the aggressive side. Rather than instinctual drives, as we are normally accustomed to think of them, I would prefer to describe the motivational sources of wishful desire and purposeful striving as drive capacities that the organism calls into operation when stimulus conditions, meaningful contexts, and purposeful initiatives require their activation. In the work context, wishes and desires come into play in setting goals and providing the context of valuation associated with a given project.

Aggression comes into play in overcoming obstacles—internal or external—standing in the way of goal accomplishment and achievement of objectives (Buie et al., 1983; Rizzuto et al., 1993). The aggressive component becomes active when the ordinary functional capacity of a particular function or combination of functions is exceeded by reason of an imposed obstacle to attaining a given objective—an extra push or effort is then required for the function(s) to operate effectively and achieve their objective. Aggression thus serves the work principle by reinforcing the work dynamic in the face of interfering factors—for example, in the extra effort required to lift a heavy weight, in the extra concentration required to accomplish a given task in the face of distractions or interruptions, in the resolve to continue the task to the end when other pressures (including conflictual or defensive) or demands or needs arise, in the determination to find a way to gain one's goal despite limited resources or opposition from others, and so on. In this sense, then, work is a major channel for the expression of aggression in a way that allows for constructive and positive input to personality organization and functioning. Along with work, the second major outlet for aggression, especially in the form of competition, rivalry, overcoming opposition, striving, and achieving mastery, is sports.

In effect, the work principle in these terms is not only a subspecies of the principle of agency (Meissner, 1993), but it broadens the consideration of such effective self-actualization to include not only intrapsychic phenomena, but the interaction between the individual subject and his external environment, both physical and social. On this macroanalytic level, then, the work principle is a function of the self and its imbrication with the surrounding environment, rather than predicated on an isolated intrapsychic agency—the ego.[1] The work of the ego has a limited intrapsychic focus, as involved in its complex defensive, executive, and adaptive interactions *vis-à-vis* id and superego. The work of the self, in contrast, is a matter of the effective integration of the respective contributions of all psychic agencies and their direction

---

[1]This construction follows the lines of argument laid down by Hartmann (1947, 1950) with respect to action. See Meissner (1986b, 1993).

to the accomplishment of external goals and purposes. The work of the ego, in this sense, is cast in microanalytic terms within the boundaries of the intrapsychic sphere; the work of the self is cast in macroanalytic terms in the framework of interaction between the self-as-agent and other agents or external objects.[2] Ultimately, it is the self-as-agent, including the tripartite agencies and their conscious and unconscious components, who is the author of work in this sense.

THE MEANING OF WORK

Before we can formulate the role of work in the psychic economy, we need some specification of the meaning of work. The term "work" does not have an univocal meaning, but rather finds analogous application in the specific contexts in which it is predicated. Work can be physical—bodily exertion in performing a task—but not all physical exertion is work. The determination of such exertion as work lies in the nature of the task and its meaning to the agent. Playing tennis is vigorous physical exertion, but for most people it is recreation and not work. But for the tennis pro, it is work because it his way of earning a living. Golf is a major recreational activity for many, but for the golf pro it is his work. The work of a scholar is to sit quietly, to read, think and possibly write—a class of activities the stevedore or bricklayer would hardly tend to regard as work, certainly not hard work. But if you have ever tried it seriously, you know that it is hard work. The work of the painter is to paint, the work of the musician to play music, the work of the intellectual to think, of the mystic to pray. The monk who spends hours quietly at prayer and meditative reflection in his cell is as much at work as when he is pouring out sweat in the field.

In these examples, the meaning of work is not defined by the level of physical exertion, by the financial rewards, by the degree of productivity however measured, or by the purposefulness of the activity. Work is not even defined by the channeling of aggression, since many recreational activities call for considerable use of aggression, but do not thereby qualify as work. If this view has any validity, it puts us immediately into tension with prevailing social and cultural norms regarding the meaning of work. Society imposes certain expectations for taking on responsibilities, for assuming a productive place in society, for earning a living and paying one's way. This is a pressing problem for males in our society for whom definition of themselves as masculine and mature has become a function of work commitment and performance—largely defined in economic terms. The developmental channels for establishing masculine identity are compromised

---

[2]The lines of this analysis are analogous to the distinction between ego autonomy in microanalytic terms (Beres, 1971) and the macroanalytic self-autonomy described by Erikson (1959). See Meissner (1986a, 1992b).

by the societal downgrading of the father's role and diminishing opportunities for young boys to live and work with their fathers (Bly, 1990;
Brickman, 1993). As Abelin (1971) and others (Chasseguet-Smirgel,
1985, 1986; Mahler et al., 1975) have suggested, the father serves an
important developmental function in drawing the child toward reality
as an arena for playful and adaptive mastery and away from the dyadic
symbiotic attachment to the mother in the interest of promoting separation and individuation.

The threats to masculine identity are compounded by the increasing presence in the work world of women, who, to that degree, displace
men from their traditional roles as breadwinners and workers (Betcher
and Pollack, 1993). Any deviation from the established stereotype, or
even wishes to modify the standard, can be fraught with conflict.
Changing sex roles and changing patterns of job involvement in the
corporate world can create stress and problems in self-definition and
identity. It does not strain the imagination to realize that these circumstances contribute to a good deal of conflict and uncertainty of identity
in many working men—whether potentially or actually working. For
some the conflict is resolved by obsessive immersion in work to the
detriment of their personal and social lives. For others the solution lies
in dropping out, giving up, promiscuous sex, drugs, and other escapes.
The failure of ambitions, the inability to live up to ideals and expectations, and the disappointments and disillusionments of wishes denied
and hopes frustrated leave ample room for despair. The fundamental
need to achieve, to find self-expression, to create, to be and feel effective, are channeled into the work situation and can put the individual at
risk of denying himself the satisfactions of home, family, and personal
desires exclusive of those imposed by the demands of work. Striving,
competing, producing, and seeking mastery are fundamental motivating forces of the human personality—and they have become culturally
endorsed and reinforced (Vaillant, 1977; D. Levinson, 1978). The cultural imperative is for a man to be "a who and a what" (H. Levinson, 1976).

If changing cultural patterns have given rise to conflictual patterns
in the male experience of work and its meaning, the same movements
have introduced a parallel ambiguity into the meaning of work for
women. If there is an upside to the contemporary women's movement
in gaining equality of opportunity in the world of work and economic
rewards for women—especially when economic pressures make it necessary for many women to work, even mothers of young children, in
order to maintain a decent standard of living—there is also a downside
in that it has created doubts and devaluation of the more traditional
feminine roles. Again, we run into the pressure of cultural and societal
demands. I would hope that the modern woman would find the work
of wife and mother and of the maintenance of a home and family as

significant and meaningful as any career or job outside the home. It is a tragedy for many women in our own day who feel the pressure to work outside the family when their desires and inclinations lie in the direction of devoting themselves to the welfare and well-being of husband, children, and family. If the women's movement opens opportunities for women in the work force as true options, along with the more traditional options that may be authentically desired and satisfying to many women, it has accomplished a valuable goal. If it creates a situation in which the traditional roles are devalued and disparaged, and women are then regarded as second-class or inferior for following more traditional paths, it will have created a modern tragedy. Here again the issue of what work is and what meaning it possesses are central.

I would like to discuss some of these issues as they present themselves in clinical experience. I shall discuss two cases. The first is a young man with whom I have had a continuing relation extending over more than a decade, and the second a psychiatric patient for whom the issue of work played a prominent and decisive role in his mental stability and ultimate suicide—Vincent van Gogh.

WORK AND THE FALSE SELF

For Arthur, the issues of work and accomplishment have been a lifelong burden and impediment. He was born to a wealthy and powerful family—his father was a highly placed corporate executive in charge of an international conglomerate. Arthur was provided all the advantages of wealth, privilege, and position. He lived in a mansion, attended by servants, was sent to the best schools, provided the best of everything. What was lacking was parental involvement and empathy. His only childhood memories of interaction with his father were episodes when he was called on the library carpet to account for his misdemeanors and failures to perform up to expectation in school. Neither parent spent much time with him or took much interest in him. There was very little in his reconstructed childhood history to suggest that they had the faintest idea of what it was like to be a little boy or any consideration for what he needed as a child. He painted the picture of his childhood as dismal, isolated, with few friends or available playmates, and increasing alienation. He had two younger sisters, but there did not seem to have been much interaction with them or much of an affectionate bond. Their experience in the family seems to have been somewhat different from his—possibly related to the fact that they were girls and did not have to bear the burden of parental expectations in the same fashion.

This mounting burden of parental expectations and disappointments dogged Arthur's footsteps as he matured. Internally the titration of impotent rage grew apace. Although he was quite intelligent and gifted, his school performance was indifferent—colored by his intense feelings of inadequacy and shame—and any suggestion of competence or success was short-circuited by the chronic devaluation and indifference of his parents and his own rebellious, if suppressed and displaced, rage. He was left feeling inferior, inadequate, unable to perform to anyone's satisfaction, and deeply resentful of those who imposed these burdens on him—parents, teachers, counselors, and so on. He was convinced that the only reason he graduated from preparatory school was that his father was a major benefactor of the school and gave the address at his graduation. His college career was equally dismal—failing courses, skipping classes and exams, barely getting by, making no effort to establish any base of competence or learning he could take any pride in. The mounting burden of frustration, bitterness, meaninglessness, and impotent rage finally reached a critical threshold. After college, he tried working for the Red Cross, but under stress of living in a foreign country and in the face of a definitive rejection from his girlfriend, suffered a psychotic episode.

He was brought back home and hospitalized. Hospitalization lasted several weeks, during which he recompensated and was discharged. He spent the next ten years drifting from one place to another, from one menial job to another, a dismal and bleak existence from which he felt there was no escape, no relief. He would spend long hours in his apartment, reading, trying to study, but feeling that it was all pointless, leading nowhere, and completely unsatisfying. He decided to seek help and made his way to my office.

There are many facets of this case well worth exploring, but my focus here is on the work issue. When we began working together, he was over thirty, had little to show for his efforts, had not established himself in any adult way, lived on a fairly generous stipend provided by a trust fund established by his parents, and felt that his life was slipping away without any meaning. Several phobias hampered his activities—especially speaking in a group of people, no matter how small. In efforts to audit occasional classes in the local adult education programs, he would become paralyzed and panic if he had to say anything in class. He would generally speak to no one, isolate himself in a far corner of the room, and devise often clever strategies to avoid having to speak or become involved with fellow students.

Work in the therapy was never a question—with a curious point of initiation. In the beginning, the agenda was clear—he undertook to tell me his life story. Once we had covered that ground, he would come in, say hello, sit down and stare out the window, saying nothing. For a while, I would try to interrupt the silence with questions or casual observations, but these found no response. I learned to wait—even to sit back, let my mind wander, thinking about matters of my own concern having nothing to do with Arthur, even occasionally picking up a book and reading while he continued to sit in silence looking out the window. For quite a few hours, the time would pass in this fashion—we would spend the hour in silence, and when the time was up Arthur would stand up, smile, and say goodbye. Then, one day he suddenly began to talk about his silence. It turned out that he found it comforting and appreciated it greatly. He recalled episodes from his early years when he would be forced to talk, to have opinions, to discuss topics of current interest intelligently, and to argue pros and cons—all of which he hated and resented. Being allowed the freedom to talk or not to talk as he wished was a relief and a liberating experience. The pattern quickly evolved in which he would enter my office, greet me, sit down and spend two or three minutes in silence. During this time I made no effort to question or initiate anything, I would simply sit quietly, not even looking at Arthur, musing about my own thoughts. Then suddenly Arthur would start talking and the flow of material did not stop until the hour ended. He turned out to be a very good patient who worked well and effectively in his therapy.

Work, it turned out, was also a wicked word for Arthur. The fact that he had never held a steady job, that he had never measured up to his parents expectations, that he lived off their support and did not earn his own way, that many of his schoolmates had all gone on to successful lives and careers, was a constant and unremitting obex that made him feel hopeless and defeated. He saw no possibilities for anything meaningful or satisfying in his life. His strong feeling and conviction was that he deserved nothing. The money he spent was not his own; he had done nothing to deserve it, and was riddled with guilt and shame on this account. A constant problem about which he complained repeatedly was that when he met people they would inevitably ask what he did for a living. The question would throw him into a tizzy of shame, confusion, resentment, and embarrassed frustration. He seemed unable to accept any of the obvious options open to him—to think that the answer to the question was nobody's business, that he could justifiably say he was a man of leisure, a student, unemployed, independently wealthy, seemed beyond him.

The problem, as far as I could see, was that Arthur had swallowed whole his parents' values and attitudes about what made a man valuable and a life meaningful, particularly their views regarding the place and meaning of work in a man's life. His functioning self, then, was a form of false self based on his conflictual conformity to his parents' and societal expectations. The false self, as Winnicott (1960) has indicated, is pervaded by a sense of futility and unreality. Modell (1993) added, ''This inability to believe in one's efficacy can pervade the entire personality. People with such feelings are convinced that they can never make things happen'' (p. 53).

The parents' ethic of work was much like the culturally conditioned attitudes I have described above, with a strong salting of the puritan ethic. For them, a man was defined by his work—and his worth was measured by the amount of money he made and by the significance of his contribution to his society. The latter was defined in their minds by the amount of public acclaim he received in the mass media or by the established social institutions in his world. If one did not receive commendations from the president or the governor, if he was not consulted by the Congress, if he were not a respected insider in the corridors of power, if he was not continually accorded the perquisites of power and influence—special hotel suites, banquets, medals, being quoted, saluted, treated as important and special—he did not amount to anything and was not worth paying attention to. These attitudes Arthur had imbibed from his earliest years.

For Arthur this code was an intolerable burden and constant source of failure and impaired self-esteem. Part of the therapeutic problem was how to help him work his way out of this elaborate psychic *cul-de-sac*. My tactic was to challenge the suppositions of this code of values. He would often mouth a principle as though he was enunciating an incontrovertible axiom. I would question and probe. Did he really believe it? What did he think about exceptions to the rule? Did everybody think like that? Where did he get his ideas from? He found the discussions stimulating and seemed to enjoy arguing with me. I had opportunities to observe how curious it was that he would find himself stoutly defending his father's principles, the very principles that had caused him such grief and which he otherwise hated and despised. Such observations would put him back on his heels. The idea that these principles were not written in stone, that one might approach matters from a different perspective, or that other aspects might be important or carry the weight of value seemed to perplex, even confuse, him—but overall I felt that some space was being cleared for Arthur to rethink some of his ideas and perhaps come to his own conclusions.

The issue of autonomy, not unexpectedly, became a major focus of our work. What risks might he run were he to distance himself from his parents' views and begin to form his own? My argument ran roughly as follows: he was financially secure, and therefore was freed from the necessity of and concern about making a living and supporting himself. This in itself was liberating. He had open options as to what he chose to do with his life. In making such choices, he had to decide on what basis he would make his decisions—was it to be the principles laid down by his calvinistic parents and the puritanical and capitalistic ideology they espoused? Or was it to be what made sense to him and offered the basis for a meaningful life on his terms?

The program was moderately successful. The issue was whether Arthur could abandon his false-self organization, rooted in his conformity to parental demands and expectations, and allow space for the emergence of his more authentic and true self. A basic question focused on whether the measure of success was monetary or in terms of productivity, whether it was better to look for what was fulfilling and gratifying to oneself and put the rewards and estimations of others in second place. This would mean that it was more important to do what one felt was interesting and satisfying rather than what was profitable or productive. Arthur understood what was at issue and gradually began to test the waters. He developed a capacity to make up his own mind about small matters—e.g., to buy a shirt he liked despite the salesman's pressure to buy a more expensive one.

Useful points along the way included his decision to invest his money and put it to work for him. I had pointed out that his simply accepting and spending the trust funds did not allow him to establish himself independently. Investing the money would be a way of declaring his ownership and building a base of financial independence. Another choice point was his decision to return to college and shore up his education. After several semesters auditing courses at the undergraduate level, he decided to undertake a graduate program for degree credit in a field of his interest—one, incidentally, that his father would scoff at and despise. His investment of himself in this effort was admirable and his hard work and concentration won him excellent marks and continuing encouragement and support from his teachers. The therapeutic effort was directed to gradually establishing and broadening these beachheads of autonomy and self-determination. Arthur has not finished his effort at self-conquest, but he is well on the way. He is still seeking work that he can value and will give him a sense of fulfillment, that will be *his* work.

L'Artiste Inconnu

My second case comes from the pages of art history. Vincent van Gogh's life bears many resemblances to Arthur's. However, Van Gogh found work to which he could devote himself without reservation and, after his death, that work achieved the status of great art.

The Art Dealer

Vincent van Gogh's towering artistic accomplishment is astonishing—especially when we realize that it was all done within a ten-year span. But Vincent's work experience otherwise was, to say the least, far from impressive. His early life experience was not that different from Arthur's—factors included his birth as a replacement child, his growing up with a depressed, unavailable and unempathic mother (Meissner, 1992a), a childhood dogged by isolation, alienation, eccentric behaviors, and uncertain school performance. He was in short a troubled and difficult child—sensitive, resentful, withdrawn, isolated, and peculiar. He dropped out of the school at fifteen without graduating, and in the following summer took a position as an apprentice clerk in the Hague branch of the Goupil art firm managed by his uncle Cent, then, in due course, was transferred to the branch of Goupil in Paris. He seems to have hit it off with Tersteeg, the manager, who was only eight years his senior, and he was soon on friendly terms with Tersteeg's family. He was enthusiastic about his work and, after four years of apprenticeship, was assigned to the London branch in May 1873. The post meant advancement and offered the prospect of an exciting adventure. Tersteeg gave him a strong recommendation and even wrote his parents that he was well liked and would be sorely missed.

But Vincent was apprehensive. He felt the pain of separation from the place he had known for nearly four years and the friends he had made there, especially Tersteeg and the painter Mauve. This assignment must have seemed like an exile or banishment. The Hague was not far from home; London was a different matter—a foreign country with a different language, and no family or friends to be with. By that June he was living in a rooming house and had begun to settle into his work. His letters to his brother Theo reflect his ambivalence, his efforts to cope with his new circumstances and put a good face on things. His circumstances were comfortable and fairly pleasant, but there was an underlying tone of loneliness and nostalgia that surfaced repeatedly. In August he moved his lodgings to the rooming house of Mrs. Loyer, where he remained for the rest of his stay in London. His prospects during this period seemed bright, and his parents were pleased by his progress and apparent good spirits—the letters home were filled with good news and good cheer (Hulsker, 1990).

An unfortunate libidinal misadventure at this juncture seemed to trip him up. He became infatuated with the landlady's daughter, Eugenia Loyer, who toyed with him and amused herself with his awkwardness and embarrassed affection, while she was already engaged to another. The disappointment was a crushing blow for Vincent. He had a strong need to see the world, not as it was, but as he wished it to be. Time and again, when he exposed his wishes to reality, they were disappointed and trampled. He assumed naïvely that Eugenia would reciprocate his love as soon as he confessed it. Her spurning his offer of love was a terrible narcissistic blow from which he could scarcely recover. His bright hopes and ambitions were in shambles.

He could only react with isolation, withdrawal from all human contact, and severe depression.

He was home for a brief visit that June and July. His parents were appalled at his appearance, so emaciated, gloomy, and discouraged he seemed. During this time with his family he remained disconsolate and withdrawn. He returned to London and the Loyers in July, this time with his sister Anna who was looking for a position in England as a French teacher. The situation in the rooming house must have been awkward, and within a month he moved to a flat in New Kensington Road where he lived alone. His family worried about his isolation and seclusion. His letters were sparse and his spirits low. More and more he turned to religion to find relief from his depression, and consolation. He read Eliot's tale of unrequited love and hopeless fidelity, *Adam Bede,* identifying with the forlorn hero. More and more the Bible absorbed his interest. He reported to Theo that his interest in drawing had ceased. Instead he had grown interested in reading, as well as a detectable turn toward religiosity and religious preoccupations.

Meanwhile his peculiar moody behavior did not escape notice at work. It was already becoming clear that the budding art dealer was losing his taste for the work. He seemed little interested in selling art works and was absorbed in the study of the Bible. The situation was delicate since he was the protegé of uncle Cent and could not be dismissed out of hand. It was decided that he should return to Paris, since London seemed to do him little good. He did not take the move well and began to resent the manipulation of his family and the burdens of following a career they had set out for him. In October 1874, he returned to Paris where he was put to work as an art salesman. But his feelings had changed considerably—he was more isolated and morose. His parents were worried about him, and the sense of estrangement from his family had begun to assert itself—his mother complained to Theo that they received no letters (Hulsker, 1990). His interest in the art trade faded; Vincent was more invested in going to church, praying, and reading—especially the Bible. After about eight weeks in Paris, he was sent back to London, and then, after another five months, he returned to Paris. His heart was simply not in the work.

DISMISSAL

By May 15, 1875, back in Paris, he was forlorn and desperate. Dismissal was a foregone conclusion. His work suffered considerably: he was sullen, indifferent, and irritable. He discouraged customers from buying any piece of art he did not think worthy. He did not think highly of the prevailing salon art, and bluntly told customers so. Despite the complaints Boussod, Goupil's successor, waited—probably not knowing what was best to do and not wishing to offend Vincent's uncle who was still an important and influential figure.

Vincent rebelled against what he regarded as fraud on the part of art dealers. His mind turned in desperation to religious ideas in a kind of fanatical religious mysticism. He became increasingly secluded and isolated, living alone and seeing no one. He even stopped writing to his family. Boussod treated him kindly and even gave him a sort of promotion, hoping to encourage him. But to no avail—he continued to concentrate on the Bible and took no interest in the vitality of Paris. Not surprisingly, he was dismissed at the end of March 1876. And so, seven years of training as an art dealer came to an end. Vincent took it stoically. He wrote Theo, "When the apple is ripe, a soft breeze makes it fall from the tree; such was the case here, in the sense that I have done things that have been very wrong, and therefore I have but little to say" (Letter 50).[3]

If he thought that his religious enthusiasm would please his father, he was mistaken. Theodorus counseled patience and moderation; he saw Vincent's fanaticism in the image of Icarus, who in his impulsiveness flew too near the sun with disastrous results. In his eyes Vincent's behavior in squandering his opportunities was totally irrational. Theo seemed puzzled and uncomprehending, but stuck by his troubled brother nonetheless. For Vincent it was, despite his ambivalence, a narcissistic blow, a defeat and a sign of his unworthiness. He felt as though he had been rejected by his family to begin with, and now he was rejected by the world as well.

ODD JOBS

He returned to England in mid-April 1876 and took a position as a teacher in a boys' boarding school at Ramsgate. The school was the embodiment of Dickens' Dotheboys Hall—dirty, infested, and harsh in discipline. Vincent worked for room and board and no salary. The food was meager and unpalatable at best, disgusting and inedible otherwise. He soon left (July 1876) for a school in Ilseworth, closer to London. The fare was no better and at least he could teach the Bible and preach occasionally at the local Methodist chapel.

In December 1876, after months of semistarvation, Vincent returned to visit his family in Etten, where they had recently moved. His appearance distressed them, so emaciated and forlorn he looked. His uncle Cent got him a job as a clerk and salesman in a bookstore in Dordrecht, but Vincent spent his time there surreptitiously translating passages of the Bible and sketching. The job lasted four months—from January 21 until April 30, 1877. The owner's son, recalling his impressions of Vincent years later (Letter 94a), described him as unattractive and unsociable, hardly speaking a word, a queer, lonely chap with little

---

[3]Citations from Vincent's letters are taken from van Gogh-Bonger and van Gogh (1959).

to do with anyone. His landlord thought he was out of his head—always alone, avoiding other lodgers, eating little if at all, never eating meat except for a tiny morsel on Sunday's, and up at all hours of the night. He lived frugally, even ascetically.

> His roommate and fellow worker, P.C. Gorlitz, described him in the following terms: He was a singular man with a singular appearance as well. He was well-built and had reddish hair that stood straight up from his head; his face was homely and full of freckles, but changed and brightened when he became enthusiastic—and that happened quite often. . . . Van Gogh's attitudes and behavior often provoked amusement because he acted, thought, felt and lived so differently from others his age: he prayed for a long time at the table, ate like a hermit—consuming, for example, no meat, no gravy, etc.—and he invariably had a withdrawn, pensive, deeply serious, melancholy look on his face. But when he laughed he did so with such gusto and geniality that his whole face brightened.
>
> He was frugal by nature and also from necessity, as his income was, like my own, limited—even more so because he was still only a novice in the business. Nor did he want to appeal to his parents for supplementary income. . . .
>
> And when he had to provide information to women and other clients, about prints exhibited by Mr. Braat, he did not take the interests of his boss into account but said precisely and plainly what he thought about the artistic value of each one. Once again, he was unsuited to business [Cited by Stein, 1986, pp. 41–42].

Even at this early stage of his career, it seems clear that Vincent had set himself on a path of abysmal failure—every enterprise to which he turned his hand resulted in dismal failure and disgrace.

RELIGIOUS MISSION

Faced with this string of failures, Vincent decided that he would commit himself to the ministry and follow in his father's footsteps as a minister of the gospel. Here again defeat followed on defeat, failure on failure. Preparation for the ministry meant theological training, so arrangements were made for him to study for the entrance examinations to the theological faculty of the university. After a year of anguished study of Latin and Greek, he failed the examinations. Still clinging to his wish to be a preacher, he enrolled in the course for evangelists in Brussels, but again failed to qualify.

Urged on by his fanatical determination, he undertook a trial of missionary work in the Borinage, the impoverished coal mining district of Belgium. But the story was not much different there either. He poured himself out in a paroxysm of self-denial, deprivation, devotion, and heroic acts of charity and missionary zeal—a scene of devotion and asceticism rarely equaled in the annals of sanctity—all for naught. His efforts made little impact on his poverty-stricken and oppressed flock, and he succeeded only in drawing down on himself the suspicions and opposition of the church authorities. They withdrew their approval and support, and his religiously inspired mission came to an inglorious end. Vincent retreated in pain and depressive defeat—possibly a psychotic depressive reaction—and was not heard of again for months.

THE ARTIST'S VOCATION

When he resurfaced, he had transformed his religious devotion into a commitment to art. He poured into his new-found vocation all the intensity, all the fanatical determination and zeal that had found expression in his religious mission. Given his immense artistic talent and genius and the undeniable judgment of history, it is astonishing to follow his footsteps on this artistic path. He struggled from the beginning and never found a secure or satisfying footing—he was able to sell only one painting during his life. His attempts to study with Anton Mauve ended disastrously in recriminations and bitterness. When Mauve tried to get him to draw from plaster casts, Vincent rebelled, angrily smashed the casts to smithereens, and broke with Mauve. He enrolled in the Art Academy at Antwerp, but with no better results. His work was unorthodox, his style vigorous and seemingly undisciplined, his attitude exquisitely sensitive to any criticism and rebellious—not the best of students!

He lasted little more than a month, and in despair turned to his brother Theo, who was established as an art dealer in Paris. He learned much and assimilated important techniques from his connections in the art world during his stay in Paris—particularly Bernard, Gauguin, Toulouse-Lautrec, and the impressionists. But to his fellow artists, Vincent was a mystery; many thought his work strange and eccentric, if not at the same time interesting. His style was direct. He was totally unconcerned with artistic conventions, unorthodox in his technique, his brushwork, his use of colors. An unbridled expression and intensity of feeling permeated his canvases. To many his work seemed rough, unrefined, unskilled, and undisciplined—as though there was little to distinguish between the works and the man. Gauzi, Lautrec's close friend, recalled: "He worked with a disorderly fury, throwing colors on the canvas with feverish speed. He gathered up the color as though with a shovel, and the globs of paint, covering the length of the paint-brush, stuck to his fingers. When the model rested, he didn't stop painting. The violence of his study surprised the atelier; the classically-oriented remained bewildered by it'' (Cited by Stein, 1986, pp. 71–72).

Later, early in 1890, Albert Aurier, a young French art critic who had examined the canvases Van Gogh had left in Theo's apartment, wrote a review of Vincent's work that seemed to capture something of the character of the artist and his work:

> What characterizes his work as a whole is excess, excess of strength, excess of nervousness, violence in expression. In his categorical affirmation of the character of things, in his often fearless simplification of forms, in his insolence in challenging the sun face to face, in the vehement passion of his drawing and color, right down to the smallest particulars of his technique, a powerful figure reveals himself, a man, one who dares, very often brutal, and sometimes ingenuously delicate. And even more, this is revealed in the almost orgiastic excesses of everything he has painted: he is a fanatic, an enemy of bourgeois sobrieties and petty details, a kind of drunken giant, better suited to moving mountains than handling knickknacks, a brain in eruption, irresistibly pouring its lava into all the ravines of art, a terrible and maddened genius, often sublime, sometimes grotesque, always close to the pathological . . . [Pickvance 1986, p. 312].

And further:

> The external and material side of his painting is absolutely in keeping with his artistic temperament. In all his works, the execution is vigorous, exalted, brutal, intense. His drawing, excited, powerful, often clumsy and somewhat heavy-handed, exaggerates the character, simplifies, leaps—master and conqueror—over detail, attains a masterful synthesis and sometimes, but by no means always, great style [Cited by Stein, 1986, p. 193].

His dedication to his art was totally absorbing and brought with it a sense of increasing mastery, of dedication to an artistic vision and a mission that seemed to replace and absorb into itself all the energy, intent, meaning, and unremitting dedication that had characterized his mission in the Borinage. No sacrifice, no deprivation, no self-denial or mortification was too much for the sake of his art. If he could not sell his work, and if he could not find the solace of recognition or acceptance from his peers, he found fulfillment and satisfaction nonetheless. He proclaimed to Theo: "In my opinion, I am often *rich as*

Croesus—not in money, but rich—because I have found in my work
something to which I can devote myself to heart and soul, and which
inspires me and gives a meaning to life'' (Letter 274).

His paintings became the objects of his instinctual power, his
loves, his sexual objects, his offspring. He told Theo, ''The work is
an absolute necessity for me. I can't put it off, I don't care for anything
but the work; that is to say, the pleasure in something else ceases at
once and I become melancholy when I can't go on with my work''
(Letter 288). His work became an all-consuming obsession for him.
He told Theo:

> I do *not* intend to spare myself, nor to avoid emotions or difficulties—I
> don't care much whether I live a longer or a shorter time.... So I go
> on like an ignoramus who knows only this one thing: ''In a few years
> *I must finish a certain work.*''... The world concerns me only in so
> far as I feel a certain indebtedness and duty toward it because I have
> walked this earth for thirty years, and, out of gratitude, want to leave
> some souvenir in the shape of drawings or pictures—not made to please
> a certain taste in art, but to express a sincere human feeling [Letter 309].

There was a quality of driven urgency to his efforts. During his
time in Arles, he worked from morning to night, and sometimes into
the night—sporting a broad-brimmed hat with candles stuck in it so that
he could see the canvas. He labored incessantly, frantically, seemingly
indefatigably. He seemed driven by a demon; he described himself as
''a painting engine.'' He lived on little, often forgetting to eat, and
when he did it was a meager meal of biscuits and milk.

The crisis came when he suffered his first psychotic episode after
the famous argument with Gauguin, when he cut off the lobe of his
ear. He was hospitalized and soon released. He hoped desperately that
his illness would not interfere with his painting. Soon after the first
attack, he wrote determinedly to Theo:

> Only a few words to tell you that my health and my work are not
> progressing so badly. It astonishes me already when I compare my
> condition today with what it was a month ago. Before that I knew well
> enough that one could fracture one's legs and arms and recover after-
> ward, but I did not know that you could fracture the brain in your head
> and recover from that too. I still have sort of ''what is the good of
> getting better?'' feeling about me, even in the astonishment aroused in
> me by getting well, which I hadn't dared hope for.... Since it is still
> winter, look here, let me go quietly on with my work; if it is that of a
> madman, well, so much the worse....

And once again, either shut me up in a madhouse right away—I shan't oppose it, I may be deceiving myself—or else let me work with all my strength, while taking the precautions I speak of. If I am not mad, the time will come when I shall send you what I have promised you from the beginning . . . [Letter 574].

We can gain from his letters some sense of the extent to which Vincent's sense of self-esteem and the justification for his existence was tied up in his painting. Without it he was worthless and his life meaningless. Only in his continuing to turn out works of art could he justify accepting money from Theo. But his illness presented a continual impediment to reengaging in his work with the same intensity as before. "The doctor had given me strict orders to go out for a walk without doing any mental work. . . . As far as my work goes, the month hasn't been so bad on the whole, and work distracts me, or rather keeps me under control, so that I don't deny myself it" (Letter 576). He continued to paint, but as his condition deteriorated slowly, the effort required grew greater. It was no longer an enthusiasm and pleasure; it was a necessity. It became occupational therapy, a way of escaping from the inner anguish and torment, an island of sanity and purpose in a troubled sea of near psychotic turmoil. His only hope was in his painting.

Nonetheless he was tormented by doubts and fading hopes. To Theo he complained: "As far as I can judge, I am not properly speaking a madman. You will see that the canvases I have done in the intervals are steady and not inferior to the others. I miss the work more than it tires me . . . " (Letter 580). He had to decide whether to continue at Arles as he was or put himself more permanently in a mental institution. He wrote to Theo:

These last three months do seem so strange to me. Sometimes moods of indescribable mental anguish, sometimes moments when the veil of time and the fatality of circumstances seemed to be torn apart for an instant. . . . even allowing for hope, the thing to do is to accept the probably disastrous reality. I am hoping once again to throw myself wholly into my work, in which I've fallen behind" [Letter 582].

And little by little I can come to look upon madness as a disease like any other. . . . The idea of work as a duty is coming back to me very strongly, and I think that all my faculties for work will come back to me fairly quickly. Only work often absorbs me so much that I think I shall always remain absent-minded and awkward in shifting for myself for the rest of my life too" [Letter 591].

THE ARTISTIC CRISIS

When he finally decided to commit himself to the asylum of Saint-Paul-de-Mausole in Saint-Remy-de-Provence, Vincent plunged himself into his art in a desperate effort to preserve his sanity and the slender threads of meaning and hope he could salvage. Works of sublime artistic merit flowed from his brush in a seeming torrent. Hulsker's catalogue (1980) lists nearly 300 works during this St. Remy period, nearly half of them in oil. To mention a few, there is the famous irises, then a series of studies of wheatfields, his well-known painting of The Starry Night, a series of powerful mountain landscapes, his studies of cypresses, a series of poignant self-portraits, other portraits of the chief orderly and his wife, the famous Pietà after a Delacroix lithograph, the Raising of Lazarus after a Rembrandt etching, his familiar paintings of sowers and reapers, and finally a series of paintings depicting scenes in and around the hospital and its environs. The list is very incomplete, but it suggests the feverish pace of his effort and the intensity of his preoccupation with it.

He struggled with his painting and the lurking awareness that his control over his medium was ebbing away. The coherence and the majestic power of the Arles period had disappeared. His work became uncertain and variable. He himself was not unaware of the change. Something had given way. Had he lost faith? Was he crazy to continue to paint and get nothing out of it? Despite his doubts, he clung to his painting desperately, hopefully, as if it were his last lifeline. He wrote Theo: "Work distracts me infinitely better than anything else, and if I could once really throw myself into it with all my energy, possibly that would be the best remedy. . . . You see that I am in a very bad humor, things aren't going well. Then I feel like a fool going and asking doctors permission to make pictures. Besides, it is to be hoped that if sooner or later I get a certain amount better, it will be because I have recovered through working, for it is a thing which strengthens the will and consequently leaves these mental weaknesses less hold" (Letter 602). With desperate hope and determination he threw himself into his work—hoping against hope that reimmersion in the only medium of salvation he had ever found would save him from the ravages of his disease. He told Theo: "I am working like one actually possessed, more than ever I am in a dumb fury of work. And I think this will help cure me . . . in the sense that my distressing illness makes me work with a dumb fury—very slowly—but from morning till night without slackening—and—the secret is probably this—work long and slowly" (Letter 604).

Some of his paintings from this period express a sense of deep melancholy, unutterable loneliness, a mournful tone of tragic presentiment. Vincent himself felt a deep sense of oppression and depression.

His need to paint became all the more desperate, urgent, imperative. To Theo, he wrote:

> I think M. Peyron [his physician] is right when he says that I am not strictly speaking mad, for my mind is absolutely normal in the intervals, and even more so than before. But during the attacks it is terrible—and I lose consciousness of everything. But that spurs me on to work and to seriousness, like a miner who is always in danger makes haste in what he does'' [Letter 610].
>
> For the moment I am overcome with discouragement. But since this [last] attack was over in a week, what's the use of thinking that it may in fact come back again? First of all you do not know, and cannot foresee, how or in what form. Let's go on working then as much as possible as if nothing had happened. I shall soon have an opportunity to go out when the weather is not too cold, and then I have rather set my heart on trying to finish the work I have begun here. . . . My work at least lets me retain a little of my clarity of mind, and makes possible my getting rid of this some day. . . . I have already started working again, and if he saw any objection, M. Peyron would probably not have let me do it. What he said to me was—''Let's hope that there will be no recurrence''—exactly the same thing as ever; he spoke very kindly to me, and as for him, these things hardly surprise him, but since there is no quick remedy, perhaps only time and circumstances can have any influence [Letter 622].

He finally was discharged from the asylum and made his way to Auvers-sur-Oise, where he put himself in the care of Dr. Gauchet. But fear, desperation, and hopelessness dogged him. He wrote poignantly to Theo: "There—once back here I set to work again—though the brush almost slipped from my fingers, but knowing exactly what I wanted, I have painted three more big canvases since. They are vast fields of wheat under troubled skies, and I did not need to go out of my way to try to express sadness and extreme loneliness. I hope you will see them soon . . . since I almost think that these canvases will tell you what I cannot say in words, the health and restorative forces that I see in the country . . . '' (Letter 649). Soon after this, he walked out into the farmyard where he fired the fatal shot that ended his life.

DISCUSSION

Both of these cases were victims, with respect to the issue of work, of the cultural and societal standards and expectations of their respective environments. For Arthur, not only were parental expectations set exorbitantly high, but they were accompanied by a constant devaluation and subtle undermining and discouragement of his capacities to perform competently and successfully. His parents seemed remarkably out of tune with his needs as a child and indifferent to any input from them that might have contributed to the development of his sense of himself as a valued and effective human being. As his therapy revealed most clearly, the devastation was even more basic—the message was loud and clear—do not show any independence or competence, because even the slightest display of such capability would threaten his parents, primarily his father, who had to find unremitting confirmation of his superiority even in the diminishing and defeat of his only son. The only acceptable standards of work performance and accomplishment were set at such a level that they not only exceeded, but were totally beyond the reach of a little boy. Any of his child's efforts to gain some sense of mastery were ridiculed, devalued, and thwarted. Work in his experience came to mean frustration, failure, humiliation, and defeat.

In Vincent's case, the circumstances were different but the outcome was not that different. His position as the replacement child (Meissner, 1992a) and as the oldest son subjected him to particular burdens of parental expectation. His early life experience was complicated by the persistence of his mother's depression, which created an ambiance in which he was not valued and embraced as a source of pleasure and satisfaction for her, but as a trial and burden. Nor was Vincent's father much of a sustaining resource for him. Theodorus was a solemn and remote figure, not harsh or punitive from what we can tell, but a sober and pedestrian man with little empathic connection or capacity to appreciate his son. By far the dominant affects coming from Theodorus were lack of comprehension, disapproval, perplexity, disappointment, and irritation. Any intonations of support, approval, or pleasure in Vincent's talent or accomplishments were completely lacking.

Vincent's early attempts to establish himself in the world of work were cast in the shadow of the opportunities provided by his parents. His ambivalence played itself out in his dalliance and indifference to these opportunities. The impassioned and fanatical turn to religion and his agony of self-deprivation and ascetical extremes in the Borinage were a last-ditch effort to find the approval and acceptance from his idolized father that had always eluded him. When that failed, he turned at last to a vocation that was held in suspicion and even some contempt by his parents—his art. But his path even there was not straight and conventional—he became an impoverished vagabond, a bohemian caricature, living with a prostitute and flagrantly rejecting and violating every canon of his father's law. In terms of the contemporary setting in which he worked, he carved out a path of eccentricity, isolation, rejection, and apparent failure. He was chronically poor, unsuccessful. He poured out his heart and soul in his frenetic painting—only to find rebuke, criticism, exclusion from all but a handful even of the marginal group of artists he associated with. As a painter he was peculiar, an eccentric, whose nobility of soul found a few isolated admirers, but for the most part condemned him to the margins even of the artistic world of his day.

But for him art was all-consuming and inexhaustibly demanding. He spared nothing of himself in the service of this demanding mistress. The motivations that drove him on were complex and deep—the driving forces were narcissistic, masochistic, ideological, and above all religious. But it was in his painting that he found escape from the hateful burdens of his painful life, and the sense of purpose, of ambition, of the meaning of life, of a sense of creating a place for himself, something that made it seem as though his existence was not wasted or meaningless. I would argue that his painting was so central to his sense of himself and the meaning of his life that when the inroads of his illness finally came to threaten his creative capacity, his life began to lose meaning and suicide loomed as an ever more poignant possibility. The connection with Theo also played a vital role in this regard, since the symbiotic linkage of the two brothers may have played a vital part in sustaining the psychic existence of both (Meissner, 1994, 1995a). Theo's marriage, the birth of his child, and finally his own precarious health—he died six months after Vincent—may have put the final seal on Vincent's precarious existence and made the possibility of suicide an inevitability (Meissner, 1992c).

The work principle in these cases came to play a central role. Both required a reversal of the societal dictate that to become an authentic human being one has to establish oneself in a recognized and accepted working context. In Arthur's case, he had to suspend the standards of monetary reward or social approval in order to find work he could commit himself to and find fulfillment and satisfaction in it. The criteria of importance, success, monetary reward, social approval, and so on, had to be jettisoned or at least shifted to a much less significant level of importance in his thinking. Only when he is able to find the freedom to determine his own inclinations and desires and to assert and implement them can the prospect of finding any meaningful involvement in work open before him. The terms of his choice, however, have to be his own interest, desire, and the meaning of whatever he chooses to do has for him personally—regardless of the opinions or attitudes others, particularly his parents.

Vincent had to fight similar battles—struggling through a series of work positions formed according to his parents' ideology. The culmination of this effort came in the Borinage when he made his last desperate effort to find parental acceptance by immersing himself in the vocation of his father. But even this effort became corroded by his ambivalence, and followed a path of inhuman excess to a devastating defeat. Only when he broke through the ring of parental demand—a task he must have accomplished in the nine months of isolation and depressive retreat after he left the Borinage—and embraced the artistic vocation, did he find the medium of self-expression and self-discovery that made his work commitment meaningful and fulfilling.

These moments of self-realization are rooted in the self-as-agent. They reflect the dynamic of achieved self-autonomy, the freedom of self-determination, of self-commitment and the declaration of identity. They require a meaningful degree of resolution of underlying conflicts, both oedipal and preoedipal, of integration of ego capacities and super-ego standards, of the modification of narcissistic ego-ideal investments to accord with the limitations of personal ability and the standards of realistic achievement, and a purposeful consolidation of desire and intention, of both the pleasure and reality principles in the service of work. The self needs and seeks meaningful and purposeful work, and it is in the process of attaining and functioning effectively within that work-related context that the self finds the functional channels of expression and meaning that contribute to its own structural integrity and evolution.

References

Abelin, E. L. (1971), The role of the father in separation-individuation. In: *Separation-Individuation: Essays in Honor of Margaret Mahler*, ed. J. McDevitt & C. Settlage. New York: International Universities Press, pp. 229–252.

Beres, D. (1971), Ego autonomy and ego pathology. *The Psychoanalytic Study of the Child*, 26:3–24. New York: Quadrangle.

Betcher, R. W. & Pollack, W. S. (1993), *In a Time of Fallen Heroes: The Re-creation of Masculinity*. New York: Atheneum.

Bly, R. (1990), *Iron John*. Reading, MA: Addison Wesley.

Brickman, H. R. (1993), 'Between the devil and the deep blue sea': The dyad and the triad in psychoanalytic thought. *Internat. J. Psycho-Anal.*, 74:905–915.

Buie, D. H.; Meissner, W. W.; Rizzuto, A.-M. & Sashin, J. I. (1983), Aggression in the psychoanalytic situation. *Internat. Rev. Psychoanal.*, 10:159–170.

Chasseguet-Smirgel, J. (1985), *The Ego Ideal*. New York: Norton.

——— (1986), *Sexuality and Mind*. New York: New York University Press.

Erikson, E. H. (1959), *Identity and the Life Cycle. Psychological Issues*, Monogr. 1. New York: International Universities Press.

——— (1963), *Childhood and Society*. New York: Norton.

Hartmann, H. (1947), On rational and irrational action. In: *Essays on Ego Psychology*. New York: International Universities Press, 1964, pp. 37–68.

———— (1950), Comments on the psychoanalytic theory of the ego. In: *Essays on Ego Psychology*. New York: International Universities Press, 1964, pp. 131–141.

Hendrik, I. (1942), Instinct and the ego during infancy. *Psychoanal. Q.*, 11:33–58.

———— (1943a), Work and the pleasure principle. *Psychoanal. Q.*, 12:311–329.

———— (1943b), The discussion of the "instinct to master." *Psychoanal. Q.*, 12:561–565.

Hulsker, J. (1980), *The Complete Van Gogh*. New York: Abrams.

———— (1990), *Vincent and Theo Van Gogh: A Dual Biography*. Ann Arbor, MI: Fuller Publications.

Levinson, D. (1978), *The Seasons of a Man's Life*. New York: Knopf.

Levinson, H. (1976), *Psychological Man*. Cambridge, MA: Levinson Institute.

Mahler, M.S., Pine, F. & Bergman, A. (1975), *The Psychological Birth of the Human Infant: Symbiosis and Individuation*. New York: Basic Books.

Markson, E. R. (1993), Depression and moral masochism. *Internat. J. Psycho-Anal.*, 74:931–940.

Meissner, S. J., W. W. (1986a), Can psychoanalysis find its self? *J. Amer. Psychoanal. Assn.*, 34:379–400.

———— (1986b), Some notes on Hartmann's ego psychology and the psychology of the self. *Psychoanal. Inq.*, 6:499–521.

———— (1992a), The childhood of an artist. *Annual Psychoanal.*, 20:147–169.

———— (1992b), The concept of the therapeutic alliance. *J. Amer. Psychoanal. Assn.*, 40:1059–1087.

———— (1992c), Vincent's suicide: A psychic autopsy. *Contemp. Psychoanal.*, 28:673–694.

———— (1993), Self-as-agent in psychoanalysis. *Psychoanal. Contemp. Thought*, 16:459–495.

———— (1994), The theme of the double and creativity in Vincent van Gogh. *Contemp. Psychoanal.*, 30:323–347.

———— (1995a), Creativity and symbiosis in Vincent van Gogh. *Contemp. Psychoanal.*, 31:641–665.

———— (1995b), The economic principle in psychoanalysis: I. Economics and energies. *Psychoanal. Contemp. Thought*, 18:197–226.

Modell, A. H. (1993), *The Private Self*. Cambridge, MA: Harvard University Press.

Pickvance, R. (1986), *Van Gogh in Saint-Rémi and Auvers*. New York: Metropolitan Museum of Art.

Rizzuto, A.-M., Buie, D. H. & Meissner, W. W. (1993), A revised theory of aggression. *Psychoanal. Rev.*, 80:29–54.

Stein, S. A., Ed. (1986), *Van Gogh: A Retrospective*. New York: Park Lane.

Vaillant, G. E. (1977), *Adaptation to Life*. Boston: Little, Brown.

van Gogh-Bogner, J. & van Gogh, W., Eds. (1959), *The Complete Letters of Vincent van Gogh*, 3 vols. Greenwich, CT: New York Graphic Society.

White, R. W. (1963), *Ego and Reality in Psychoanalytic Theory. Psychological Issues*, Monogr. 11. New York: International Universities Press.

Winnicott, D. W. (1960), Ego distortion in terms of true and false self. In: *The Maturational Processes and the Facilitating Environment*. New York: International Universities Press, 1965, pp. 140–152.

4

INFANCY AND THE ESSENTIAL NATURE OF WORK

Annie Reiner, L.C.S.W., and Bernard W. Bail, M.D.

Psychoanalysis shows us that the answers to our most profound questions about human beings can be found in their early development. Since Freud began his excavations into the mind and soul of mankind, others have continued to move our perspective further back in time. Melanie Klein afforded us an earlier view of the infant's mental life, which deepened with the work of Wilfred Bion and the object-relations theorists. In that same spirit, this paper examines a very fundamental level of our relationship to work in the service of understanding its meaning to us later in life. In the process it will be necessary to present something of the basis of the authors' perspective, specifically as regards the development of the self and the mind in infancy. Clinical examples illustrate these ideas as they relate to the capacity to do meaningful work. Our focus is on the earliest precursors of that capacity, with the understanding that the capacity to do *any* work, and to do it genuinely, depends first of all on the development of a true self. Without this, neither one's work nor one's life can ever truly be one's own.

THE INFANT'S FIRST JOB

At the most fundamental level, the work of every human being is to survive. The healthy infant undertakes this work with gusto, adapting to his new gaseous environment with a hungry gulp of air and a loud cry. He searches for the nipple and sucks at it with energy and concentration, for like any animal he knows instinctively that his life depends on it. Being a different kind of animal, however, he has other instinctual needs as well. Since the potential for consciousness is part of our human equipment, we also need to consider the development of the mind as a basic drive.

The precursors of the authors' concept of the mind can be found in Bion's (1962) theory of "container and contained." The interaction between the mind and its contents ("container and contained") creates the dynamic psychic energy necessary for creative thought. This is in contrast to the mental flotsam and jetsam which too often fills our heads, and which may be mistaken for thinking. In these terms, it is not real thought, and that which contains it is not, in these terms, a real mind.

The seeds of the capacity to think are sown in the relationship between the mother and the infant. Her ability to *understand* her baby, not just his physical needs, but his mental needs as well, serves as a container for the contents of the child's mind—his feelings, experiences, etc. This understanding provides the infant with the model for consciousness—an intrapsychic relationship between the contents of his mind and that which contains them. These work together to create the unity of an integrated mind, just as he once worked together with his mother (Bion, 1970).

We shall use the term "mind," then, in a very specific sense, to describe this unity. It may be seen as a unity between intellect and emotion, between thoughts and feelings, or between conscious and unconscious modes of perception, but it is always a function of the personality capable of bridging the gap between the dualities of human nature. This capacity for integration also defines a unified self, capable of fluid movement between conscious and unconscious modes of perception.

We may be relatively unfamiliar with the vicissitudes of this kind of mind, but it asserts itself with great force in every infant. The infant cries to be fed but also to be *mentally* nourished. The latter is far more problematic for there is still widespread confusion as to what constitutes good nutrition for the mind. Consciousness is a hunger of the mind and self to which infants are especially attuned, however, for their mental potential still exists untrammelled by the considerable obstacles to consciousness which later come into play. By the time one reaches adulthood, the infant's pure instinct for consciousness is often severely clouded. As we shall see later, primary among the obstacles are the behavior and expectations of parents and societies not yet cognizant of the true nature of the mind.

The infant is impelled toward a sense of his self and his mind as passionately as he is toward food or air, and so the work of achieving consciousness becomes his earliest, most fervent occupation. All future work that the individual will undertake has its roots in this fundamental task of living. For the human being with his vast potential for a higher mind it is a striving of the greatest power, one that fuels the noblest achievements of mankind.

While this may seem to be an impractical level at which to begin our explorations, we need to ask ourselves if there is really any other level at which we *can* begin. If we are to find answers to the knotty problems in which mankind is embroiled, we need first to have a firm foundation upon which to stand, and that means finding a way to connect with what is most essential in us.

THE SELF AS A PROCESS OF INTERACTIONS

At the deepest level, *the self is not a singular entity but rather the product of a relationship*, originally between the infant and the mother. It is not a fixed entity, but an exchange of energy. The true self continues throughout life to be a *process of interaction* of two energies rather than a discrete ego, completely separate from the other person. It is a self that is always changing and capable of development.

We have called this approach "quantum psychoanalysis" because of the similarities we have found between these interacting energies of the self and the interacting energies of subatomic particles. At the deepest level of matter we now know that matter actually ceases to exist, and in its place are continuous exchanges between fields of energy. Einstein showed that physical reality had to be seen in terms of continuous functions in space rather than material points. Likewise, in psychic reality, the concept of a rigidly defined ego can no longer be used to define the self. The idea of continuous functions in mental space, a kind of fluid reality, should really be quite familiar to psychoanalysts, for the unconscious has always been understood to have these characteristics. It is a timeless realm beyond the usual strictures of logic and reason, a breakdown of time and space as dreamers travel to distant places and times in the flash of a neuron. An integrated self and creative mind depends upon incorporating this realm into our consciousness in a much more general way than we have so far.

Just as matter and energy were shown to be interchangeable at the deepest level of matter, at the deepest level of the mind comparable laws seem to apply. A true understanding of the self does not depend on the individual alone, but on the interactions in which he or she is engaged. As we learn more about the complexities of internal object relations we see that the inner landscape is filled with various mental images representing various different identifications in constant interaction with each other within the personality. In order to understand the self, we need to understand these relationships. This makes the analyst's job considerably more complex, for at any particular moment the individual may not actually be the person he appears to be. Intrapsychically, he may be his mother, father, siblings, grandparents, etc., and the analyst must be mentally agile and perspicuous if he is to keep up with these ongoing mental shifts.

Still, on a physical level, we are obviously only one person, and the authors hold to the idea that at an even deeper level there does exist an essential self that allows the individual his separate identity and the creative use of his mind. But the line cannot be too strictly drawn, and it might be more accurate to call it an "essence of self," an essential energy. The self has a paradoxical nature—separateness and interconnectedness simultaneously—and between the two sides of this paradox, the self must find its balance.

Our entire view of the mind has to shift to accommodate a deeper perspective, and many of our psychoanalytic theories need to be reexamined from that perspective.

THE WORK OF CONSCIOUSNESS

This brings us finally to the topic of our relation to work. As we have stated, the self is always dependent on an interaction for its existence, but we have seen in countless dreams that few mothers, few *people*, are in contact with that fundamental unity of the self. While it may then seem to be a lot to ask, to the infant it is nonetheless a requirement. He senses intuitively that if he is to develop his mind and his true self, he must make real contact with the unified self in the mother (or other).

Consciousness or mental unity is the capacity to integrate conscious and unconscious modes of thought and perception. Lacking the developmental capacity for this kind of integration, the infant must borrow his mother's capacity for consciousness. As *her conscious attention* is brought to bear on *his preconscious perceptions*, he will have a moment of mind and selfhood. The first job of the infant is this collaborative work with his mother.

If the mother is *not* capable of doing this kind of work, the infant is, in a sense, fired from his job, perhaps after only a few days of life. Without someone to understand his as yet unconscious experiences, he will lose touch with those experiences, and with his potential for a mind. This loss, though it may never become conscious, is devastating, and strips the essential meaning from his life.

Unfortunately, this situation is *not* a rare affliction that occurs only in severely dysfunctional families. On the contrary, it is a most common experience for infants, and is congruent with the general principles by which most of society abides. Widespread understanding of consciousness and the mind that would enable us to understand infants, simply does not yet exist.

These ideas should not be used to condemn mothers and fathers, any more than psychoanalytic interpretations should be used to condemn. Human beings are a work-in-progress whose current level of mental evolution has not yet allowed them to realize their considerable potential. Nonetheless, mothers who are out of touch with their own unconscious states are hard-pressed to help their infants to make contact with theirs, and the infant in such a situation is forced to take another job. No longer able to do the work of consciousness and realization of his true self, the infant will search frantically for other means of mental survival. Since the infant exists largely in an unconscious mode and has a mother who is divorced from hers, *his* unconscious becomes a ready receptacle for all of *her* repressed unconscious thoughts and feelings.

Klein's (1946) theories of splitting and projective identification show us that the infant projects his feelings of envy and jealousy into the mother. While this has certainly proved to be true, we can now see that it works both ways.[1] Any unresolved feelings of envy or jealousy contained in the mother's unconscious, will inadvertently be projected into the infant. He is called upon to digest these alien emotions and experiences, and this becomes his new job. It is a job he is unequipped for, and the energy of his incipient mind is quickly overtaken by the cast off debris of his mother's (or father's) unconscious.

While it is true, as Klein (1946) has shown, that the infant projects into the mother, it is also true that the parents inadvertently project into the infant. Dreams show that much of what the child projects is actually the introjection of what *has first been unconsciously projected into him by the parents.* Unfortunately, they may have a considerable burden of unconscious emotions to pass on to the child, having themselves been burdened with projections from *their* parents. In our view, mental illness is an outgrowth of these conditions, as the infant is filled with mental debris that divert him from his true work—the natural development of his own mind.

CLINICAL EXAMPLES

In the first clinical example, the patient's dream shows how her own mind very early on became supplanted by her parents' minds, diverting her from her essential work of realizing her mental potential. In the second example we will see how these earliest infantile states determine the nature of the patient's future and his relation to work.

Our method of working is a development of Freud's technique of dream interpretation, taking care to get associations to every aspect of the dream. Putting aside all one's theories, his safety net of stored knowledge is, of course, an exceedingly difficult discipline, for to work strictly in this way, "without memory or desire" (Bion, 1970), is to

---

[1]This idea of Dr. Bail's is an important one in understanding our theories of the mind and the self.

enter the fluid world of one's own and the patient's unconscious, the egoless world of the infant. Only here can a true meeting of minds and selves take place.

EXAMPLE 1

The patient, Dr. R., is a psychologist, a bright, engaging forty-five-year-old woman from a good family. Her father was a wealthy businessman and her mother, though distant, was kind to the patient and her sister as children. Dr. R. has always had a feeling of emotional dissatisfaction, and has never stopped searching for answers and help in various kinds of therapy and analysis. Her marriage is fraught with problems, and she works hard, long hours without having achieved the kind of success in her work she feels she should have by now. In this session, we get some insight into the problems in her early life that affected her in her personal relations and her work later on, as well as a clear illustration of the *mental dilemma* in which infants often find themselves.

Dr. R. had been in analysis for only a short time when she reported the following fragments of three dreams:

[1.] I was in Phoenix at 14th Street and A_____. I was getting a room in a boarding house for $59 a night. My office phone was hooked up to the phone there.

[2.] In the next dream I was in a house with my husband. There was a huge TV screen and I couldn't turn it off. My husband said to use the remote button, but I couldn't find it.

[3.] Then I was in a big house like my friends', Ella and Jim. There was another huge TV screen . . . and something about not knowing what channel was on. That's all I can remember.

Associations

Phoenix: My home town.

14th Street and A: We used to live on 13th and A_____. That's the house we lived in when I was born. It was a beautiful house. But it's not a nice neighborhood now. I wouldn't want to walk there at night. No, I wouldn't feel safe. My father's office was also on A_____.

$59: My friend's house burned down last week. She's staying at a hotel for $59 a night. It looks nice from the outside but inside, well, it's pretty bad.

Ella and Jim: I saw them at a party this weekend and they both seemed distant. Ella usually gives me a big hug, but she didn't this time, she was sort of cold and remote. Maybe something was going on with them. It's funny though, *their* house is torn down now, too.

Huge TV: I don't have one, but Jim and Ella do.

Remote button [no associations].

Later in the hour Dr. R was silent and then, looking teary, she said:

I'm having a lot of feelings. This is the first time I've ever felt that I can just tell the dream to an analyst or therapist without having to figure it out myself. I always had to work so hard, as if *I* had to interpret it. [Pause] I feel angry and depressed at all those wasted years but it feels good to know I can trust you to interpret it.

Interpretation

Since the first dream is set in her home town and childhood home, we are dealing with early feelings in relation to her parents. It feels good to her now to be taken care of because she never had a chance then to be a baby or be taken care of. I showed Dr. R. that even though her parents and their home may have been beautiful from the outside, her dreams indicate that the experience she had there did not *feel* beautiful at all. Like her friend who has lost her house, Dr. R. lost her "house"—her own personality—as a child, and was forced to live in her parents' personalities. We see more evidence for this in dream 2. The huge TV that could not be turned off represents her parents' unconscious. Their emotional coldness (as she describes her friends Ella and Jim) filled *her* with coldness. She was overtaken by *their* unconscious and could not turn it off.

In dream 3, we see a confusion of identities. She "didn't know what channel was on," for once her parents' "channels," *their* unconscious, had supplanted her own, Dr. R. could no longer tell who was who. Furthermore, in dream 2, she cannot find the remote button—a triple play on words. She could not turn off her parents' *remoteness* and coldness, a part of the *remote* past, which is now, in addition, a *remote*, repressed part of her personality. With these remote parents hidden inside her, she could not find her self.

Discussion

As she said in the hour, Dr. R. always felt she had to do the therapist's work, to interpret her own dreams. Clearly, if the patient could do this he or she would not need an analyst. The child, likewise, cannot contain or understand his or her own mental experience. The child whose mother (like Dr. R.'s) is unavailable and cold cannot do the work of a child for the feelings have no home, no one to hold or understand them. This is why all the houses in Dr. R.'s associations are torn down.

The child will always continue to try to find the connection to the mother that is necessary in order to develop a true self. As we see in Dr. R.'s dream, she began to do the mother's work, carrying her mother's unconscious when it should be the other way around. This determined her choice of a career. As a therapist she is the mother, doing the same work she had always done. Despite her hard work and innate talents, Dr. R. feels unable now to do the job as effectively as she would, unburdened of those early parental projections.

The implications of these ideas are far-reaching for these were not abusive parents, but well-meaning, "normal" people. It is the parents' *internal states of being* that so profoundly affect the child, as he is forced to carry the parents' unconscious thoughts and feelings and is robbed of the work of his own development.

The course of one's work is determined at this early stage, for one cannot really be satisfied or do *any* work if one is lacking one's real self. If the most essential work of any human being is to be who he is, to survive mentally as well as physically, it becomes clear why even with the apparent advantages Dr. R. has enjoyed, her relationships and her relation to work would have been troublesome, and why so many people have similar dissatisfactions in their lives. The "lives of quiet desperation" about which Thoreau spoke may be traced to this fundamental level at which the true work of one's life is derailed.

EXAMPLE 2

Dr. A. is a sixty-five-year-old psychoanalyst with a successful practice. In addition, he works in a hospital two nights a week, leaving little time for a personal life. His recent bitter divorce followed years of complaints from his wife and three sons about his physical and emotional absence.

Dr. A.'s mother was a controlling, depressed woman prone to hostile rages. His father was a weak man who, when angered, sometimes became violent and beat his son.

Dr. A. felt that neither of two previous analyses helped him to deal with his problems. He was aware of something missing from his personality, and was plagued by depression, sleeplessness, and anxiety. He has also had a lifelong problem with asthma which began in early childhood.

After one year of analysis Dr. A. reported this dream:

[1.] I was in bed with seven other people, four on each side of the bed, lying head to foot. There was an attractive young woman to my right and an older woman to my left. Someone was discussing a book and the older woman said, "The writing is hard to understand." I answered, "That's because it's about the unconscious, that's why the writing is turgid and condensed and hard to understand."

[2.] Suddenly I realized it was ten of eight and I was late for class—my first day of medical school as a junior. I was upset because it would take a half-hour to drive to school, and where would I park? I had tremendous anxiety.

[3.] The young woman came in the bathroom and noticed I had an erection. She said, "Oh, we can't waste that." She wanted to fuck, but of course I didn't have time.

[4.] There was one more fragment I remember. I was sitting on a bench with a group of people. There were other people walking by. Somewhere I saw a map of Europe, then one of China.

Associations

Dr. A: I had dinner with my girlfriend Sally yesterday. We had been getting along well and feeling affectionate the day before, but she got upset last night because I was distant. I think she wanted to make love and I guess I did too, but I felt tired so I wasn't really interested.

Head to foot in bed: It reminds me of my brother, Sam. Sometimes just playing around we would lay that way.

Attractive woman: She had dark hair. I guess she looked like Sally. I suppose the older woman to my left is my mother.

Book: It was about the unconscious. I think about Freud's [1900] *Seventh Chapter*—the one about the metapsychology of dreams. I never quite got it—it's too theoretical.

Junior in medical school: I was very anxious in those days, scared I couldn't do the work. By the time you're a junior you know you've made it, but I went to a hard medical school—I didn't have time for girls. Maybe like the part of the dream in the bathroom, I had to get to school, I couldn't think about fucking. I didn't want to end up like my brother. He didn't even finish high school. All he did was hang around, drink, and fuck girls.

Europe: I was there last year with Sally; we also went to China. It should have been wonderful, but it was pretty awful, I guess; I was depressed, going through a bunch of emotional crap and just couldn't have any fun. I felt very bad that I ruined her time.

People walking by: I don't know, but the map was there—I think they were all going on the trip to Europe and China. I was just sitting there.

Interpretation and Discussion

In part 2 of this dream, Dr. A.'s anxiety about being late for school is a way of saying that he is anxious, so late in his life, finally to be finding out who he really is. After 60 years, two analyses, and much searching he is grateful for it but also very anxious about whether he can find his real self. The "school" represents his analysis; "a place to park his car" would be a place to put his self, a place to *be*. His real self has been hidden for so long that there is also great anxiety about what he will find when his real feelings return to him.

The reason Dr. A. knows nothing of his real self is revealed in the first part of the dream. Although he is in bed with Sally, his whole family is there as well—his mother is the older woman to his left. The dream, then, is one of infancy and the "book about the unconscious" which he cannot understand is really his mother's unconscious which, as an infant, he kept trying to "read." Her deep depression and cruel rages kept her child attached to her in a pathological way, for he felt compelled to understand her, as every child does. In part it is self-defense, as protection from her rages, and in part the hope of figuring out how to get from her the kind of love he needed. This was Dr. A.'s first job—he was employed in trying to understand his mother. In a very real way, it was his first job as an analyst, delving into his mother's unconscious to try to discover what had obstructed her from giving him the care necessary for his mind and self to thrive. The dream says that her mind was to him an incomprehensible book—as it would be for any child.

On one side of the bed were Dr. A., Sally, his mother, and probably his father. There were no associations to the four other people in the bed, but we might conjecture that they are his two sets of grandparents. The burden of his mother's pathology, and his father's, would ultimately be the residue of projections they received from *their* parents—their own internal objects passed on to Dr. A.

The patients in these two clinical cases both happen to be mental health professionals, but the human being is an innately curious, scientific animal, and we have found that *all* children apply that curiosity first of all to the task of understanding their mothers. As a psychoanalyst, Dr. A. has devoted his entire life to it, and the specific nature of his first job has determined his choice of his career and the course of his life. His relationships have been pale ghosts of that earlier attachment. His marriage ended destructively and his relations with his children are strained and distant. He had been too consumed by his attention to his mother to attend to anything or anyone else. As we see in parts 2 and 3 of his dream, although he loves Sally, after the initial sexual excitement dies away, he is too "busy" for sex, too busy, that is, fulfilling the work of understanding his mother for any real sexual *or* emotional intercourse.

As an analyst Dr. A.'s preoccupation with the unconscious is appropriate, and has even brought him success. Every patient represents his mother, whose unconscious he studies as if his life depends on it which, when he was an infant, it *did*. His self depended on his mother having a healthy self. Unfortunately, his devotion to his task left him no time or mental space for an adult life in the present. The dream shows the etiology of his obsession with analytic work—the child who could not withdraw his attention from his mother's unconscious.

Part 4 of the dream repeats this theme. He had been unable to enjoy his trip to Europe because he was completely occupied with the work of attending to his internal mother. As a result he is sitting there "benched"—he cannot participate in his life. The other people walking by are going on the trip, so they are felt to be on the journey of life which he has, thus far, been unable to begin.

All of this explains why there is so much anxiety in the dream about being late for school and why, more generally, he has been plagued by anxiety all his life. Unconsciously, Dr. A. always knew that he had not yet started his life, that he was too concerned with reading his mother's book to have written his own. It is the mother's job to "read the child's book," to understand *his* mind, not the other way around. Because of the inability of Dr. A.'s mother to do this, *he* had to care for *her*, a task that is impossible for any infant, and which robs him of his self.

EXAMPLE 3

This next example from Dr. A.'s analysis takes place two weeks later. The dream shows a development of these ideas and reveals how the self is further repressed by being kept from the fundamental work of infancy.

Dream

[1.] I was with a woman and another couple. We saw a man with a small briefcase jump in the river. I somehow knew that in the briefcase there was stolen money.

[2.] Then we all went into a hotel, but it was in the neighborhood I grew up in, near my old house. When we checked in, the desk clerk called me by name and I was surprised he knew my name. I asked him to get my bags, and he said he didn't know what to do because it was his first day on the job. Then I asked him how I could get my jeans cleaned and he handed me a packet of soap. I wondered, "How am I going to clean my underwear and my shirt?" Suddenly I was carrying a briefcase just like the man who jumped in the river.

[3.] After that I walked past the hotel restaurant on the way to my room. The restaurant manager got a phone call from a woman in Paris, and she asked him to come there for a visit. He seemed pleased and said, "Yes, great," but then he hung up and shot himself in the throat with a gun.

This long dream is worth our efforts at understanding for it gives us important insight into the infant's psychological reactions to being overwhelmed by parental projections.

Associations

Briefcase: It was very thin—more like a lap top computer.

Jumping in the river: It reminds me of that movie, *Butch Cassidy and the Sundance Kid*. They were being chased and escaped by jumping in the river.

The two couples: In the army, there were a lot of times we'd pick up girls, go to a hotel and fuck. Maybe it was like that, except that this hotel was right around the corner from my parents' house.

Hotel: I went away with Sally for the weekend . . . we stayed in a hotel.

Desk clerk: He looked like my old friend, Fred C. from medical school. I saw him at our reunion a few years ago and he looked very young. It was amazing, he hadn't changed a bit. He's a nice guy, his wife is lovely, too; they have a good relationship, they seem to be in love.

First day of work: That makes me think of something I read about the Kabbalah. It said that on the first day God created everything on earth. All the elements were there.

Clean my clothes: I don't know how I was supposed to clean them. I thought someone would do it for me, help me with it.

Restaurant manager: He looked like Ed Asner, who I saw on TV last night talking about the war. His father was killed in the camps . . . he was sent away as a child.

Paris: I was first there during the war and loved it. It looked somehow familiar to me, as if I'd been there before. I was always interested in France—I'm sure my interest came from the fact that I was in love with my French teacher in college. I had a terrible crush on her for years.

Shot in the throat: It was the same spot as a tracheostomy . . . when you can't breathe you need a tracheostomy. Of course I have terrible trouble breathing sometimes because of my asthma . . . it's been bad this week.

Dr. A. went on to say that he had been feeling very weak at work that day, almost sick. It reminded him of his war experience, of going into a state of collapse after having been in battle. He also said that he and Sally had been getting along beautifully last week, they had been very loving and sexual, closer than they had ever been. But then, a few days ago on their trip, "all hell broke loose and there's been nothing but hostility since then."

Interpretation and Discussion

The first thing we see in this dream and in the hour as a whole, is a confusing mélange of love and war. The dream reveals that Dr. A.'s early experience of love for his mother is equated with war, for although the hotel is in his childhood neighborhood near his parents' home, his associations are to his wartime experiences. It is his internal war he is remembering, the nature of which we can now learn more about.

As we know from the earlier session, Dr. A. was so occupied tending to his mother's mind that he had no room for his own mind to develop. As with all infants, Dr. A.'s mind was no match for the force of his mother's unconscious projections, and as his real self was drowned by them he had little choice but to jump into her unconscious, abandoning his own. In the dream, the man who jumps into the river therefore represents his real self. He notes that he "somehow knew the man had stolen some money." We can understand this if we consider that as the infant identifies so totally with his mother, he *becomes* her, in a sense he "steals" her personality when his own is lost to him. In the dream, Dr. A. (like all infants in this predicament) inadvertently becomes a thief and makes off with his mother's personality. We see further evidence of this later in the dream, when Dr. A. is carrying the same briefcase as the thief, clearly identifying himself *as* the thief.

The association to *Butch Cassidy and the Sundance Kid* further supports this notion, denoting Dr. A.'s unconscious awareness that he is a fugitive, and has *been* a fugitive since infancy. Unable to do the work of developing his own self and mind, he has appropriated his mother's. Since the briefcase looked like a computer, we can also say that Dr. A.'s mind, his mental computer, as it were, was forced to store the contents of his mother's mind.

There is a fundamental confusion in thinking for which we can see the source in this part of the dream. The burden of carrying the mother's mind deprives the infant of his opportunity to have a self, but nonetheless comes to be felt by the infant to be a cache of stolen wealth. It is a reversal and denial of his profound pain and loss, and the source of mania and omnipotence, as the infant begins to view his identification with his mother as strength. It is a false strength, however, for the energy of his true self which is capable of genuine growth has become unavailable to him.

The hotel clerk who reminds him of his old friend, Fred, represents Dr. A. as a baby. The evidence for this is built on several associations, first the fact that Fred looks so young—"he hasn't changed a bit"—and that it is his "first day on the job." Furthermore, Fred is a loving man with a loving marriage and in our view we can say that babies are naturally available for love, *if* love is available. The dream therefore states that, like Fred, the internal baby is still there, still able to love. As a result of the work we have done in the analysis, the adult Dr. A. is just now meeting his infant self for the first time; in the dream he is surprised that the clerk knows his name; he is surprised finally to be introduced to this ancient, loving part of himself.

The dream further shows that his infant self is already dirtied by his mother's projections—he has the stolen "dirty money" of his mother's personality in his briefcase/computer/mind. How, he wondered, is he to wash his "underwear"—that is, rid his *inner* self of his mother's unconscious? All his life he would have sensed that he was dirtied through and through, down to his underwear—the underpinnings of his psyche. He would have known too, that he could not clean it by himself, that he would need someone like an analyst to help him.

In the last part of the dream Dr. A. sees the restaurant manager who receives the enticing offer to fly to Paris to meet the woman. Since he seems pleased, how can we explain his violent behavior—shooting himself in the throat? The answer becomes clear if we understand the confusion that took place in his infancy, between his natural need for love and mental development, and the experience of war against his mind.

Dr. A.'s association to Paris is to his love for his French teacher, and so the woman in Paris represents love. This is stimulated by his new feelings of closeness and love for Sally, an unusual experience for Dr. A., and while it would seem to be desirable, like any change within the personality it arouses serious anxiety and resistance. We can understand why, for if he experiences love again he reactivates his fundamental infantile capacity for love, which in Dr. A.'s case became quickly associated with war. Because of his mother's emotional problems, love became a casualty of the war for his self. The loss of the self and the mind is therefore also linked to the loss of the genuine capacity for love.

For Dr. A. to open himself to love is to open himself as well to the suffocation of his true self that occurred when he first loved, and it is for this reason that the wonderful offer to "go to Paris" moves him to shoot himself in the throat. As he points out in his associations, it is in the exact spot of a tracheostomy, which would enable one to breathe if there were a blockage in the nose and throat. Here we see the etiology of Dr. A.'s lifelong problems with asthma. With his true self suffocated by his mother's overwhelming presence in his internal world, and with no one to help him "clean the underwear" of his inner self, he is forced to resort to emergency measures to help that buried self breathe. It is significant, however, that these measures could be lethal. Likewise, for the infant, the very means he adopts to try to save his self further endanger his mind and self.

SEX AND AGGRESSION AS SUBSTITUTES FOR THE SELF

This last point touches more generally on some important aspects of relationships. Buried in the mother's personality, the infant's true self cannot breathe, and the child feels himself to be dying, as indeed, mentally he is. The emergency "tracheostomy" that Dr. A. does on himself in the dream gives us an understanding of the common measures infants use to try to save their buried selves and make contact with something vital.

Like Fred in the dream, with his loving wife, the infant's essential self is the part of the personality capable of love. Once it is suffocated, and lacking the means to revive mentally, the only alternative open to the child is to deal with the problem physically. He tries to arouse feelings in himself, *any* feelings, trying to get in touch with something visceral in order to feel alive. This, he vainly hopes, will bring that essential self to the surface.

The ways in which people try physically to arouse and resurrect their lost selves are through aggression and sex, both of which we see in Dr. A.'s dream. Of course, the visceral feelings stimulated by these activities do nothing whatsoever to resurrect *true* feelings of love, which are always a product of the mind and the self. They *simulate* their pleasure and/or excitation. In wartime, the fear for one's life can cut through the numbness of a self unavailable for more genuine intimate emotions, but it is only a temporary reminder that one *has* feelings, that one is alive, a fact that is forgotten when the self is lost. Like many men, Dr. A. felt he could leave his mother and become a "man," become himself, cleaning her out of his personality by going off to war. But however stimulating they may be, feelings of fear and anxiety are not love, and do nothing to resolve the early confusion. Despite these efforts the infant self remains buried.

The use of sexuality (going to "fuck some girls") as an attempt to feel meets with the same fate, for sexual stimulation of the body does nothing to touch the mind in which the true capacity to love resides. In fact, the use of either of these physical methods to stimulate emotion actually drives the self further into hiding for they are destructive to the genuine capacity to love. This use of sexuality is as dangerous a "cure" as violence, for the needs of the mind simply cannot find satisfaction in the stimulation of the body. These kinds of defenses represent a fundamental confusion between the mind and the body and are a direct result of the repression of the self.

Conclusions and Theoretical Implications

Samuel Beckett's work provides insight into a deep level of unconscious reality which can help us visualize the preceding ideas. In his play, *Endgame*, the protagonist's (Hamm's) parents live in garbage cans in his room, a room he is unable to leave because he can no longer walk. This room corresponds to the infant's unconscious, so filled with the "garbage" of the *parents'* unconscious, that he can no longer use his mind. The infant's uncluttered psyche is capable of the movement and activity of true thought, but this becomes unavailable to him, its energy buried under old thoughts and feelings that are not even his own. His essential mind, like Hamm's body, can no longer move.

These psychological realities found a voice through Beckett's genius, and show us that once burdened with the parents' old thoughts and feelings, the true movement of the mind and true creative thought is blocked, replaced by a false mind and static thinking fettered by the parents' mental debris.

Bion's (1970) theory of "thoughts without a thinker" is relevant to these ideas for it distinguishes between real thinking and the unwitting lies we take to be the truth. Higher truth simply exists, with or without us to think it; all we need to do is be open to it. On the other hand, lies require a thinker, and these unconscious lies constitute a lamentably common means of communication.

Bion (1962) uses the term "beta elements" to represent projections, which are inadequate for use in thinking. These are distinguished from "alpha elements" and "alpha function," which form the basis of the capacity to think. The purpose of these theories is to call attention to the higher mind and to distinguish it from lower forms of mental functioning. The authors have added to this a perspective on the etiology of the obstacles to higher thinking and creative thought. Through patients' dreams we can observe the disruption of the infant's capacity to work at the development of his mind. Instead he has to work at cleaning his mind of his parents' unconscious projections, and this ushers in a use of the mind for purposes alien to its natural task. The projections, the "beta elements" that Bion saw as an indication of mental illness, may be more common than we normally suppose. The parents' unwitting projections of their own past psychological troubles may render our usual conception of the "normal" mind something with many similarities to a pathological state.

The picture is not as bleak as it seems, however, for through deep work with dreams we can make contact with the higher mind and the essential self so that the self can begin to do its own work. This is difficult work indeed, for as we know, the resistance to change is formidable—a mental "catastrophe" (Bion, 1970, 1992)—and the deeper the change the more violent the resistance.

We have proposed a very basic idea—that there can be no real work unless there is a real self to be doing it. This simple notion becomes very complex, however, in its requirement that we first understand the nature of an essential self. Because of the way civilization has developed, and the way human beings have developed, the necessary conditions that could enable a true self to come into existence have not been met.

If the mother lacks awareness of and ability to contain her own unconscious thoughts and feelings, she cannot contain the infant's, and his true mind, capable of creative thought, cannot come into being. It is upon that true mind, however, that the capacity for any kind of work is based, for clearly, one cannot work if one does not mentally exist. The awareness necessary for a true mind to come into existence must still be considered rare knowledge. Though the child may develop physically and intellectually along "normal" lines, there is something missing in his capacity to think creatively and in his capacity for a unified self. In most cases, the parents will not notice any problem, for there is no awareness of any other way of being.

Psychoanalysts are people who grew up in this same society under similar circumstances, and most current theories of psychoanalysis are based on this same level of consciousness. As a result, many psychoanalysts would likely be unable to detect any problem at this deeper level of the self. We should not be led to believe, however, that this knowledge, although rare, is too esoteric or out of reach to strive for. Each of us begins with the potential for this knowledge and wisdom, and so to the infant it is *not* rare. Nor is it forgotten by us as adults. Consciousness is a drive in the human animal, although it is one of which we have less understanding than our other animal instincts. It would be unwise to allow our current unfamiliarity with consciousness to determine our efforts to achieve it in the future, for as we have shown it can be detected and dealt with in analysis. An awareness of its existence, together with a better understanding of its origins in infantile life, should rather inspire us to work with greater energy and devotion toward discovering it in our patients and in ourselves.

References

Bion, W. R. (1962), *Learning from Experience*. New York: Basic Books.
———— (1970), *Attention and Interpretation*. London: Tavistock.
———— (1992), *Cogitations*. London: Karnac.
Freud, S. (1900), The Interpretation of Dreams. *Standard Edition*, 4 & 5. London: Hogarth Press, 1953.
Klein, M. (1946), Notes on some schizoid mechanisms. In: *Envy and Gratitude and Other Works*. New York: Delacorte Press, 1975, pp. 1–24.

5

FREUD: MAN AT WORK

Patrick J. Mahony, Ph.D.

Iamque opus exegi quod nec Iovis ira nec ignis
nec poterit ferrum nec edax abolere vetustas.
[And I have carried out my work that neither Jove's wrath nor fire
Nor iron weapon nor age will be able to destroy.]
—Ovid, *Metamorphoses*, Bk. 15, lines 871–872

The folly of that impossible percept, "Know thyself," till it be translated into this partially possible one, "Know what you canst work at."—Thomas Carlyle, *Past and Present*, Bk. 4, Ch. 7

Where and how to begin? And how to end? Such unending questions about beginnings and endings confront us when we attempt to approach the subject of Freud at work. Though I shall touch on Freud's theory of work, my focus is on the practical place of work in his life.

It is platititudinous to say that Freud was a genius. Better to say that he lists among the world's dozen or so greatest geniuses ("When Nature has work to be done," Emerson mused, "she creates a genius to do it"). With his gigantic mind Freud worked incessantly to discover and elaborate a world paradigm of revolutionary dimensions. His was even the rarest accomplishment to reveal new facts, to set forth a method for uncovering them, to organize them into an overarching theory and, beyond that, to speculate on the unprovable in his time (see Jones, 1953, pp. 51–52). Indeed, Freud counts among those who belie the generalization that in philosophy the questions remain the same and only the answers change. He gave us questions, endless.

And he worked and he worked and he worked. And miles to go before he slept. He peeked into his dreams and found he worked there too, and then told us that we all do dream work. And he wrote about his baby self, a mere nineteen months, self-enlisted into child-labor—mourning the death of his still younger brother Julius—and he wrote that we all do mourning work not only at death, but also at the high noon of life. And he wrote another Genesis valid for tomorrow as well as for yesterday. In the beginning there was work: a drive is "a measure of the demand made upon the mind for work in consequence of its connection with the body" (Freud, 1915, p. 122). And then there was wish: "Nothing but a wish can set our mental apparatus to work" (Freud, 1900, p. 567).

One of Freud's finest insights as well as memorable quotations shows the incomparable premium he laid on work: "No other technique for the conduct of life attaches the individual so firmly to reality as laying emphasis on work; for his work at least gives him a secure place in a portion of reality, in the human community" (Freud, 1930, p. 80n.). It is not accidental that in leaving hypnotic for psychoanalytic treatment, he was opting for a praxis that necessitated much more working by the patient—working and working through. The latter term ties in with a value Freud assigned over and over to a particular type of work—in German, he called it *Leistung*, which means efficient work, achievement, or performance. Thus we should nuance Strachey's Freud who says that the doctor merely aims to restore "some degree of capacity for work and enjoyment" (Freud, 1912, p. 119; cf. *G.W.*, 8:385: *Leistungs-und Genussfähigkeit*).[1]

Sometimes one hears that today's analysts are Freud's lengthened shadow. Those who are prone to take such a statement as demeaning might pause to imagine how Freud would have understood it. An idle fancy? Here is the answer in Freud's spellbound wish for a memorial: "When you think of me, think of Rembrandt, a little light and a great deal of darkness."

---

[1] See also Strachey's translation about the aims of psychoanalytic treatment to make the patient "as efficient and as capable of enjoyment as possible" (Freud, 1923a, p. 251; cf. *G.W.*, 13:226: *und ihn so nach die Möglichkeit leistungs-und genussfähig zu machen.* Elsewhere Strachey's translation respects the qualitative denotation of *Leistung*: "A neurotic is incapable of enjoyment and efficiency—the former because his libido is not directed on to any real object and the latter because he is obliged to employ a great deal of his available energy on keeping his libido under repression and on warding off its assaults" (Freud, 1915–1917, pp. 453–454; cf. *G.W.*, 11:472: Der Neurotiker ist genuss-und leistungsunfähig" (cf. also p. 457 and *G.W.*, 11:476). Freud was aware, incidentally, of the forgeable oneiric link between *Leistung* and *Leiste*, the German word for groin (Freud, 1900, p. 412).

To understand what work personally meant for Freud, we might set out by first clearing up a confusion. Erikson once reported that upon being asked what mental health consists of, Freud responded that it involved working and loving well. Sometimes, with echoes of a Winnicottian orientation, critics have said that in his response Freud neglected play. To counter such a charge, we must examine Freud's personal definitions that characterize his idiolect. Let us note that play was part of Freud's work, both theoretical and practical. For Freud creativity was play, as he made plain to Pfister, "I could not contemplate with any sort of comfort a life without work. Creative imagination and work go together with me; I take no delight in anything else" (Freud, 1963, letter of March 6, 1910, p. 35). Freud could not be plainer: he could not live without play of the mind. True to his surname (*Freude* in German means joy), he lived in creative enjoyment, by that enjoyment, and for it. In that larger sense, he lived out the rich meanings of *ludus*, which in Latin means play and school, and of *schole*, which in Greek means school and leisure.

Apart from sheerly creative work, Freud had a restlessness and enormous energy, it appears, for any kind of work. Jones (1955, p. 32) observed that "Walking fast used to stimulate the flow of Freud's thoughts, but it was at times breathtaking for a companion who would have preferred to pause and digest them." When climbing stairs, it was his habit to go two or three steps at a time (Freud, 1900, p. 238). As a tourist Freud had restless energy, so much so that according to Minna his ideal was to sleep in a different place each night (Jones, 1953, p. 332; 1955, p. 395). In 1921 the sixty-five-year-old Freud met with the Secret Committee in the Harz mountains; he had occasion to do some hiking with his colleagues, his juniors by a quarter-century. To their amazement, he excelled them in endurance and speed (Jones, 1953, p. 18; 1957, p. 81).

But in my estimation, the most spectacular evidence about Freud's energy that can be found in the available literature concerns one of the two occasions in Freud's first forty years of married life when, according to Jones (1955, p. 391), he was confined to bed. Jones's curt report merits amplification from other texts. During the period in question, which lasted less than two weeks, Freud had difficulty breathing and yet was studying the topography of Rome and had examined Kassowitz's *Allgemeine Biologie*. On October 23, 1898, Freud wrote to Fliess that he was suffering from influenza, but there was more that Freud did not mention; on November 6, he informed Fliess that he had been operated on for "a large furuncle on the raphe scroti" (Freud, 1985, pp. 331, 334). Now within that near two-week period Freud dreamt about riding a horse, which he commented on this way:

> For some days before [the dream] I had been suffering from boils which made every movement a torture; and finally a boil the size of an apple

had risen at the base of my scrotum, which caused me the most unbearable pain with every step I took. Feverish lassitude, loss of appetite
and the hard work with which I nevertheless carried on—all these had
combined with the pain to depress me. . . . It was a remarkable *feat*,
too, to be able to carry on my psychotherapeutic work for eight or ten
hours a day while I was having so much pain. But I knew that I could
not go on long with my peculiarly difficult work unless I was in completely sound physical health [Freud, 1900, pp. 230–231].

The excerpt has no need of comment save to say that the Freud at
work was a Freud afire.

A few particulars about Freud's work schedule might be of some
interest. During his teen years, he would eat alone so as to have more
time for study; when his friends visited him, he would receive them
in his study rather than in the family quarters (Jones, 1953, p. 21). We
can well imagine when Freud reached his twenties and served six and
a half months in the clinic of the internist Nothnagel, he adapted more
than most to Nothnagel's strict counsel to his pupils: "Whoever needs
more than five hours of sleep should not study medicine. The medical
student must attend lectures from eight in the morning until six in the
evening. Then he must go home and read until late at night" (Jones,
1953, pp. 63–64).

Once on his own as an analyst, Freud (1900, p. 523) lived out
the cherished motto of another hero, the French physiologist Claude
Bernard: *travailler comme une bête* (to work like an animal). The work
schedule maintained by Freud was truly intense:

> He would rise soon after seven and have his first patient at eight and
> work until the lunch break from one to three; then he resumed analyzing
> until supper usually at nine, though sometimes at ten; finally he went
> to bed never before one in the morning, and often later. Sunday was
> his favorite day for writing [Jones, 1955, pp. 382–385].

It might be added that even on vacation Freud could be a workhorse,
as this unpublished letter to his daughter indicates: "I have so much
to do with writing, corresponding, correcting and conceptualizing that
I can not sufficiently appreciate the beautiful weather" (letter of
August 10, 1920—located in the Library of Congress).

A primary thrust in all of Freud's life work was to plumb the
secrets of nature that for him, at a deeper level, represented a maternal
object. In this regard we might recall Freud's contention that a child's
brooding and doubting about sexuality "becomes the prototype of all
later intellectual work directed towards the solution of problems"

(Freud, 1908, p. 219). Significantly, when the adolescent Freud referred to girls in his correspondence, he used "principles," a code word with glorific ethical and scientific denotations (Freud, 1990). Listening to the lecture entitled "Nature," the young Freud was moved to drop his philosophical studies for medicine. Pertinently, that lecture contains these eroticized identifications of nature:

> She dwells in none but children; and the mother, where is she?—She is the sole artist: from the simplest stuff to the greatest contrasts; without apparent effort, to the greatest perfection . . . She enacts a drama . . . There is an eternal life, a coming into being, and a movement in her . . . She loves herself and through eyes and hearts without number she clings to herself. She has analyzed herself in order to enjoy herself . . . She has set me within. She will also lead me without. I commit myself to her [in Wittels, 1931, pp. 31ff].

Somewhat later, in a telling letter to Martha, Freud identified science as female:

> I know a beautiful fairy tale which I have experienced myself, and as for lofty science and say: "Your Highness, I remain your humble, most devoted servant, but please don't hold it against me; you have never looked kindly upon me, never said a comforting word to me; you don't answer when I write to you, listen when I speak . . . You will understand if I now devote myself to the other so undemanding and gracious lady. Keep me in pleasant memory until I return. I have to write to Martha" [Freud, 1961, letter of June 6, 1882, p. 29].

Later, Freud avowed to Martha that science "could become your bitterest enemy" (Letter of March 29, 1884). In brief, nature is female, science is female, and likewise, as Freud told Jung, "Lady Psychoanalysis" (Freud, 1974b, letter of February 2, 1910, p. 292).

Those identifications were at the heart of Freud's own investigations. In many ways, Freud's ego ideal as an investigator was Leonardo da Vinci, considered by him to be the first modern man and the first since the Greeks to use only his observation and judgment to explore the secrets of nature. Freud's praise of the antiauthoritarian da Vinci seems autobiographical: "If we translate scientific abstraction back again into concrete individual experience, we see that the 'ancients' and authority simply correspond to his father, and nature once more becomes the tender and kindly mother who had nourished him" (Freud, 1910, p. 122). Freud's comments on da Vinci to the Vienna Psychoanalytic Society were in the same vein: "But this absence of prejudice too is determined by his relationship to his parents: all along he endeavors to free himself from old age [i.e., father] and to return to Mother [!] Nature—principles that he repeatedly advocated in public" (Nunberg and Federn, 1967, p. 348).

Erotized factors served as incentives to Freud's explorations, which he executed with an overall successful sublimation and in a total commitment to work. Freud counseled in one of his early lectures: "This is the only way to make important discoveries: have one's ideas exclusively on one central interest" (Sachs, 1944, p. 69). Freud lived this counsel intensely, even libidinally. He spelled it out this way:

> I am well aware that it is one thing to give utterance to an idea once or twice in the form of a passing *aperçu*, and quite another to mean it seriously—to take it literally and pursue it in the face of every contradictory detail, and to win it a place among accepted truths. It is the difference between a casual flirtation and a legal marriage with all its duties and difficulties. "*Epouser le idées de . . .*" [to marry the ideas of] is no uncommon figure of speech, at any rate in French [Freud, 1914, p. 15].

And so in talking of *Totem and Taboo*, Freud could write: "Sometimes I feel as though I only wanted to start a little liaison and at my age discovered that I had to marry a new wife" (Freud, 1994, letter of November 30, 1911, p. 317). A better example is Freud's (1900) masterpiece, *The Interpretation of Dreams*, whose epistemological investigation is set in a narrative framework of traveling through nature. Insofar as nature symbolized the female body for Freud, he married his scientific presentation to an oedipal and then preoedipal journey through the maternal corpus (Mahony, 1987)—symbolic marriage, symbolic incest, and a labor that produced the child of psychoanalysis.

For the sake of coverage, I shall mention but not digress on another libidinal strain in Freud's investigations. He was propelled by the fantasy of being his own progenitor. A variant of the Oedipus complex, that narcissistic fantasy of being one's own parent stands aside the other variants—the Abraham or filicidal myth and the Cain or fratricidal myth. Let it be said that the fantasy of self-fecundation, although of decisive import in Freud's life, has not been sufficiently examined up to this time. Freud's conflicts over scientific priority, involving Fliess as one among others, testifies to Freud's anxiety over influence and his investment in the fantasy of self-fecundation. He did not like to be worked on.

Among the factors determining Freud's mode of work, physical stimulus enjoyed a major function. This reflection leads us straight to Freud's experience with cocaine, which will give us a new opportunity to uncover his attitudes to work. One part of the story of Freud's missing out on fame is well known—he was on the verge of discovering the anesthetic qualities of cocaine. But other parts of the story tell us new things about our subject. On account of his cocaine experiments, Freud incurred the risk on being an accomplice in what a contemporary called, "the third scourge of humanity" (Jones, 1953, p. 95). In a twist of fate, not many years later he would disturb the sleep of the world and not many years later again—in 1909—he would bring his version of pestilence onto the New Continent.

Freud's cocaine connection begins in 1884. His interest in the drug, be it said, was aroused by its effect more on energy for work than on mental acuity. While declaring that he was still drug-free in the same letter, Freud interjected: "An explorer's temperament requires two basic qualities: optimism in attempt, criticism in work" (Freud, 1961, letter of April 21, 1884, p. 40). Within two months later he had taken the stimulant about a dozen times. In the letter of June 19, 1884 we hear Freud, as if proclaiming from the ramparts: "This must continue to be my way of life: risking a lot, hoping a lot, working a lot. To average bourgeois common sense I have been lost long ago" (Freud, 1974a, p. 41). In "Über Coca," an essay finished in the same month, Freud explained:

> One senses an increase of self-control and feels more vigorous and more capable of work; on the other hand, one misses that heightening of the mental powers which alcohol, tea, or coffee induce. . . . I have tested this effect of coca, which wards off hunger, sleep, and fatigue and steels one to intellectual effort, some dozen times on myself [p. 60].

Seized by the impact of the magical substance, Freud (1974a) announced in his "Contributions to the Knowledge of the Effect of Cocaine" (completed in January 1885), that he frequently took cocaine (p. 104). The quest for magic continued: in March 1885, Freud published "On the General Effect of Cocaine," which reports his observing a writer who for weeks had literary inhibition and who was able with the help of cocaine to work fourteen hours without stop (p. 114). The next year in Paris presented the occasion of the most powerful existential encounter in Freud's life, as he never forgot the few months with Charcot and even named his very first son after the Parisian; it hardly goes without saying that Freud's experience urged him to cocaine consumption (Freud, 1961, letters of January 18, 1886, p. 161; January 20, p. 162; February 2, pp. 164, 166). The tide turned by July 1887 when Freud penned "Craving for and Fear of Cocaine." The essay contains Freud's disingenuous avowal that limited his cocaine consumption to "some months" (1974a, p. 173). Exit cocaine, enter

Fliess, re-enter cocaine in the service of a curious pan-nosology—the nose was all. In July 1895, when Freud gave birth to his Irma dream and to scientific dream interpretation, he was under the impress of Fliess and prescribed cocaine—in the form of nasal applications. He took it in 1895 (Freud, 1900, p. 111).

In the light of the etymology of Freud's first name (Sigmund: victory-mouth), it is a sad irony that his cigar smoking became a veritable addiction which, however contributory to the creative process, accelerated if not caused his lethal oral cancer. Freud's daily consumption of cigars approximated twenty (Jones, 1953, pp. 309, 385), and as his massive correspondence to Eitingon recurrently testifies, he tolerated deprivation with enormous difficulty. For one sample, I cite a poignant complaint to Eitingon: "The sum of my various infirmities raises the question as to how much longer I shall be able to continue my professional work, especially since giving up the beloved habit of smoking has brought about a great reduction of my intellectual interests (letter of March 16, 1926—located in the Library of Congress). And yet, although Freud's smoking became a necessity in his creative theorizing, he realized that his smoking habit prevented him from working out certain psychological problems (letter to Abraham of February 13, 1916, cited in Jones, 1955, p. 189).

Freud's self-destructive dependence on nicotine brings us the question of his general reliance on pain. In exploring Freud's working alliance with pain, we could well take as our motto a precious aphorism from near the end of the *Project*: "Unpleasure remains the sole means of education" (Freud, 1895, p. 370). With the aid of Freud's aphorism, we can dispute the regret by many analysts that Freud had to work too hard for a living and that if he were less economically burdened, he would have had more time to exploit his creativity. Ample evidence exists to dispel such pious reflections. In fact, for optimal achievement, Freud needed disgruntlement, whether it be from physical fatigue or psychic misery, and he described that necessity time and again. It seems as if he feared the regressive pull of full contentment and hence thrived on irritation, which drove him to expunge it in creativity. A month before the appearance of *Studies on Hysteria*, Freud (1985) described his tyrannical desideratum this way: "A man like me cannot live without a hobby-horse, without a consuming passion, without—in Schiller's words—a tyrant. I have found one. In its service I know no limits" (letter of May 25, 1895, p. 129). In sum, irritation was Freud's requirement not just for working, but for *Leistung*, performance—working well, writing well. Let us listen again to Freud:

A failure [in research work] makes one inventive, creates a free flow of associations, brings idea after idea, whereas once success is there a certain narrow-mindedness or thick-headedness sets in so that one always keeps coming back to what has been already established and can make no new combinations [letter to Martha, October 31, 1883; in Jones, 1953, p. 196].

During an industrious night last week, when I was suffering from that degree of pain which brings about the optimal condition for my mental activities, the barriers suddenly lifted, the veils dropped, and everything became transparent—from the details of the neuroses to the determinants of consciousness [Freud, 1985, letter of October 20, 1895, p. 146].

I returned to a sense of too much well-being and have since then been very lazy because the modicum of misery essential for intensive work will not come back [Freud, 1985, letter of April 16, 1896, pp. 180–181].

My style has unfortunately been bad because I feel too well physically; I have to feel somewhat miserable to write well [Freud, 1985, letter of September 6, 1899, p. 370].

I have long known . . . that I can't be diligent when I am in very good health, but I need a bit of discomfort from which I have to extract myself [Freud, 1994, letter of April 2, 1911, p. 265].

The summary conclusion is that in the last years of the nineteenth century Freud was at his most creative and at the same time was suffering most from his neurosis (see Jones, 1953, p. 305). For sure there was a threshold in Freud's suffering past the painful stimulus that hampered his creativity. Yet that threshold was peculiar to him, for the amount of suffering that could stimulate him would dampen the creative capacity of most.

There are two common misconceptions about Freud's creativity that are worthy of mention. The first is part of a popular belief which assumes that intellectual geniuses are blessed with continuous inspiration and create works that spring ready-made from their brain—a fantasy akin to the Greek myth of Athena, the goddess of wisdom, who bolted in birth from the head of Zeus. And indeed, Freud himself (1900, p. 613) lent credence to the account that Goethe and Helmholtz (like Mozart) created almost ready-made wholes. Researchers in creativity have done much to demystify the generalizations of such accounts. Gruber's (1982) magisterial study of Darwin shows that his insight was gotten through hard work and was much more gradual than supposed. The same process obtains for Freud, the month of October 1897, being exceptional (see Jones, 1953, pp. 241–242, 321, 324, 326, 392; 1955, pp. xii, 5).

The second misconception about Freud's creativity is more perni-
cious in that it intrinsically affects the meaning of his works. Attention
has often been called to Freud's dualistic rather than pluralist way of
thought. In a startling reflection on this cognitive feature, Jones wondered whether Freud's pan-dualism was a defense against oedipal strivings (Jones, 1957, p. 267; see also 1955, pp. 320, 422–423; 1957,
pp. 306–307). But the allegation is only partly true, for in fact Freud's
oppositional procedure that seems at times to be a simplifying quirk
covers up a fundamental complexity which pervades his texts. It would
be more accurate to say that Freud's *initial* analytic moves are dualistic,
which he then typically proceeds to undercut. Suffice it to say that his
elaborations of continuity between previously proposed opposites are
legion: the pleasure and reality principles, normality and abnormality,
Eros and Thanatos.

There are aspects of Freud's anxiety during workaday performance that have escaped commentators up to now. One of Freud's
techniques to control anxiety was to think of some idea to serve as an
electrical grounder which would distract him from the task at hand.
Thus, before embarking on the journey to Clark University where
Freud trembled upon receiving an honorary doctorate, he told his colleagues that he was going to the States for the compound purpose of
lecturing and catching sight of a wild porcupine (the technique and
motto "to find one's own porcupine" were adopted in Freud's early
circle [Jones, 1955, p. 59]). So great was Freud's anxiety, however,
that the porcupine strategy did not suffice. He therefore had recourse
to a second containing measure. As he wrote to Jung, "When my turn
comes [to lecture], I shall comfort myself with the thought that at least
you and Ferenczi will be listening" (Freud, 1974b, letter of July 19,
1909, p. 243).

Freud's measure for controlling anxiety was not merely aimed at
unfamiliar audiences. Even when lecturing to the small group of the
Vienna Psychoanalytic Society, he sought out Lou Andreas-Salomé as
a pacifying target:

> I missed you in the lecture yesterday . . . I have adopted the bad habit
> of always directing my lecture to a definite member of the audience,
> and yesterday fixed my gaze as if spellbound at the place which had
> been kept for you [Freud, 1966, letter of November 10, 1912, p. 11].

> I am very sorry that I have to answer your letter in writing, i.e., that
> you were not at my lecture on Saturday. I was thus deprived of my
> point of fixation and spoke uncertainly [Freud, 1966, letter of March 2,
> 1913, p. 13].

To say it otherwise, one of the two ways Freud employed to control anxiety was rooted in object relations. He would fantasize a reassuring closeness. Expressive of that need for closeness was his style of delivery, which was not oratorical but conversational, talking intimately and gathering the audience close to him (see Jones, 1953, p. 342). As a writer too, he wanted closeness, as readers readily appreciate in Freud's engaging dialogic style; that effect was a spillover from the intimate audience Freud had to have. In truth, Freud's power as a writer is that he managed to have his second audience, the general readership, imagine itself as the sole and intimate audience.

As Freud wrote, however, with Fliess's disaffection, he lost his "only audience" (Freud, 1985, letter of September 19, 1901, p. 450). Later the select audience grew to a handful—Freud admitted to Ferenczi that he wrote for five people (letter of December 15, 1914; located in the Library of Congress). To conclude: Freud's particular need of object constancy during productivity proved to be but an aspect of his more general need of object constancy. For example, when traveling for a few weeks, Freud would often be homesick; he had to send home a card or telegram nearly daily, and a long letter once every two or three days (Jones, 1955, p. 395).

The time has come in my exposition to approach a feature of Freud's work life that is the hardest to discuss, precisely because it has attracted so much psychoanalytic commentary that borders on the pietistic and saccharine. I refer to Freud's courage in its obvious and not so obvious traits. A consideration of Freud's courage can lead us into many byways: his being wrecked by success dating back to the time when he was still a child and his brother Julius died at eight months (see Jones, 1955, p. 375); his martial ideal traceable to his first three years when he was fighting with his year-older nephew John (Freud, 1900, p. 198; cf. Jones, 1953, pp. 8, 14); his two greatest fears identifiable as helplessness and poverty (Freud, 1965, letter of December 30, 1914, p. 208). But how does courage refer to work, and if so, how so?

Let us set out with Freud's self-insight contained in the first entry (January 1883) in the secret record, which he and Martha wrote together about their engagement:

> There is some courage and boldness locked up in me that is not easily driven away or extinguished. When I examine myself strictly, more strictly than my loved one would, I perceive that Nature has denied me many talents and has granted me not much, indeed very little, of the kind of talent that compels recognition. But she endowed me with a dauntless love of truth, the keen eye of an investigator, a rightful sense of the values of life, and the gift of working hard and finding pleasure in doing so [in Jones, 1953, p. 118].

Somewhat short of three years later, he came back to this self-insight shared with Martha:

> My whole capacity for work probably springs from my character and from the absence of outstanding intellectual weaknesses. But I know that this combination is very conducive to slow success ... [Breuer] told me that he had discovered that hidden under the surface of timidity there lay in me an extremely daring and fearless human being. I had always thought so, but never dared tell anyone [Freud, 1961, letter of February 2, 1886, pp. 215–216; see also Freud, 1985, letter of December 8, 1895, p. 155; and the letter of April 4, 1915 to Ferenczi; in Jones, 1953, pp. xiii, 320, 404].

The cost of such courage is considerable, especially as it entails a forthrightness that disturbs one's addressees at the very worst moment—when they are asleep:

> I belonged to those who have "disturbed the sleep of the world," as Hebbel says, and ... I could not reckon upon objectivity and tolerance. Since, however, my conviction of the general accuracy of my observations and conclusions grew and grew, and as my confidence in my own judgment was by no means slight, any more than my moral courage, there could be no doubt about the outcome of the situation. I make up my mind that it had been my fortune to discover particularly important connections, and was prepared to accept the fate that sometimes accompanies such discoveries [Freud, 1914, pp. 21–22].

Freud's courage, nevertheless, was neither pure precious metal nor mettle. He cultivated his natural bent to a manneristic degree. Thus, in one of his betrothal letters, Freud declared that since prestigious men around him possessed a characteristic "manner," he too would adopt one; he would exploit his native propensity to honesty and turn it into a "mannerism." But again, we may ask ourselves, how does Freud's courageous "mannerism" relate to work? We may not be far off the mark if we begin remembering that in Ludwig Börne's work, just before the momentous text on free associations that lastingly impressed Freud, the following thesis appears: "Sincerity is the source of all genius, and man would be more intelligent were he only better" (Jones, 1953, p. 247). Freud's sincerity was a combined raw and finished product. It seems that his fascination with the novel force of his sincerity egged him on to produce more in the partially mannered persona.

Assisted by his hybrid courage and honesty, Freud stamped his own coin and caused those around him to deal with its currency. He displayed his dislike of ceremonies, even his marriage. He carried this reaction to the meretricious into his social communication. As a speaker, he had a persona that in some ways resembled Goethe and Samuel Johnson, who avoided banal expression and spoke in memorable phrases that impressed their audience. As a writer, he imposed his personal style in whatever he wrote; his letters possess a distinctive style, not only as in their entirety, but also as epistolary collections addressed to someone in particular (see Jones, 1955, p. 155). Even when he returned repeatedly to write up a familiar topic such as dreams, Freud managed to fashion a freshness in his work (cf. Jones, 1953, p. 362; 1955, pp. 155, 420).

A rather delicate issue remains to be considered under the rubric of courage. Although Freud did not say it directly, and for the sake of the survivability of his scientific movement could not say it directly, he held most analysts to be unworthy and cowardly, with a carryover of that deficiency in the quality of their work. For organizational psychoanalysis the brutal, unwelcomable fact is that Freud used a secret committee to rule the International Psycho-analytical Association from 1912 to 1926, at which time he withdrew from administrative tasks. In other words, unknown to most of his contemporary colleagues, for the entire period when Freud was administratively active, he wielded power in a covert manner. Despite his discovery of psychoanalytic treatment that has brought solace to so many, Freud made no bones about his general contempt of humankind. Given his remarkable courage, that contempt was in good measure based on what he perceived as a lack of courage—and he included most analysts in that judgment: "My worst qualities, including a certain indifference towards the world, have no doubt had the same share in the end result as my good ones, e.g., a defiant courage in the search of truth. In the depths of my being I remain convinced that my dear fellow creatures—with few exceptions—are a wretched lot" (Freud, 1966, letter of July 28, 1929, p. 182).

Gesindel—wretched lot, trash, rabble—the depreciative utterance did not arise from an isolated moment of irritation, for it echoes throughout Freud's texts. It should not be confused with Freud's one-shot impulsive, self-contradictory remarks that are frequently misrecognized in the babble of critics bent on making a towering mountain from the hill of some mole. Seldom did Freud voice with repeated insistence an idea such as his devaluation of people as *Gesindel*. We hear it from the teenage Freud and from him as a young, middle-aged, and elderly adult as he addressed a variety of interlocutors—patients and colleagues, men and women, his juniors and seniors. These included the youthful Silberstein, Martha as fiancée, Pfister, Jung,

Ferenczi, Putnam, Jones, Lou Andreas-Salomé, and so unfortunately on. The work has yet to be written on courage in the history of organized psychoanalysis—one even wonders that were Freud himself the author, he would have written about the overall history of organized psychoanalysis as one of cowardice.

As part of its due credit, the role of writing in Freud's courageous self-analysis should be used to sound his rite of passage. The unknown story is as follows. In May 1897 Freud sat down to compose his *Interpretation of Dreams*, but rapidly fell into a writing block. It was precisely in response to that inhibition that he began a prolonged systematic self-analysis starting in June 1897. Yet to say that first came writing, then inhibition, then self-analysis is erroneous, for the self-analysis that focused on dreams was itself in writing!

To the detailed documentation of that historical procedure (see Mahony, 1994), I add these supplementary comments. Writing was more than just a medium for Freud; it informed his professional organizing experience. That private experience in turn was guided by the tenet that dreams as psychic transcriptions are recoverable *par excellence* by their externalized transcription and scriptive interpretation. The homebred practice became a family heirloom, as we read in Anna's letter to her father: "Now finally I also believe your idea that if one is alone, one can analyze dreams only by means of writing" (letter of August 8, 1921, located in the Library of Congress; her letter of August 4, 1921 is also pertinent). In the case of analyzing others, writing involved greater activity for Freud. As he stated to Abraham, "I have to recuperate from psychoanalysis by working, otherwise I should not be able to stand it" (Freud, 1965, letter of July 3, 1912, p. 120; see also Freud, 1993, letter of April 15, 1910, p. 51).

Writing is one thing, but working it up into a publication is another. Psychoanalytic historians have not realized how much the concept of work as *published* achievement was decisive in Freud's crucial early years as an analyst. Freud even attributed his break with Breuer to publication: "I believe he has never forgiven me for having lured him into writing the *Studies* with me and so committed him to something definite" (Freud, 1985, letter of March 1, 1896, p. 175). The case with Fliess is different. If we examine the years 1887 to 1900, the period of the relatively positive friendship between Freud and Fliess, we shall be able to trace Freud's disillusionment with his friend not only because of theoretical issues in the abstract, but also because of publication as such. It is not appreciated that even if we discount Freud's psychological writings, his neurological ones for that period far surpass Fliess's in quantity. From 1887 to 1900 Fliess published a pair of monographs and four brief articles, all totaling no more than 400 pages. During that same span Freud published his book on aphasia; a volume of 220 pages co-authored with Oscar Rie; a text of 168 pages on the central diplegias; and a massive treatise of 327 pages with 14 pages of bibliography. Added to that there were Freud's translation of three books, his numerous neurological articles, and—just between 1898 and 1900—83 abstracts and reviews of neurological literature in the *Jahresbericht über die Leistungen und Fortschritte auf dem Gebiete der Neurologie und Psychiatrie.*

In 1897 itself Freud completed his last work on neurology, and Fliess's volume, finished the previous year, saw press. Yet, from 1897 to 1900, Fliess could write up only a short article. Fliess could not keep up with Freud, nor could he underwrite their scriptive ego ideal any more. Meanwhile Freud was bristling with impatience to receive concrete evidence of scriptive performance. Let us open three of Freud's letters:

[June 1897: I hope] that instead of a short article you will within a year present to us a small book which solves the organic secrets [Freud, 1985, p. 254].

[May 1899:] A contented letter from you containing evidence of your being well and the promise that you will attempt a first presentation of your earthshaking formulas were a long-missed pleasure [Freud, 1985, p. 351].

[June 1899:] The announcement that you are engaged in research perhaps may mean, [that] instead of writing? And [thus the] postponement of the date on which I can read something of yours? [Freud, 1985, pp. 365–366].

Jung was a horse of another color—he manifested his scriptive efficiency, but that, in Freud's lights, slowly became dissociated from achievement. We go back to 1909 where we can begin to follow, like the rise of a neurosis, the burgeoning tensions between Freud and Jung. Upon their return from the United States, Jung bespoke his aim to write a psychoanalytic study of mythology and asked Freud for "a beam of light"; Freud's rejoinder was: "I am glad you share my belief that we must conquer the whole field of mythology. Thus far we have only two pioneers: Abraham and Rank" (Freud, 1974b, letters of October 14, 1909 and October 17, pp. 251–252 and 255). By November, to Freud's delight, Jung was plunging into archaeology and the phylogenesis of neurosis. All through that year, the adulating Jung was calling Freud a hero and demi-god, and even "father creator," an epithet composed on Christmas day (see Freud, 1974b, letters of June 4, 1909, p. 229; December 14, 1909, p. 275; December 25, p. 279).

On the first day of the New Year, Freud conveyed to Ferenczi the related conceptions that he had been thinking of uniting his co-workers into a closer bond and that religion depended on the infantile

helplessness of mankind (Freud, 1994, pp. 118–119). But by the end
of that same year, in a lecture about his forthcoming book to the Zurich
Psychoanalytic Society, Jung expressed his fear of Freud's objections.
Freud pleaded innocent: "I don't know why you are afraid of my
criticism in matters of mythology. I shall be very happy when you
plant a flag of libido in that field and return as a victorious conqueror
to our motherland" (Freud, 1974b, letters of December 23, 1910,
p. 383; January 18, 1911, p. 385; January 22, 1911).

Then lo and behold, as if returning from a covert night march and
raising banner on high, Freud announced that he was working on a
larger synthesis, though not identifying it as *Totem and Taboo* (Freud,
1974b, letter of February 12, 1911, p. 438). Months passed, many
months, before Freud came out with a missive sounding like serendip-
ity, but mocking the last two syllables of that word:

> Since my mental powers revived, I have been working in a field where
> you will be surprised to meet me. I have unearthed strange and uncanny
> things and will almost feel obliged *not* to discuss them with you. But
> you are too shrewd not to guess what I am up to when I add that I am
> dying to read your "Transformations" [*Psychology of the Uncon-
> scious*]. [Freud, 1974b, letter of August 20, 1911, p. 438].

In his disquieted retort, Jung was on the same wavelength as Freud's
message but could not read it:

> Your letter has got me on tenterhooks because, for all my "shrewd-
> ness," I can't quite make out what is going on so enigmatically behind
> the scenes. Together with my wife I have tried to unriddle your words,
> and we have reached surmises which, for the time being at any rate, I
> would rather keep to myself [Freud, 1974b, letter of August 29, 1911,
> p. 439].

In the meantime the first half of Jung's mythological *Psychology*
appeared. The battle alarms in the background blared louder, but in
the foreground we hear that Freud paid a visit to Zurich in September
though never mentioned his interlocutor's opus. Jung continued on the
second half of *Psychology*, which Freud was sensing as a declaration
of independence. The ominous last chapter of Jung's opus, "The Sacrifice," passed off unconscious sexuality as merely symbolic. Jung realized that his mimetic writing was equally performative: "When I was
working on my book about the libido and approaching the end of the
chapter 'The Sacrifice,' I knew in advance that its publication would

cost me my friendship with Freud . . . I realized that [it] meant my own sacrifice'' (Jung, 1961, pp. 167–168).

The specter of corpses lay on the battlefield. Should they be attended to, and if so, what then? So Freud answered in a letter about parricide, priority, and gloom:

> It is a torment for me to think, when I conceive an idea now and then, that I may be taking something away from you or appropriating something that might just as well have been acquired by you. When this happens, I feel at a loss. . . . Why in God's name did I allow myself to follow you in this field? [Freud, 1974b, letter of November 12, 1912, p. 459].

In a response bordering on anticlimax, Jung told Freud that he was ''a dangerous rival.'' But unbeknownst to Jung, the climax was yet to come.

Freud's *Totem and Taboo* was also performative, not only describing the primal psychology, but also figuring as a symbolic gesture in the contemporaneous history of the psychoanalytic primal horde. Freud felt that the last part of his masterpiece would be a vital sign offsetting the homicidal wishes of his Viennese foes; more than that, his masterpiece would signal rupture with Zurich. And more than that again, he traced his progression from wish to deed: from the wish of parricide in his Dreambook to killing the father in *Totem and Taboo* (Jones, 1955, p. 354).

The end of the affair fell into suit. Wittels (1923, p. 191) and Stekel (1950, p. 143) felt that Freud's book dealt Jung a damaging blow. The happy brothers of the secret committee danced to a victorious beat. They invited Freud to a repast which they named a totemic feast (Jones, 1955, p. 355). Truly Freud's book was efficient work, performance, enactment—was corpus.

How many worked to write as much? If we take the 14,000 extant letters out of the putative 20,000 that Freud wrote, and if each were edited to occupy an average, quite modest estimate of a page and a half in print, we would have an edition of 21,000 pages or three times the length of the *Standard Edition*. I opine that the publication of Freud's entire extant work—pre-analytic and psychoanalytic texts, translations, correspondence, notes, the many drafts[2] and notebooks and registers of all sorts, and corrections of others' manuscripts—will comprise some 150 volumes. That authentic *Standard Edition* will not

---

[2]In an astute lecture given in London on June 5, 1994, Ilse Grubrich-Simitis elaborated on the three stages in Freud's creative process: taking succinct notes, drawing up drafts, and writing final copy.

see light in our generation or in the next, and I doubt in that of our children's children. When we add to our consideration that Freud destroyed considerable amounts of his scriptive production on three occasions in his life, we can begin to glimpse the endless importance that writing had for him, one among the handful of the most prolific great writers in all of history.

A rumination of the elderly Freud seems custom-designed for my essay: "The one bright spot in my life is the success of Anna's work" (letter of February 13, 1935, to Arnold Zweig; in Jones, 1957, p. 195). Freud's fatherly reflection, however, is ill-fitting in that it tempts us to ignore his work, indeed, his scriptive work at the time. In spite of his twenty-three operations, he wanted to prize mental alertness, and to that end the only analgesic he took was aspirin; as he said once to Stefan Zweig: "I prefer to think in torment than not to be able to think clearly" (Jones, 1957, p. 245). Despite the ever-increasing pain, Freud wrote copiously—much more than we realize today; even within the month of his arriving in England in 1938, he occupied himself, *inter alia*, with correcting a series of lectures by Simmel (Jones, 1957, p. 233). Inexplicable exceptions like Rimbaud aside, a born writer does not want to suffer the hell of being without that activity. To our good fortune, it was a hell that Freud could not tolerate, running as he did to his own demons who pushed him to write.

Just as the manifest dream has an importance all of its own, as Freud belatedly stressed, so also does the written text. Freud was caught in the hedonic and ascetic pull of writing—compulsively drawn to a practice in which the written text is intermediate space, representing and distorting, satisfying and not satisfying. For example, Freud complained that due to the recalcitrancy of the material in *The Ego and the Id*, the chapter headings were somewhat beyond his control (Freud, 1923a, p. 48). In similar order he criticized his *Civilization and Its Discontents:*

> The book does not deal exhaustively enough with the subject [namely, the discomfort in our culture], and on top of this rough foundation is put an overdifficult and overcompensating examination of the analytic theory of the feeling of guilt. But one does not make such compositions, they make themselves, and if one resists writing them down as they come, one does not know what the result will be. The analytic insight into the feeling of guilt was supposed to be in the dominant position [Sterba, 1982, pp. 113–114].

It was in *Moses and Monotheism* that Freud voiced his more general comment on the tyranny of the ongoing work on the mind: "Unluckily an author's creative power does not always obey his will; the work proceeds as it can, and often presents itself to the author as something independent or even alien'' (Freud, 1939, p. 104).

So he mourned about writing, took to writing as a mourning, and also carried out a simultaneous mourning-through in a writing-through. A disappointment and regret (note the anticipatory pain that Freud had before writing and the sadness he always had after writing); pain that what was inside became uttered and othered. The fraternal twinship between utterance and otherance, Cain disabled. Words are parables, thrown next to; texts are parables of parables, throws upon the thrown, never the thing.

> Workman
> where thou goest
> that is thrown
> through and
> through

REFERENCES

Freud, S. (1895), Project for a scientific psychology. *Standard Edition*, 1:283–398. London: Hogarth Press, 1966.

———— (1900), The Interpretation of Dreams. *Standard Edition*, 4&5. London: Hogarth Press, 1953.

———— (1908), On the sexual theories of children. *Standard Edition*, 9:205–226. London: Hogarth Press, 1959.

———— (1910), Leonardo da Vinci. *Standard Edition*, 11:59–138. London: Hogarth Press, 1957.

———— (1912), Recommendations to physicians practicing psychoanalysis. *Standard Edition*, 12:109–120. London: Hogarth Press, 1958 [*Gesammelte Werke*, 8:375–388. Frankfurt: Fischer Verlag, 1945].

———— (1914), On the history of the psychoanalytic movement. *Standard Edition*, 14:3–66. London: Hogarth Press, 1957.

———— (1915), Instincts and their vicissitudes. *Standard Edition*, 14:109–140. London: Hogarth Press, 1957.

———— (1915–1917), Introductory Lectures on Psychoanalysis. *Standard Edition*, 15&16. London: Hogarth Press, 1961 [*Gesammelte Werke*, 11. Frankfurt: Fischer Verlag, 1944].

———— (1923a), The ego and the id. *Standard Edition*, 19:3–68. London: Hogarth Press, 1961 [*Gesammelte Werke*, 13:235–290. Frankfurt: Fischer Verlag, 1940].

———— (1923b), The resistances to psychoanalysis. *Standard Edition*, 19:213–222. London: Hogarth Press, 1961.

———— (1930), Civilization and its discontents. *Standard Edition*, 21:49–148. London: Hogarth Press, 1961.

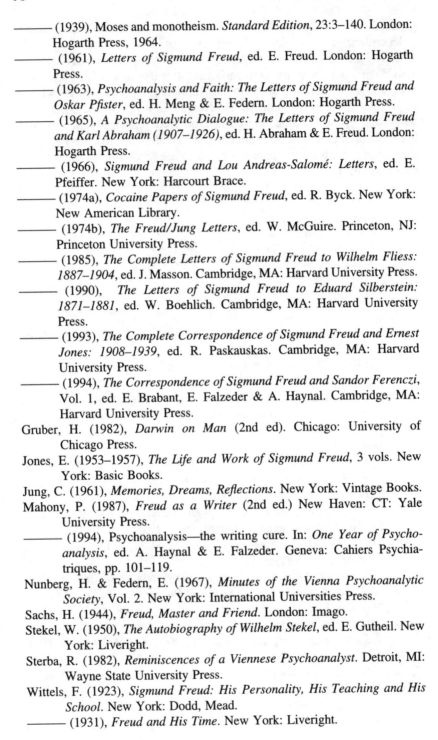

—— (1939), Moses and monotheism. *Standard Edition*, 23:3–140. London: Hogarth Press, 1964.

—— (1961), *Letters of Sigmund Freud*, ed. E. Freud. London: Hogarth Press.

—— (1963), *Psychoanalysis and Faith: The Letters of Sigmund Freud and Oskar Pfister*, ed. H. Meng & E. Federn. London: Hogarth Press.

—— (1965), *A Psychoanalytic Dialogue: The Letters of Sigmund Freud and Karl Abraham (1907–1926)*, ed. H. Abraham & E. Freud. London: Hogarth Press.

—— (1966), *Sigmund Freud and Lou Andreas-Salomé: Letters*, ed. E. Pfeiffer. New York: Harcourt Brace.

—— (1974a), *Cocaine Papers of Sigmund Freud*, ed. R. Byck. New York: New American Library.

—— (1974b), *The Freud/Jung Letters*, ed. W. McGuire. Princeton, NJ: Princeton University Press.

—— (1985), *The Complete Letters of Sigmund Freud to Wilhelm Fliess: 1887–1904*, ed. J. Masson. Cambridge, MA: Harvard University Press.

—— (1990), *The Letters of Sigmund Freud to Eduard Silberstein: 1871–1881*, ed. W. Boehlich. Cambridge, MA: Harvard University Press.

—— (1993), *The Complete Correspondence of Sigmund Freud and Ernest Jones: 1908–1939*, ed. R. Paskauskas. Cambridge, MA: Harvard University Press.

—— (1994), *The Correspondence of Sigmund Freud and Sandor Ferenczi*, Vol. 1, ed. E. Brabant, E. Falzeder & A. Haynal. Cambridge, MA: Harvard University Press.

Gruber, H. (1982), *Darwin on Man* (2nd ed). Chicago: University of Chicago Press.

Jones, E. (1953–1957), *The Life and Work of Sigmund Freud*, 3 vols. New York: Basic Books.

Jung, C. (1961), *Memories, Dreams, Reflections*. New York: Vintage Books.

Mahony, P. (1987), *Freud as a Writer* (2nd ed.) New Haven: CT: Yale University Press.

—— (1994), Psychoanalysis—the writing cure. In: *One Year of Psychoanalysis*, ed. A. Haynal & E. Falzeder. Geneva: Cahiers Psychiatriques, pp. 101–119.

Nunberg, H. & Federn, E. (1967), *Minutes of the Vienna Psychoanalytic Society*, Vol. 2. New York: International Universities Press.

Sachs, H. (1944), *Freud, Master and Friend*. London: Imago.

Stekel, W. (1950), *The Autobiography of Wilhelm Stekel*, ed. E. Gutheil. New York: Liveright.

Sterba, R. (1982), *Reminiscences of a Viennese Psychoanalyst*. Detroit, MI: Wayne State University Press.

Wittels, F. (1923), *Sigmund Freud: His Personality, His Teaching and His School*. New York: Dodd, Mead.

—— (1931), *Freud and His Time*. New York: Liveright.

6

A SELF PSYCHOLOGICAL PERSPECTIVE OF WORK AND ITS INHIBITIONS

ERNEST S. WOLF, M.D.

> What is work? And what is not work?
> Questions that perplex the wisest of
> men—*Bhagavadgita*, 4.

I

Somewhat surprisingly, the human activity we call work defies a generally satisfactory definition. To be sure, everyone knows what is work just like everyone knows what is love or what is fun. What everyone knows is the subjective experience that he or she as an individual attaches to these concepts. Clearly, that is not good enough for serious science, and numerous authors in a wide range of social science disciplines have attempted to arrive at generally acceptable definitions. A useful summary might define work as the sum of all human physical and mental activities aimed at creating desired goods and services. Among the definitions in the *Oxford English Dictionary* I found most relevant " . . . something that is or was done; an act, deed . . . effort directed toward a definite end."

It may be an appropriate occasion to briefly look backwards to the roots of our thinking about work. In ancient times these activities were apparently beneath the dignity of Greek aristocrats and of most educated citizens who spent their time in "superior" social activities, leisure, and recreation, including the arts, sciences, and business, and, of course, military enterprises. This was not work. Work was done by slaves and manual laborers. The ancients did speculate on the phenomena of work and leisure. Aristotle divided the serious activity of men into two types: labor, toil, and business which is the kind of work that creates wealth and earns subsistence, and leisure activities by which he meant the creation of the goods of the spirit and of civilization, not the production of the material goods, comforts, and conveniences of life. Both labor and leisure are hard work because they leave one tired. Aristotle prescribed play and recreation for the relief of the fatigue of hard work. Labor and business are necessary for earning a living but do not ennoble human life. Leisure, however, allows man to grow morally, intellectually, and spiritually and thus makes life worth living. Working—in our modern sense of this activity—did not do much for Greek self-esteem. For society to prosper and feed its increasing population required a different, more positive attitude toward labor and making a living.

Judaism and Christianity seemed to redefine the work concept to make it a more positive and rewarding experience by setting before men and women the image of a God who worked six days to create the world and rested on the seventh day. Emulating God became a guide to morally correct behavior. A life full of work had the highest ethical value, while mere play and entertaining leisure were thought to lead straight to hell. The work ethic, particularly the Protestant variety, generated a powerful spirit of enterprise. It was only the general weakening of the authority of the church and of religious beliefs that seemed to diminish the sinfulness of pleasure, leisure, and fun. But the old morality was saved by psychologies that pronounced the disinclination to work as sickness.

Galatzer-Levy and Cohler (1993) sum up our contemporary preoccupation with work:

> From the student who was perversely satisfied by the number of hours spent in study, to the factory worker anxious to accumulate overtime hours, to the physician taking pride in the long hours devoted to service, Western society is unique in reckoning work time as a virtue in itself [p. 232].

While this condensation of over two thousand years of history is no doubt an oversimplification, the moral of the story has not been diluted by time passing. Whatever the reason for the tenacity of its message, whether in the service of society's or of individual's power or economic interests, it has found its reflection in the psychological theories built, or perhaps shunned, to explain motivations for working. Even this present volume, with its underlying theme of work and its inhibitions takes for granted a normal, healthy urge to work so that an absence of this urge almost automatically assumes an unhealthy inhibition.

II

In his "Recommendations to Physicians Practicing Psychoanalysis," Freud (1912, p. 119) cautions us to be "content if one has won back some degree of capacity for work and enjoyment." Freud intended to guide his colleagues and students toward an aim of treatment rather than to simply define psychological health by the capacity to love and to work. Anna Freud (1965) spelled this out more clearly: "The adult patient strives for normality since this holds out to him the promise of pleasure in sex and success in work" (p. 27). Yet, though not explicit, a definition of psychological health seems implied and most of Freud's followers have so understood the injunction to aim for a capacity to love and to work. Within the framework of the present paper, I shall mainly leave aside the varieties of fates that can befall the act of loving, and reexamine the vicissitudes of working. Still, we might benefit from a first comparison of these two types of human activities. In the Freudian world loving is the expression of an intrapsychic dynamic fueled by and subject to the destinies of the instinctual drives. Working, however, is not an expression of an inner-motivated necessity, but a response to a compelling environment. Normality might be characterized by the ego's uninhibited capacity to freely respond to libidinal demands presented by the id or to demands for work presented by the pressures of external reality.

Freud (1917) clearly saw the societal coercive influence:

> The motive of human society is in the last resort an economic one; since it does not possess enough provisions to keep its members alive unless they work, it must restrict the number of its members and divert their energies from sexual activity to work [p. 312].

and, even more explicitly, in 1927:

> It seems rather that every civilization must be built up on coercion and renunciation of instinct; it does not even seem certain that if coercion were to cease the majority of human beings would be prepared to undertake to perform the work necessary for acquiring new wealth . . . For masses are lazy and unintelligent [p. 7]; . . . To put it briefly, there are two widespread human characteristics which are responsible for the fact that the regulations of civilization can only be maintained by a certain degree of coercion—namely, that men are not spontaneously fond of work and that arguments are of no avail against their passions [p. 8].

Freud thus comes squarely down on the side of society and its need to coerce men to do the work it deems necessary. If left alone, men will not work but indulge their passions instead, whether sexual or aggressive, or, at best, lazily and self-indulgently fritter their time away. However, Freud (1930, p. 80n.) does recognize that work relates men to society and allows them to acquire not only material goods, and avoid the pains of coercion, but also to obtain the libidinal satisfactions that can be sublimated into professional activities.

> No other technique for the conduct of life attaches the individual so firmly to reality as laying emphasis on work; for his work at least gives him a secure place in a portion of reality, in the human community. The possibility it offers of displacing a large amount of libidinal components, whether narcissistic, aggressive or even erotic, on to professional work and on to the human relations connected with it lends it a value by no means second to what it enjoys as something indispensable to the preservation and justification of existence in society. Professional activity is a source of special satisfaction if it is a freely chosen one—if, that is to say, by means of sublimation, it makes possible the use of existing inclinations, or persisting or constitutionally reinforced instinctual impulses.

But Freud does not credit his fellow men with much pleasure and happiness from work:

> And yet, as a path to happiness, work is not highly prized by men. They do not strive after it as they do after other possibilities of satisfaction. The great majority of people only work under the stress of necessity, and this natural human aversion to work raises most difficult social problems.

Freud recognized a conflict between the individual's drive for pleasure and the biologically as well as societally imposed need to make a living. He accepted a natural human aversion to work. Does he see the pursuit of leisure and pleasure as healthy or pathological? He does not say. His own personal feelings about work hint that he experienced leisure as a cause of restlessness and that he habitually cured this misery by working. In his letters to Fliess, Freud (1887–1904) writes:

> Essentially I am well, because plenty of work and newly arising possibilities of resolving hysteria satisfy my inner unrest'' [December 4, 1896].
> . . . as far as condition is concerned, you are certainly quite right; strangely enough it is far easier for me to be productive when I have mild troubles of this kind [March 8, 1895].

During an industrious night last week, when I was suffering from that degree of pain which brings about the optimal condition for my mental activities, the barriers suddenly lifted . . . [October 20, 1895].
I returned to a sense of too much well-being and have since then been very lazy because the modicum of misery essential for intensive work will not come back [April 16, 1896].

Do we detect here traces of the sinfulness of leisure that demands it be balanced by the goodness of work? Or do we conceptualize in a contemporary self-psychological manner that Freud's misery was evidence for a state of fragmentation which even interfered with his work capacity? Perhaps, the satisfying prospects of helping his patients and solving the mystery of hysteria, when placed in front of his friend Fliess, elicited such a positive experience of friendly responsiveness that Freud's fragmentation was transformed into a cohesive self-experience with accompanying feelings of well-being. As Kohut recognized:

Freud used to say that intellectual work was one of the best safeguards for mental health . . . He never explained it . . . I think this is what it must mean—the self-confirming effect, the capacity to confirm yourself [Elson, 1987, p. 60].

Galatzer-Levy and Cohler (1993) come to similar conclusions:

For many adults work is an extremely important essential other supporting the experience of a cohesive, valuable, and stable self. . . . In our society personal worth is organized around the self as worker to the extent that many people cannot find meaning in any other context [p. 231].

III

More than fifty years ago Lantos (1943) pointed out that disturbances of working capacity come next in importance to disturbances of sexuality. One might expect, therefore, that the investigation of work, its disturbances and its distortions into work obsessions, as well as into work inhibitions, would have proved a fruitful field for psychoanalytic research. To be sure, there has been much discussion in the psychoanalytic literature of work inhibition. Fenichel (1945) points out that "many an occupational inhibition turns out to be actually an inhibition of aggressiveness, since under our cultural conditions, aggressiveness is necessary for a healthy career" (p. 178). But not only aggressiveness becomes a target for inhibitory influences, but also sexuality. Thus when some organ or activity has been sexualized it becomes by displacement a victim of the inhibition of sexuality. As Freud (1926) says, "It has been discovered as a general fact that the ego-function of an organ is impaired if its erotogenicity—its sexual significance—is increased" (p. 89). Fenichel (1945) mentions various types of inhibitions that affect work performance. Since work is the way to independence and success, all conflicts around dependence and independence and ambition may present themselves in the form of work inhibition. Children often are unpleasantly pressured to perform actions as a duty that is demanded by authorities as the opposite of pleasure. Consequently, conflicts around authority, rebellion, and obedience may be expressed in attitudes toward work. And, more generally, persons with reactive-type characters, who feel compelled to repress any instinctual demands by becoming uninterrupted robotlike hard workers without any pleasure in their activities, may eventually rebel with disturbances in their work patterns. Those people who associate laziness or even leisure with forbidden libidinal enjoyment, or who need to conceal pleasure in dirt or disorganization, may respond with an excessively reactive and compulsive type of work pattern that is devoid of pleasure or of a sense of accomplishment. Thus psychoanalysis has addressed neurotic work inhibition and neurotic work compulsion. But Lantos (1943) calls attention to an important omission in the psychoanalytic investigation of work. She comments, "Although we have to deal extensively with disturbances of work, the question of what work is is not treated as a problem" (p. 114). What does work mean? What do we work for? She concludes that man is forced to work in order to earn a living. This is true, she says, even if some people have independent incomes as a result of former work or of work by others. Thus Lantos avoids addressing the question of why individuals work, by reminding us that for mankind as a whole, i.e., society, work is a necessity, and apparently she implicitly extrapolates from this basic condition of human existence to the individual without further identifying the specific factors involved. Indeed, the question of what is work, the question of a definition, is not raised at all. In an aside, Lantos mentions that the concept of work can only be used in connection with adults. "A child is not concerned with what a grown-up regards as his most important activity—although the child is in no way less active than the adult" (p. 114). Lantos distinguishes the child's activity itself, e.g., walking, as initially uncoordinated, back and fro, enjoyable for the activity itself, an autoerotic activity. Eventually, the child gains mastery over its motion and then can become goal-directed. "We call play what children do in order to enjoy themselves, we call work what adults do in order to earn a living" (p. 115). For children most activities, e.g., eating, walking, looking, talking, are all performed as pleasurable games. But gradually the child feels an impulse to perform some useful, purposeful activity; it wants to assist in the household activities and in caring for other children. "It is quite clear that what matters is not simply the pleasure of the activity but the fact of achievement" (p. 115). One might add here to Lantos's formulation that the child's motivation to assist in household activities may neither just be simply the pleasure of the activity nor the fact of achievement, but the experience of being a participant in a relationship of mutual responsiveness with other members of the household, a relationship that confirms for the child its very existence and its acceptance by the others, in short, being a person in his own right as well as being part of a larger whole.

Placing the above scenario into a larger, developmental perspective, it becomes clear that Lantos has omitted a crucial goal in the gradual transformation of some of the child's activities from sheer playfulness into something more purposeful. One can surmise that, consciously or unconsciously, one goal for the child is to elicit certain responses from the significant adults. A beginning definition of work seems to emerge from these considerations: work are those purposeful activities of an individual that are motivated by achieving needed responses from the human and nonhuman environment. This approaches the definition given by Hendrick (1943), though Hendrick remains locked into considering only constituents of soma and psyche, since he lacks a concept of a unified cohesive self.

> I shall suggest that work is not primarily motivated by sexual need or associated aggression, but by the need for efficient use of the muscular and intellectual tools, regardless of what secondary needs—self-preservative, aggressive, or sexual—a work performance may also satisfy. I shall call this thesis the *work principle*, the principle that primary pleasure is sought by efficient use of the central nervous system for the performance of well-integrated ego functions which enable the individual to control or alter his environment [p. 311].

Hendrick also implies an instinct of mastery without explaining the need for or the sources of such an instinct. But both Hendrick and Lantos have broken new ground by no longer taking the activity called work for granted, but by attempting to examine the conditions and motivations that result in what we call work.

A modern thinker, such as Habermas, appears close to Hendrick when he categorizes work as concerning the technical mastery of the natural and social environment (McCarthy, 1978).

> . . . work or purposive-rational action in the narrow sense would include not only action oriented toward inanimate objects but also action oriented toward other human beings, where the orientation is predominantly one of technical control [pp. 28–29].

Similar thoughts were expressed already by the French philosopher
Montaigne (1569):

> Being is something we hold dear, and being consists in movement and
> action. Wherefore each man in some sort exists in his work [p. 279].

Benedek (1950) sees work as a psychic organizer. She formulates
a self-concept that she sees as an unstable structure during development. Benedek's "achieving self" seems closely related to what in
contemporary self psychology we term the efficacy selfobject experience.

> Parents recognize that "activity-lust" (pleasure in activity) in the three-
> to-six-month-old infant; they proudly recognize the glow of satisfaction
> on the face of the one- to two-year-old toddler when he has reached the
> spoon or the toy that he wanted. The psychology of this is that the
> child's ego registers the satisfaction of having achieved a self-set goal.
> The affective experience of achievement becomes incorporated in the
> self-image as the "achieving self." Self-esteem originates in such mi-
> nute experiences, leading to a self-concept, e.g., "I am a good, lovable,
> capable, achieving self." The ego thus becomes cathected with "sec-
> ondary narcissism." But the self-concept is not a stable structure in
> one's psychic apparatus. Through the same processes by which it is
> established, it is also measured [p. 346].

IV

The emergence of self psychology in recent decades has led to a new
look at the role of work in the psychological household of men and
women. Such a reassessment was to be expected with the downgrading
of classical psychoanalytic drive-and-defense theory. Kohut clearly had
moved the traditionally central focus of psychoanalytic concern with
instincts and their vicissitudes toward a peripheral role in psychoanalytic theory. Indeed, all experience-distant theory became somewhat
less important with the greatly intensified interest in the experience-
near clinical situation that cast so much doubt on the theory-bound
constructions. As reported by Elson (1987) Kohut made a deliberate
choice to be guided by empirical data:

> The theoretical concepts I am presenting to you are not derived induc-
> tively. They are derived empirically. They are not deduced from purely
> theoretical concepts. It is on the basis of a variety of clinical observa-
> tions that concepts gradually peel themselves out. They are not deduced
> from some basic axioms [p. 27].

Like all good analysts Kohut set out on his new investigations propelled by some insights into his self:

> ... certain things one can do for oneself to boost self-esteem when it has been shattered. For example, an individual can sit down and do good work by himself. Nobody else knows it, but he will feel better. This is one of the best means I have to regulate my self-esteem when I am low. To sit down and work, after some blow to my self-esteem, and then, come up with something I consider to be good—this experience makes me feel better [p. 60]

In principle the relation of the capacity to work to the structure of the self can be stated quite simply: a strong self, i.e., a self that consists of cohesively structured constituents, in harmonious balance and energetically vigorous, is a self that performs well in all its intrapsychic and its interpersonal functions. Work is one of such a list of functions of the self. A person's ability to work thus represents a manifestation of a strong cohesive self. A serious interference with the capacity to work may well be the result of a disturbance in self function that may be related to the structure of the self, to (1) fragmentation of the self, or (2) an imbalance among the constituents, e.g., to a hypertrophic overidealization of the work, or (3) a lack of energic vigor, e.g., a weakened tension arc due to insufficient idealization of the pole of values and ideals of the self. I shall illustrate these configurations with some clinical vignettes.

1. It is a rather common clinical experience during the analysis of a self disorder that an analysand will come to a regular analytic session looking somewhat unkempt and in a listless or grumpy mood. While at first glance one might suspect a depressive episode, it often turns out that the analysand is rather irritable and jumpily awkward. Usually there has been fitful sleep, and work performance that day has been poor and sloppy. Uncoordinated in appearance and in action might be an applicable description. A state of fragmentation of the self explains the clinical picture. Its cause may be found in some disturbing ripple in the relation to one of the analysand's significant others, whether that be the spouse, the boss, the parent, the lover, the child, the friend, the analyst, or whoever. Such fleeting fragmentations are by their very nature self-limiting through the restoration of the relationship and, concomitantly, the recohesion of the self can be speeded by appropriate interpretations. Work performance will be restored simultaneously with self recohesion as the mirroring selfobject experience in the transference to the analyst functions to enhance the structure of the self (Wolf, 1988).

Such transference-like experiences are ubiquitous in daily life. Mentors frequently serve as the source of self-enhancing selfobject experiences. Galatzer-Levy and Cohler (1993) have called attention to the importance of the mentoring relationship in the workplace. Levinson (1978) writes:

> Mentors are essential others who strengthen the resolve to work at difficult tasks. . . . In a "good enough" mentoring relationship, the young man feels admiration, respect, appreciation, gratitude, and love for the mentor. . . . The elder has the qualities of character, expertise, and understanding that the younger admires and wants to make part of himself. The young man is excited and spurred on by the shared sense of his promise [p. 100].
>
> The mentor need not always be an actual sponsor. He may be someone the protégé has studied. Admiration of Freud's intellectual and scientific integrity, his relentless pursuit of truth even when confronted by stigma and resistance, has fostered the careers of many younger psychoanalysts who never met him [Galatzer-Levy and Cohler, p. 243].

2. Some persons compensate for a basic fragility of the self by totally identifying with their work and its achievements. A college student with superior intellect but poor social skills invested himself so totally in his studies that he became increasingly isolated from his peer group, his fellow students. Without at first noticing it, he gradually had fewer contacts with his classmates and consequently fewer confirming selfobject experiences of the mirroring variety. Thus starved of needed selfobject responsiveness, his self weakened with slowly diminishing self-esteem while greatly overvaluing his intellectual products. Unconsciously aware of his reliance on the approval from teachers for his work as the main remaining basis for any self-esteem, he no longer dared expose his work to the teachers' criticism. No longer would he submit his written papers, and he also began to miss examinations. Finally, he failed to complete the required course work. The imbalance between his regard for himself as a person and his regard for the products of his work was so tilted in the latter's direction that it paralyzed his formerly excellent performance.

In a more general vein, it is useful to point out here that one of the most frequently noted disturbances among young people are these so-called work inhibitions of students. The clinical picture is of a young man or woman in high school, college, or graduate school whose usually superior academic performance begins to deteriorate for no apparent reason. Closer examination reveals a person who is somewhat depressed. However, the depression seems to be more of a surface phenomenon since it is neither deep enough to account for the observed

inability to do the required academic work, nor does it reflect adequately the seriousness of the threatening situation of impending academic failure and dismissal from school. Analysis often reveals the
deeper reason for the clinical picture. We are likely to find a young
person of high intelligence whose self-esteem has been supported almost solely by an illusion of having a near perfect intellect, that is, by
a secret conviction of being some kind of genius. Praise and admiration
for intellect and high achievement from parents, peers, and teachers
have helped create and support this illusion. Indeed, during the early
years of the educational experience these youngsters do perform almost
flawlessly. As they get older the material to be mastered gets to be
more difficult and they encounter occasional lapses in their heretofore
unblemished ability to achieve and shine. This sudden failure is experienced as an unbearable narcissistic injury, an affront to the self-image
that has sustained them. They become very reluctant to expose themselves to a repetition of the nonsuccess. Instead they procrastinate in
doing what needs to be done, they can no longer finish their assigned
work, they sit and stare at the blank page, unable to go further. The
risk of failing again is too great. Their self-esteem collapses in a situation that would appear to most people as an expected imperfection.

The analysis usually also uncovers a developmental trauma. There
may be any number of patterns of parent-child relationship that all
have in common the parents' expectation of an exceptional child. The
child's imperfections are not accepted, but overlooked or dismissed.
There is no recognition that human beings have human limitations.
Expression such as ''you can do anything if you want to'' create false
expectations that are incorporated in the youngster's developing system
of values and ideals, especially regarding the self. Indeed, that is the
only acceptable self to parents and child alike. In the coming years
tragedy inevitably lurks around the corner.

Kohut (1971, p. 120) reports:

> Many of the most severe and chronic work disturbances of our
> patients . . . are in my experience due to the fact that the self is poorly
> cathected with narcissistic libido and in chronic danger of fragmenta-
> tion, with a secondary reduction of the efficacy of the ego. Such people
> are either chronically unable to work at all, or (since their self is not
> participating) they are able to work only in an automatic way (as the
> isolated activity of an autonomous ego, without the participation of a
> self in depth), i.e., passively, without pleasure and without initiative,
> simply responding to external cues and demands. Occasionally even the
> patient's awareness of this rather frequent type of work disturbance in
> narcissistic personality disorders comes about only in the course of a
> successful analysis. The patient will one day report that his work has

changed, that he is now enjoying it, that he now has the choice whether
to work or not, that the work is now undertaken on his own initiative
rather than as if by a passively obedient automaton, and, last but not
least, that his approach has now some originality rather than being
humdrum and routine: a living self in depth has become the *organizing
center of the ego's activities.*

A variety of work disturbance that may superficially resemble the isolated self working in an automatic way is the self with a work obsession, which I shall discuss below.

3. In contrast to the above clinical examples, the developmental
vicissitudes during the childhood of some youngsters may result in
atrophy or nondevelopment of a sufficiently strong pole of idealization.
The cause here is often found in the severely traumatic disappointment
in the idealized selfobjects of early life. A son's experience of being
closely merged into an idealized image of his father—such as admiration of father's strength, goodness, and wisdom, which is necessary
for the boy's being able to develop those qualities in himself—may
come to a traumatic end by the father's sudden illness or untimely
death. If the boy sustains such a loss during his most vulnerable years,
perhaps around age three to six, the pain and weakness associated with
such a tragic disappointment may be so severe that the youngster may
never again allow himself to have such idealized selfobject experiences. As an adult he will probably be chronically somewhat depressed,
and he is not likely to endow his work and his achievements with the
pride of being associated to these products of his self. Kohut (1971)
reports:

> So long as he felt accepted and counseled and guided by such [idealized]
> men, so long as he felt they approved of him, he experienced himself
> as whole, acceptable, and capable; and under such circumstances he
> was indeed able to do well in his work and to be creative and successful.
> At slight signs of disapproval of him, however, or of lack of understand-
> ing for him, or of loss of interest in him, he would feel drained and
> depressed, would tend to become first enraged and then cold, haughty,
> and isolated, and his creativeness and work capacity deteriorated [p. 58].

V

A few words need to be said about work obsessions. For many individuals in our culture work becomes something more than either joyful
self-fulfillment or an activity motivated by the need to make a living.
It is as if life would lose its meaning and its flavor if one stopped

working. Indeed, statistics seem to support the impression that many men die within a few years of their retirement from regular work. Perhaps they would have died anyway, or perhaps their retirement was speeded by their awareness of impending demise. No causal relationship has been proven. Still, one cannot escape the impression that the psychological effect of retirement or, more precisely, the sudden loss of the meaning work gave to their lives, has had a decisive influence. Mainly these are individuals who have successfully substituted the satisfactions of work for those of close and intimate relationships with people. Their success depends on their ability to identify almost completely with their work and its products. The motivation for such a shift is their experience and, perhaps, their awareness of their sensitivity to the inevitable self-fragmenting slights and perceived insults of the social intercourse of everyday life. Their vulnerability is probably related to predisposing early experiences. Psychoanalytic treatment may reveal the etiology of the significant dynamics of self-forming relationships of infancy and childhood. The inescapable disruptions of the transference during treatment present opportunities for curative interventions that can repair the damaged self. Thus these analysands may finally achieve some relief from their compulsion to work excessively, and begin to really enjoy other aspects of life, especially their relationships with others.

Kohut (Elson, 1987) comments on a particular variety of creative individuals:

> There are many geniuses who clearly have a disturbed sense of self, as we can see from their disheveled appearance and the neglect of their clothes and bodily needs. Beethoven is an example, with his enormous need to perfect the work he was composing. It seems to me that the self-esteem regulation that relates to one's own person is surrendered to one's work.
>
> In other words, work becomes the true carrier of self-esteem, particularly in the perfecting of it. Once the work is done, it can be an enormous loss for the person to let it go. There is a peculiar jealousy toward the work taking on its own life and being admired by others. While the creator works on it, it really belongs to him, the creator [p. 277].

VI

Anecdotally, Freud has been reported to characterize the state of mental health by the ability to love and to work. To live a life of leisure would generally be considered not just as undesirable but as a sign of some sort of psychological illness. But the word leisure defined as the absence of work does not capture the positive, assertive aspects of a life that is not devoted to working but instead actively devoted to a kind of enjoyment of living. Let us note that the opposite of the activity we call working is not leisure but playing. Sometimes playing as the major occupation of an individual may be the result of a work inhibition, in other words, symptomatic of psychological disturbance. But playing may also be the normal activity of a healthy person. Children normally play, and their play often reveals much of their preoccupations in fantasy and in affects. Lichtenberg (1994, personal communication) regards play as an activity involving exploration, problem-solving and rules-based games accompanied by an affect of "playfulness."

It may be useful to try to approach work as well as play in the spirit of contemporary self psychology from the point of view of subjective experience. We have already noted that Freud often was able to banish a subjective self experience of "misery" by intensive work. Indeed, Freud thought he needed such misery in order to not be lazy and get to work (letter to Fliess of April 16, 1896, quoted above). Many people experience the absence of an assigned or required task, not having anything to do, with a feeling of uneasiness. Not to be occupied in useful endeavors is often thought of as a pleasure forbidden, or at least disapproved, by the idealized selfobjects of one's early formative years. Such a pleasure evokes a judgment of moral deficiency and, therefore, of being less than fully in harmony with one's ideals and values. In the subjective self-judgment of many adults there seems to be only a short path from the absence of work via laziness to sin. Playing is all right for children, but adults should work. "In the sweat of thy face shalt thou eat bread" (Genesis, 3:16). This moralistic posture is easily generalized and displaced onto others, resulting in a powerful work ethic by which we judge societies and our fellow citizens. Great crimes can be hidden underneath slogans such as the one over the entrance to some Nazi concentration camps: "Arbeit macht frei" (work makes one free).

Is it the individual who is responsible for creating such an ethic, or is it society that, by way of education and training, installs such systems of values in its citizens? (Cf. Freud, 1930, p. 80n. quoted above). One can find examples of both sources for the origin of the work ethic. The pressure to identify with one's essential selfobjects and their values is enormous for both children and adults. Most people unconsciously accept and absorb the value system of their surrounding selfobject milieu. They become aware of the extent of their identifications with their group's ideals only by the unpleasant experience of affective dissonance when suddenly immersed in an alien culture. On the other hand, some people use the adoption of a system of values and ideals in opposition to their milieu as a preferred way to delineate their self and its boundaries. That may boost self-esteem by creating an illusion of autonomy, though it is really just as reactive as the compliant self.

But what about the individual who does not experience this inner pressure to work? Is the absence of a feeling of being driven to work evidence of some self defect? Is he sick? Of course, this individual could be developing and growing up in a subculture of wealth that is taken for granted. The healthy norm here would be a life of leisure. Clearly, it is the environment that has shaped the idealized expectations and that thus has determined the trajectory of the tension arc from ambitions to ideals. It is therefore quite easy to conceive of individuals whose dedication to their own leisure and pleasure would be quite in harmony with their healthy self structure. No inhibition of the capacity to work need be postulated. Shakespeare's Prince Hal represents a fictionalized version of such a character type. It is noteworthy that Prince Hal was able to assume the full burden of work, of the royal duties, as soon as his accession to the throne demanded it.

As a psychoanalyst in the developing tradition of self psychology, I find the definition of work as an effort directed toward a definite end not very helpful in making clinical judgments. Instead, a metapsychological definition of a self state describing an uninterrupted tention arc from ambitions to ideals appears more useful in distinguishing healthy from impaired activities, regardless of whether the activity is labeled work or play. Leaving aside an obviously fragmented, anenergic or imbalanced self, how is the observing psychoanalyst to judge whether the analysand's self state includes a completed trajectory toward an idealized goal or whether the tension arc is incomplete? Here the analyst's empathic sensitivity becomes a decisive factor. A completed tension arc from ambitions to ideals is experienced by a person as more than passively enjoyed pleasure, but includes actively having fun. Fun implies the pleasure of vigorous and enjoyable but not serious amusement. Fun, like work and like play, defies precise definition, but everyone knows what it is like to have fun. As a marker for a damaged self, an impaired capacity to have fun is a significant signal. Rather than objective observations of the analysand's behavior, it is the analyst's empathic attunement to the analysand's affective state that is more decisive for assessing psychological health.

References

Benedek, T. (1950), Climacterium: A developmental phase. In: *Psychoanalytic Investigations*. New York: Quadrangle, pp. 322–349.
Elson, M., Ed. (1987), *The Kohut Seminars on Self Psychology and Psychotherapy with Adolescents and Young Adults*. New York: Norton.
Fenichel, O. (1945), *The Psychoanalytic Theory of Neurosis*. New York: Norton.

Freud, A. (1965), *Normality and Pathology in Childhood. The Writings of Anna Freud,* Vol. 6. New York: International Universities Press.

Freud, S. (1887–1904), *The Complete Letters of Sigmund Freud to Wilhelm Fliess,* ed. J. F. Masson. Cambridge, MA: Harvard University Press, 1985.

——— (1912), Recommendations to physicians practicing psychoanalysis. *Standard Edition,* 12:111–120. London: Hogarth Press, 1958.

——— (1916–1917), Introductory lectures on psycho-analysis. *Standard Edition,* 16:243–276. London: Hogarth Press, 1963.

——— (1926), Inhibitions, symptoms and anxiety. *Standard Edition,* 20:87–147. London: Hogarth Press, 1963.

——— (1927), The future of an illusion. *Standard Edition,* 21:5–56. London: Hogarth Press, 1961.

——— (1930), Civilization and its discontents. *Standard Edition,* 21:64–145. London: Hogarth Press, 1961.

——— (1933), New introductory lectures on psycho-analysis. *Standard Edition,* 22:5–182. London: Hogarth Press, 1964.

Galatzer-Levy, R. & Cohler, B. (1993), *The Essential Other.* New York: Basic Books.

Hendrick, I. (1943), Work and the pleasure principle. *Psychoanal. Q.,* 12:311–329.

Kohut, H. (1971), *The Analysis of the Self.* New York: International Universities Press.

Lantos, B. (1943), Work and the instincts. *Internat. J. Psycho-Anal.,* 24:114–122.

Levinson, D. (1978), *The Seasons of a Man's Life.* New York: Knopf.

McCarthy, T. (1978), *The Critical Theory of Jürgen Habermas.* Cambridge, MA: MIT Press.

Montaigne, M. de (1569), Essays. In: *Complete Works,* trans. D. Frame. Stanford, CA: Stanford University Press.

Wolf, E. S. (1988), *Treating the Self: Elements of Clinical Self Psychology.* New York: Guilford Press.

Lucy Daniels Inman

① Brief Statement
about writing about
oneself ~~as~~ with
performance inhibitio[n]
as an example of uncons[cious]
conflict in performance
(my opening perhaps ok as
is).

7

A ROOM OF ONE'S OWN REVISITED

Lucy Daniels Inman, Ph.D.

In her 1928 essay, *A Room of One's Own*, Virginia Woolf blamed the dearth of women writers and artists over the centuries on women's confinement to roles of childbearing and nursing the sick and the aged. Woolf's solution: provide to every woman who wants to write a room of her own and an annual stipend of £500.

My Thesis: More Is Needed

As a therapist and a writer who has overcome writer's block, I know that both men and women require more than adequate income and a room of their own to be able to write. Despite having treated a number of writers, in this paper I shall address specific problems in my own writing inhibition. This is because I know these problems in intimate detail, am not limited by confidentiality concerns, and have been financially able to have more treatment and resolution of conflict than our patients, unfortunately, are typically allowed. The details, while uniquely mine, are typical of the unconscious conflicts creative individuals have to face.

Writing inhibitions (and probably creative inhibitions of all kinds) take many different forms, such as flight from success, crashing after success, inability to work, failure to produce, failure to complete, failed completions, etc. These different forms may also be disguised in a variety of ways, including psychiatric disorders. In addition, continuing to work productively can advance a writer and his work to new levels of success and associated problems. Growth of this kind is often painful at some level and frequently requires the capacity to see and deal with new conflicts in order to face more daunting levels of freedom. For the creative artist who disdains repetitive stereotyping in even very popular work, this can be a lifelong process. At times, as Rothenberg (1990, pp. 126–132) and Gedo (1983, p. 59) have noted, such individuals need therapeutic assistance in order to continue.

Truly alive creating has to do with projecting innermost feelings and conflicts outward into a work of art that reflects the artist not only to the world, but also back to the self. But can the creator bear this truth? If he can bear it, can he find the *form* of its reflection acceptable? At what level is he prepared to deal emotionally with both these challenges and that of the world's response to his innermost self? Furthermore, creating transforms very personal material into symbolic form that may hide the "true" meaning from its creator until it is out there to be observed objectively, sometimes with surprising pain. Thus, the capacity to tolerate symbolic expression of one's own material is essential.

IMPORTANCE OF SYMBOLIZATION

Symbolization's crucial role in the creative process has been the focus of several writers. Melanie Klein noted how violent feelings disrupt the capacity to symbolize. Deri (1984) looked in detail at distortions of symbolization resulting from unconscious conflicts. In *Neurotic Distortion of the Creative Process*, Kubie (1958) emphasized the crucial role of the preconscious and potential interference from both conscious and unconscious rigidity. He considered free association the essential liberator. Winnicott (1966) saw trust as necessary for the capacity to form and use images in cultural as well as the mother-child and therapy situations. He referred to such mutual trust as "potential space." Winnicott's (1953) concept of the transitional object has provided us with a means of "seeing" the baby's first symbol (created to bridge the gap with mother) through its external aspects. In his discussion of dreams as transitional objects, Pontalis (1977) has demonstrated the illumination possible when one symbol can be used in a variety of ways.

Psychoanalysts are accustomed to providing a therapeutic context sufficiently benign to allow the free flow of thoughts and feelings that comprise free association. With traumatized individuals, establishing this sense of safety can take considerable time, but only with it in place is it possible to put unconscious conflicts into the symbolic form (dreamable, viewable, speakable, thinkable) needed for consideration and resolution. In this chapter, I shall use the phrase, "a room of one's own," to refer to the state of being free to symbolize. And, in fact, there often *is* a direct relation between these two internal and external rooms. Sometimes finally getting a room of one's own in Woolf's sense only confronts an individual with his lack of emotional freedom. And from my experience, psychological and creative success require that the inhibited endeavor be resumed during treatment so that the conflicts inherent in it can be encountered and dealt with.

HISTORY OF MY WRITING AND ITS PROBLEMS

The aim in presenting my own writing and analytic journeys is to demonstrate the symbolic representation of conflicts made possible by trying to write while in analysis. Dreams proved to be a most valuable and growth-producing aspect of this capacity to symbolize. As a result, my conclusion is that creative endeavors labor at the manifest level with the same unconscious wish, resistances, and related conflicts as are represented in dreams and as psychoanalysis addresses at a deeper level through transference and interpretation.

My wish to be a writer surfaced early—from enjoying being told stories and read to as a preschooler by my eight-years-older half-sister and because writing was the way to have worth in our family. Both my father and my grandfather were writers who made word power something to envy and aspire to. Furthermore, I felt an intense need to make myself more valuable because of the strong expectations for the birth-order slot I held. My father's first wife had died bearing their second child, a son, who also died. My mother's father had died one month prior to my birth. The first child of my parents' marriage, I was born a cross-eyed girl instead of the son they needed to compensate for their losses and to insure future succession in the family-owned newspaper of which my grandfather and, later, my father was editor.

At four, when my mother was pregnant with the youngest of her three daughters, I was shocked to learn from my half-sister, Bibba, not only that we had different mothers, but also how her mother had died. I pictured this as the baby having broken her belly open. As luck would have it, I also learned in time that her mother had been something of a writer. Seeking the truth following Bibba's revelation, I directly confronted my father, "Did you love Babs?" only to be further overwhelmed as he confided his grief and love for his first wife with emotional intensity I had never heard him voice about my own mother. At the dinner table afterward with him carving the meat and exulting about "live life to the hilt," I took a silent oath not to.

As far as I know, no one but Father and I ever knew about that conversation. Our household was riddled with urgings for secrecy: the servants and Bibba did not want my mother to hear certain things; my mother did not want them to hear others. Probably my precocious verbal ability worried them all. It definitely tormented me, because words were so powerful in our house and because my mother typically reacted vengefully if she learned that her order had been violated. My two younger sisters never learned about the circumstances of Father's first wife's death until I told them as adults.

Perhaps not surprisingly with all these motivating circumstances, as a child, I never had any trouble with schoolwork and writing. Fearing failure and wanting worth, I was driven to excel. My grandfather proudly printed a war poem I wrote at age eight on the editorial page. Nor, as an adult, have I ever been unable to complete the writing assignments for college, graduate school, or my psychological practice. However, in early puberty a pattern commenced which I would now call *crash-after-success*. The form it took then (just before my twelfth birthday) was anorexia nervosa. At the time I was making top grades and a strong social adjustment in seventh grade, after having skipped the sixth on returning to North Carolina from Washington, DC where my family had lived during World War II. Secondary sexual development was also proceeding—"normally" I would have said then. But now, post-analysis, I can add that it was *not* "normal," that Father unpredictably verbally bludgeoned me in relation to both my academic success and my sexual development.

This *crash-after-success* pattern was repeated at the Quaker boarding school in Pennsylvania where I was sent in ninth grade. Despite shyness, terrible homesickness, and continuing anorexia (which was diagnosed early but not treated due to my parents' wish for me to attend boarding school), I managed again to achieve superior academic and successful social adjustment. But by the end of my junior year, following publication of my first short story in *Seventeen Magazine* and early acceptance at Vassar, the school was so concerned about my health that they insisted my anorexia be treated before I returned.

I never did return, however—because that next year at home nearly killed me. At that point my parents did seek treatment for me, but I was unable to talk about the extreme guilt that drove me to starve myself. I did not recognize, and received no proddings from others to recognize, the similarity of my condition to that of Father's first wife. There were other seemingly innocuous but extremely significant issues never alluded to then as well. These include: Father's talking all my childhood about how he resented having to live in the shadow of my renowned editor and statesman grandfather; my mother's effusive and humiliating praise of my accomplishments that I consciously felt made others dislike me and that I unconsciously felt amounted to her proclaiming me her "favorite son"; the facts that Father could not tolerate

competition and that our mother could not tolerate anyone being autonomous; and, finally, that Father, during that year of my severe illness,
not only refused to visit the doctor, but alternated between screaming
obscenities at me for not eating and holding me as a bundle of bones
on his lap, sometimes kissing the back of my neck while calling me
his "wonderful libidinal boy." Compulsive calorie counting obliter-
ated these issues and everything else from my mind but could not
protect me from fear of death by starvation.

By April 1951, weighing under 60 pounds and unable to make
use of psychotherapy, I was hospitalized in the northeast and received
most of the radical physical treatments of the day. For nearly five years
I was locked away and forced to keep my weight up in a variety of
traumatic ways while receiving no significant psychotherapy to help
with the emotional agony experienced in the process. Mental hospitals
were without schools and psychotropic medications in those days; I
was fortunate in not being leucotomized. But in that grim setting, I
resumed writing—not for publication; that was far from my
mind—rather, just because writing was something I *could* do there.

That effort more than paid off, but in a manner that now, nearly
40 years later, I can see thrust me back into the same emotional dilemma as had initiated the anorexia. "Let out" at age twenty-one, I
was a terrified emotional wreck, still harassed by fat fears about which
I had no insight. Furthermore, having been traumatized with ECT,
insulin shock, and tube feeding, I not only felt hopelessly untreatable,
but "crazy" from having been locked up so long, and "stupid" for
being a high-school dropout. I went to work as a newspaper reporter,
saw a psychiatrist weekly, and struggled to live despite feeling worthless. However, before I was out four months, J. P. Lippincott bought
a novel I had written in the hospital. By the time of its publication,
nine months after my discharge, that novel, *Caleb My Son*, was a
bestseller, praised critically in all the major newspapers and published
in several foreign countries as well.

Despite feeling fake and not as good as the writing the reviewers
said I had done, I received a Guggenheim fellowship and went on to
publish articles and short stories. I married 18 months after leaving
the hospital. At twenty-seven, though still plagued by anorexic worries
and writing doubts, I published my second novel, *High On A Hill*,
shortly after the birth of my second child. It was well reviewed, but
not a bestseller. After that I felt almost constantly that my writing was
not good enough. My husband started up the management ladder at
our family's newspaper, and at twenty-nine, following the birth of our
third child, I gave up writing altogether. I consciously did this because
I felt inadequate and that my writing was only serving my parents'
unrealistic and grandiose wishes—perhaps, too, because my husband
could be the son they needed. The pressures and pleasures of being

wife and mother (eventually of four children) certainly contributed; they also overshadowed my continuing, but by then much less intense, fat fears (reduced, I think, by bearing and caring for babies). But years later, in analysis, I came to see *that* swearing off as similar to both the anorexia and my four-year-old oath to not live life to the hilt. All had been *both defiance of and surrender to the distorted identities my parents needed me to have.* In analysis I also became able to see that the symbolism failure in both the anorexia and the writing had to do with my unconscious's desperate need to keep me a writing cripple who could make my father love my mother for giving him an heir, but not upset him by really succeeding, or her by being sexually alive.

Except for a newspaper column on books for children and the various papers and dissertation one has to write in college and graduate school, I never tried to write creatively again until 17 years later, after having completed college, clinical training, and the first years of postdoctorate employment. Only then, divorced and in private practice with an ongoing personal psychoanalysis, did I yield to my analyst's queries of "What about your writing?"

Then the capacity for symbolization made possible by psychoanalysis became a major vehicle in my pursuit of freedom. This capacity had not been available to me earlier due to strong inner prohibitions and repeated external trauma from parents, the medical world, and my own successes. By the ninth year of my analysis, when the dream symbolizations began to become most freeing, the understanding process was largely my own intense pursuit, with the analyst being mainly a listening, nonintrusive, but supportive travel companion who was willing to ask or answer questions when he could. In retrospect, Dr. H.'s relative silence also seems to have fostered my capacity to symbolize; not only was I dreaming and analyzing, but my voice was filling the consulting room.

INTERNAL CONFLICTS AND SOLUTIONS MADE VISIBLE IN ANALYSIS

Due to simultaneous dream representation of writing problems and deeper personality problems, both writing and dreaming became soul-saving aspects of my analysis. In the ninth year of treatment I also began writing regularly (as I felt the need) in a series of college-ruled composition books which I called my "copy book." These writings expanded over time from recording dreams to recording new awareness of thoughts, feelings, and insights, and eventually included writing about connections between these elements and deeper insights that came to mind in the process. Sometimes written words preceded thoughts.

Prior to analysis, my dreaming had been less frequent and rarely attended to. During analysis dreaming increased and developed into a depended-on source of information. But with the copy book, dreams and gleaning new insights from them became a driving enterprise. They taught me to picture the resistance (in both life and writing)—within my body, my feelings, or my manuscript and often in relation to my history—so as to be able to combat it.

Even more exciting, however, is the method I thus discovered for utilizing dreams and dream images. This "mountain-climbing grapple" approach amounts to embellishing Pontalis's concept of dreams as transitional objects so as to utilize dream images in more active pursuit of freedom. It involves seeing what is "wrong" in the picture and focusing consciously on how to make the dream image "right" through making changes in one's creative work and life. Such intense examining and imagining result in very active (though still considerably unconscious) efforts at conflict resolution and ego defense revision. But since dream images are much closer to life's ambiguity and complexity than our cognitive concepts of conflicts and defenses can be, such "dream climbing" is continually surprising and often liberating. Now years of employing this approach have revealed further benefits from "back-grappling." By reaching back and comparing dream images recorded years apart, it is possible to see and understand significant similarities and differences. With ego strength, insight, and life accomplishments growing in the course of analysis, "back-grappling" permits seeing new things in old dreams after it has become possible to use images from earlier dreams to much greater advantage. Thus, the copy book served as an extension of myself which facilitated my freedom to write and dream in the presence of the analyst, whose love and hatred I had abundant transference reasons to fear. In the material that follows, I shall use a few crucial dreams to demonstrate the importance of their symbolic function in increasing both creative and living freedom.

For several years after I began to write again, the quality of my writing was far from what I needed it to be. However, because it was not the source of either my livelihood or my respect in the world, and because of psychoanalysis, I not only continued writing, but also did considerable reading about creativity and its adversities. Able to observe specific problems in my manuscripts, I considered what characteristic in me would be "served" by such writing deficiencies. Often I could label a destructive quality—say, "woodenness" in writing particular scenes—and connect it to a long-term discomfort and object relationship—say, needing to appear perfect for my mother. Then I could labor consciously in the present to not allow myself and my work to be handicapped by this hated and well-known condition of my childhood. In addition, my dependable dream capacity presented images I could use and reuse in the interwoven process of self- and writing liberation.

My painful ambivalence first became visible in a 1983 dream depicting me as unable to urinate on a high, thronelike toilet in a doorless cubicle like those on the mental hospital's acute ward. Clad only in one of those short gowns assigned to acutely ill patients, I was ashamed for others to see me as, keyless, I entreated them to unlock and let me through the door from the acute ward into the chronic ward.

This was my first recognition of urination and writing being associated for me. Besides highlighting the idea of writing as excessively exalted in my view, and inherited like a kingdom, this dream clearly reflected my shame about being both a female and an ex-mental patient. But out of all the details that presented themselves for pondering both at the time of this dream and years later, the problems that most pressed to be solved for my writing's sake seemed *how to become able to urinate freely and how to get my own keys*. The main changes accomplished after studying this dream were rearranging my clinical schedule so as to have regular hours to write in the early morning and turning out considerable amounts of manuscript, deliberately barring myself from being critical. The project, written longhand as is my preferred mode, developed into an autobiographical novel. Later in this period, I also remarried.

With expanding manuscript the need to be self-observant and even self-critical came to the fore, and in working to improve the manuscript, I learned to study parts that were poor with a sense of relief. Being able to discover what made them ineffective, how that ineffectiveness made me feel, and, sometimes, that that feeling and its fantasy (and, therefore, *that* ineffectiveness) could be given up provided a new sense of self-capacity. There was a variety of shortcomings, but the three that bothered me most early on were "weak," "shallow" and "wooden." Recalling these qualities as the cause of my having abandoned writing earlier was painfully discouraging. But eventually, I had another most helpful dream:

April 1989

I was on Dr. H.'s couch, telling him about having drunk two-and-a-half glasses of wine. Suddenly I noticed that my right hand was in a cast and, then, that this was responsible for a good feeling all over my body, a kind of white-light goodness that enveloped me. But different from analysis, in the dream I was lying on my left side, looking at the wall beside the couch and turned away from Dr. H.

So there I was feeling good about myself due to being a crippled writer! But it took a long time and lots of work to make this identity-shaking image something I could consciously try to overcome. The

earlier steps in this process involved seeing that the compulsive goodness I had to maintain all my life (despite feeling it was only a cover
for shame and guilt associated with being praised by my mother) was
really reaction formation—driven love for parents I also hated, and a
way to keep me bad and them good in my world view. I also had little
difficulty seeing my wrist in a cast as representing sexual crippledness.
Since two-and-a-half glasses of wine was an amount I considered a
little too much, I began to think of a little too much in many ways
(wine, food, work, exercise, too many words, etc.) as something I did
to keep myself feeling dead or ''good''! With that equivalence, I could
also see goodness all over my body as a way of feeling like my father's
dead wife. Needing to be loved by Father might be keeping my writing
''perfectly dead'' or in a ''cast'' that preserved me as his small
''copy.'' Seeing these multiple meanings marked the start of a burgeoning capacity to manipulate symbols, ultimately the key to both
personal and writing freedom.

What followed from this dream and its associations was a lot of
analytic work (on my own and in the copybook, as well as with Dr.
H.) to shed the reaction formation. My conception of this task took
the form of trying to understand *how to remove the cast from my wrist
and the white goodness from my body*. It did not take long to see my
crippled wrist as also representing anorexia, and the goodness all over
my body as the reduction of guilt not eating too much still assisted.
That made freeing myself and freeing my writing seem synonymous.
Equating my boring, too-packed writing problems with the cast and
the straitjacket of goodness was not hard either, but again doing what
was required to eliminate them seemed daunting.

The only tangible result in the short run was deciding to have a
writing room where I could leave my work all scattered about. This
was especially needed because I did not like sharing the dark library
where my husband wrote. Six months later, after converting a bedroom
to my writing room, I had another dream:

Fall 1989

Going back to the Shamrock Drive house where we raised the
children, and where I both went back to school and got divorced, I
found a team of laborers renovating it. On the second floor, I entered
the writing room Father used after the War. Sunny, high room that had
been the nursery before we went to Washington. My own black analytic
couch was under the window looking west in the same position as my
desk is in my writing room now. I lay on it face down, while Father
worked at his writing table across the room. Strong sexual feelings in
my vagina indicated to me that I had to leave. Standing up to do so, I
was weeping. Father turned out to be Dr. H., dressed in the kind of suit

Father wore, and a smaller, identical copy of Dr. H. was with him. It made me even sadder to see that his boy could stay while I had to leave.

Obviously, being sexually alive was something I associated with having to separate from both Father and Dr. H. Also, my wonderful marriage of three years and now my private writing room seemed concrete evidence of such aliveness. In analysis we had been talking for a long time about how Father had called me his boy in terms of my being a writer and the replacement for the son he had lost. We had also talked about my ashamed willingness to regard my intelligence as masculine, as defense against Father's sexual provocativeness, and meshing with his need to keep me his boy—a copy who wrote like but never surpassed him. However, besides conceptualizing the problem of confusing my writing room with Father's, this dream integrated many significant details I never would have been able to consider consciously. For instance, Father's writing room replacing the nursery pictured how my sisters and I had been raised to treat him like a baby, another prohibition against competing with him. I got the idea that a struggle would have to ensue between Father and me before I could ever claim my own writing room. But two details did not take on full significance until four years later—that the powerful vaginal feelings were also symbolic of mouth power and that, as I was leaving, Dr. H. and his boy were utterly silent.

Working to effect the separations represented in that dream, I understood that pain and grief were inevitable. My ultimate ability to write with power seemed far from certain, but going the extra mile for my own integrity and emotional freedom had by then become a conscious shaper of life. I was already at that time in the process of negotiating to sell my share of our family newspaper, a sale that would give me the funds to provide my children with graduate education and to establish the Lucy Daniels Foundation and Center for Early Childhood.

But the grief I had to face came in more than one form. The changes in me resulting from analysis and my work in writing and in life led to both the consciously worked-for separation from my family of origin and the unexpected end of my cherished second marriage due to my husband's becoming explosively and implacably enraged. The results of selling my shares of our family newspaper had been foreshadowed in a dream that depicted me as no longer recognized by my family, and my writing as frozen but melting. But, as with the terrible pain around the end of my marriage, I had no capacity at that time to anticipate the gratification possible with freedom.

Several months after receiving my money and the end of my marriage, I had a dream on the birthday of my next younger sister,

Adelaide, which depicted me alone in a girls' dormitory. Sitting in a church pew, facing high-up sunshine, I realized I had urinated on my beautiful red dancing skirt. I put a white skirt on over it to hide the wet, but looking in a mirror, I realized that the white one was not long enough to cover the red one. Also, I was wearing high black walking boots whose stolid plainness ruined the dancing effect of both skirts. I was worried about an exam because I had not prepared in the usual way. Due to already being proficient in the subject matter, I had made a deliberate decision to not study like a "greasy grind" (as Father had labelled my hard work in latency and adolescence), and that made me suddenly frantic that I had nothing to write with. But in the bathroom drawer in the packet that used to hold my diaphragm I found two substantial black pens—black and plain, looking like the boots.

Since I had come to understand by then that my husband's emotional disintegration had, like Father's attacks in my adolescence, resulted from his not being able to tolerate my increasing good fortune, success, and sexual aliveness. I had no trouble seeing how sitting on the worshipping seat messed up my sexuality. There I was, still trying to cover up angry, alive, sexual me with saintliness. But fortunately it no longer worked. A new and surprising discovery from this dream was the idea of being anxious *because* I was experienced and not making "greasy-grind" preparations. However, it took some time to realize that the "test" before me then was writing without the protection of feeling inadequate and overworking to compensate. The fact that the two pens in the diaphragm pouch looked staid and substantial like the walking boots added to my wishful question about how to trade those boots in for dancing shoes. And the whole business occurring on Adelaide's birthday made me wonder how this test was related to that of her birth. Two possible answers: I remembered having lost my voice (become hoarse) the day she first arrived home when I was twenty months old. And, when I was still quite small, Father had hurt me, while carrying her, by saying I was "big enough to walk." That hurt had been the greater because Adelaide, as a baby, had gleefully participated in Father's raucous sexual games, while I had "hidden" from them in the shadows of furniture. In response, Father had declared me "an intellectual with no feelings and no sexuality."

The analytic work after this moved more substantively into how both my parents had, in different ways, forced penises on me. I had exerted tremendous effort to prevent this in earliest childhood, while at the same time straining to be valuable as both the nurse-mother our family needed and the intellectual success that represented family boy. In the period following this dream I had to reduce the length of the novel from about 700 pages to about 500. Upon discovering a major way to do this, an itching, burning rash developed that helped me recognize my intense unconscious need for insulation.

In early November 1991, I mailed the revised novel to my former literary agent. This felt especially important because I had been voted Distinguished Friend of Psychoanalysis by the American Psychoanalytic Association and did not want that honor for serving others to interfere with taking care of myself. Anticipating meeting with the agent while in New York to receive the award, I dreamed:

> November 24, 1991
>
> I went to see Murphy Evans (a former neighbor). Directly in front of me sitting like a Buddha, he seemed fine. But looking closer, I could see his wrists were bandaged. . . . Then, in my office (only it was in our house on Garfield Street in Washington), I was going out at 6:00 p.m. to play with the analysts. But I stashed my wallet in the back of the bottom desk drawer along with my pretty blue denim dancing bootlets. Clear, maybe bullet-proof plastic covered this drawer. Outside I could see the analysts I normally did not know, because this was the only time they came out of their offices.

Murphy Evans, who had selflessly devoted his life to a family business, had recently been attacked by a thief. I thought the dream depicted confronting the good son in me whose writing had been injured but was no longer in a cast. Pleased to note that the walking/writing boots had been replaced by durable but pretty dancing ones inspired by the dream of one year earlier, I wondered why my valuables (writing, sexuality, self-esteem?) had to be hidden in the bottom drawer under bullet-proof plastic. For preservation's sake?

That December two agents judged my book not publishable in its present form. Both saw it as having two different stories that interfered with each other, and suggested a memoir would work better if I felt up to the exposure. Returning home pretty devastated, I dreamed about a crotchety old lady kept in solitary confinement by a sinister man, possibly a doctor. He was going to kill her. Horrified, I could not decide whether to tell anyone or not. I was afraid that if I did, the keeper would charge me with libel or get me charged as an accomplice. But I was also afraid that if I did not tell, the authorities would charge me with murder, too. And not telling would make me feel *terribly, terribly* guilty.

I had no trouble seeing the confined woman as me. On the couch, I realized that Dr. H. was right: he, by working with me, *was* killing that isolated person. But my most sensational insight was recognizing the dream's intense terror and guilt as the exact same feelings as had tormented me during anorexia. Deciding that they must also be the confiners of my writing, I wondered about the relation of fear and guilt to the bottom drawer (degraded writing and self-esteem?) and bullet-proof cover (see-throughable but untouchable?) of my earlier dream. The next challenge seemed to be getting out. But how?

Some insight into what was keeping me confined came from a dream about a clinic where I went to receive "heart medicine," but was prevented from having an appointment by a brute of a doctor. I decided that this heart medicine was something like Drano, needed to clean out the love for Father that still clogged my writing equipment. During this period I began doing more public speaking, and on one occasion spoke as a writer for the first time in decades. By chance, this speaking engagement was accompanied by such severe pain in my left thumb that I subsequently consulted a hand specialist who X-rayed it, gave me a splint and a steroid injection, and told me this problem could be corrected with surgery if it continued to bother me. Associating this pain (in the thumb I had once sucked to silence myself as a child) with my speech as a woman writer connected it, also, with my dream about having my right wrist in a cast. Despite the doctor's X-ray and physiological explanation for my problem, I was able to use this pain (which waxed and waned over the next few years) to think about the painful losing of that thumb by my unconscious. If I became free to speak and write as I chose, this "stopper" would no longer be needed.

That summer I hired an editor to read for me. Then, after completing and rewriting a short story, I resolved to convert the novel to memoir. In a few weeks this dream followed:

July 12, 1992

I gave up an important suitcase or pocketbook—like my neat, versatile, roll-aboard suitcase-luggage carrier. Then I was kneeling down naked and all folded up on myself on the floor of Dr. H.'s office. Wet all over and weeping mightily about this loss, with my back to Dr. H., my scrunched-up-ness was like from having been inside the suitcase myself. . . . Next, I was with my artist friend, Eleanor, outdoors beside a pair of trees a few feet apart. A board was nailed to and joined them. Looking at the board, Eleanor saw this scary children's art work (clay monster faces) on it that she loved. A little boy who lived with elves under the roots of one tree had made this art. Eleanor wanted to leave a note to him on the back of one of her pictures, to say how much she liked his work. I knew this boy and suggested to Eleanor that she tell him in her note that she was a friend of mine. But she did not want to. . . . Then I went out in the garage of our Shamrock Drive house, in a nightgown you could not see through, to meet a friend. But before she arrived, a cute little four-year-old blond girl came up with this long-haired, pimply-faced, flaky-looking pedophile. He introduced both of them to me, "I'm a bigamist who lives up the hill there by Adelaide, and she's the daughter of my neighbor, the kidnapper".... Then, riding to the airport at night in a van with lots of other people, I feared I had forgotten my bags. We stopped and turned on the lights to look. I *had* left the roller one, but I still had the red canvas carry-on one with two handles. As we drove away, there were long lines of traffic at the pay booths, but the middle lane was clear for us.

Out of the *suit*case used to ward off attacks by trying to please both parents at once, it was obvious that I was going to feel like a vulnerable, skinned, and deformed creature, unequipped to function in the world. The board nailed to the two trees was at the same height as when the hammock in the yard of my childhood had been pushed hard enough to enable us to exhilaratingly bring back "money" in the form of leaves. I soon recognized that board as "bored," which I had used much of my life to ward off the terrifying parental emotional attacks that inevitably followed moments of success and exhilaration. I wondered, but did not understand why the artist-in-me would not let present me be in touch with the boy artist under the roots. The bigamist would be my father, in my child's mind married to my mother and his first wife all at once and, therefore, available to me in identifying with the latter. The nightgown that could not be seen through suggested, however, that other things continued to be kept out of my awareness. Still, the ease of getting through toll booths suggested I had grown able to take more for granted the losses that had to be "paid."

This "suitcase" dream, like the "wrist-in-a-cast" one, has turned out to be an even more valuable source of understanding than was evident at the time. It sensitized me to preconscious and unconscious issues that otherwise might have remained unattended to in physical feelings and symptoms, writing with increased competence and confidence, and other dreams. As these other experiences broadened and deepened my awareness, I repeatedly looked back into this dream as a mirror of truth. Thus, over time, a multitude of symbolizations interacted with each other enlighteningly. For instance, close on the heels of the suitcase dream came one about bringing a tiny girl or white elephant to life. In it people were saying that she was going to need lots of guidance due to not having judgment about heights and taking care of herself, a premonition that proved to be extremely helpful in waking life. After removing the novel's outer shell (a surprisingly easy task), and interweaving past and present in the memoir so that each informed the other, my new experience of writing effectively was paired with intense aching of a depressive and almost physical flulike nature. The pain would cease at the completion of each rewrite, but loom up to possess me again at the next resumption of the process. However, the sense of myself or the writing as weak or dead was gone.

After the first of these rewrites and before beginning the second, I had my first dream in which me writing was represented as me actually writing, not urinating. Not long after that there were several dreams that I later concluded had to do with both the wish to and terror of losing myself as in changing psychologically. Reflecting on these dreams drove home how necessary it had been for me to dissociate my mind and my body in adolescence. As pain continued to accompany my productive writing, I began to think of it symbolically as well—as, perhaps, due to breaking out of solitary confinement, anticipating the loss of parental love I had sought to preserve by staying small and silent. Only several months later did another dream show me vividly how much I experienced my productive writing as extorted by my parents. And projecting these new awarenesses onto the out-of-the-suitcase dream repeatedly allowed fresh focusing, so that new or previously overlooked details could be dealt with.

Freedom to symbolize effectively, which I call "a room of one's own," comprises both the passive capacity to "show" a concept (as in a dream) and the active capacity to focus on it consciously. Focusing precisely only becomes possible when the concept to be dealt with is both bearable and necessary. Analysis with its progress toward acceptance of emotions makes focusing increasingly bearable. The need to create more effectively or on a higher level provides the necessity. Along the way, many seemingly insignificant things can contribute to this capacity to focus. These include dreams, physical feelings and symptoms, creative work, and life experience.

While planning this chapter, and continuing to work effectively, but painfully, on the memoir, I began to think about the need to let go of and "lose" myself if I was ever to be free to write fiction again as I wanted. Once completed, the memoir had to be cut 40 percent before a New York literary agent would undertake selling it. Doing this cutting proved to be a great confidence builder, but its success was accompanied by a distressing dream in which I, as a child, was made to say the right thing in a way that I was incapable of and that could kill me. I strangled on these words while my parents stood over me, cruelly demanding that I say them "right," even though they could see I was going to die from trying.

Once the book had been turned over to the agent, I suddenly noticed how much the pain in my left hand (not my writing hand) had increased. A reevaluation by the hand doctor indicated that there had been further deterioration that could be corrected surgically. Opting for this, I anticipated some form of strong feelings due to the wrist-in-a-cast dream and the fact that the thumb involved was the one I had sucked as a child. The splinted, six-weeks recovery period did prove to be further enlightening. During it a combined sense of painful confinedness and resistance to writing followed by release did lead to a whole string of revelations: due to my parents using me as a narcissistic extension, I had felt secretly "married to" and possessed by each. I suddenly realized that in the out-of-the-suitcase dream the artist beside the left tree had been pregnant, and then that that pregnancy and the boy artist's being under the roots of the right tree were both ways of keeping secrets. By then I had come to see that continually working on a book without giving it up for publication resembled prolonging pregnancy by avoiding the loss associated with giving birth. Considering how to correct this brought to mind integrating the pregnant female artist and the buried boy artist, which, in turn, made me think about how their dissociation seemed to be supporting the two trees (each of my parents). The two artists merging in the dream would cause the trees and the "bored" holding them up to collapse in the same kind of catastrophe as I had experienced at three when one day the exhilaration of swinging high in the hammock had ended with my falling and breaking my left collarbone.

Seeing all this did not resolve everything, but it did help me take the next step, i.e., to actively pursue the capacity to "lose" myself in writing fiction. It enabled me to understand that the loss I feared was speaking out strongly as my full self, which would cause me to lose the parental "love" I had clung to unconsciously by trying to be what each parent wanted.

CONCLUSIONS

A creative individual driven to pursue artistic risks and development is destined to times of either encountering intense, often dismaying emotions or being blocked by defenses against such feelings. Contrary to Deri's (1984) belief that the strength of talent determines whether an individual becomes blocked (pp. 283–284), in my view, creative individuals are as subject to neurosis as other people. Some may be exceptionally prolific, in part because the creative endeavor offers a way to unload unacceptable feelings or to symbolically correct pain from the past while not consciously recognizing this in the work. However, at times even such prolific individuals may collide with emotional issues that stop and distress them. (Examples include Dylan Thomas, William Faulkner, William Styron, etc.) Others may be severely blocked early on due to unconscious prohibitions against symbolization, inability to bypass their own awareness when symbolizing, and/or the emotional issues unconsciously associated with creativity. A strong talent identified with unacceptable objects and/or drives may be especially barred from symbolization.

In my experience, a psychological "room of one's own" *is* a necessity for effective creating. Not only does the creative person need to have autonomy and authority in addressing the medium, he or she also needs to have the confidence that putting one's innermost self out before the world will not result in humiliation due to characteristics clung to unconsciously. For this to be possible, the creative person must feel free to claim his or her own inner space and have the courage to sweep it clean (through symbolizations that permit increasing internal separation and individuation) of characterological hindrances. Thus, having a "room of one's own" also requires the fortitude to stand alone and weather the emotional losses and surprises inherent in this process.

REFERENCES

Deri, S. K. (1984), *Symbolization and Creativity*. New York: International Universities Press.
Gedo, J. E. (1983), *Portraits of the Artist*. New York: Guilford Press.
Kubie, L. S. (1958), *Neurotic Distortion of the Creative Process*. Lawrence, KS: University of Kansas Press.
Pontalis, J.-B. (1977), Between the dream as object and the dream text. In: *Frontiers in Psychoanalysis*. New York: International Universities Press, pp. 23–55.
Rothenberg, A. (1990), *Creativity and Madness*. Baltimore, MD: Johns Hopkins University Press.
Winnicott, D. W. (1953), Transitional objects and transitional phenomena. *Internat. J. Psycho-Anal.*, 34:89–97.
——— (1966), The location of cultural experience. *Internat. J. Psycho-Anal.*, 48:368–372.
Woolf, V. (1928), *A Room of One's Own*. London: Hogarth Press, 1984.

8

IN PRAISE OF LEISURE

JOHN E. GEDO, M.D.

The invitation to contribute a chapter to a volume about "work" could not have reached me at a more appropriate juncture: I had only recently decided that I no longer wished to work. I am now almost free of professional responsibilities, and I have never enjoyed life as much as I do at present. These circumstances have given me the opportunity to indulge my contrarian tendencies: I offered to write an essay about people who do not have to work in order to earn their living. Clearly, I am not in agreement with the oft-quoted aphorism attributed to Freud that mental health involves the capacity to love and work. Had he said that it requires freedom from any *incapacity* in these spheres, Freud's statement would have been an unarguable truism; as he allegedly put the matter, however, it amounts to the elevation of a personal opinion, narrowly based on the customs of a particular social class in a specific community, into a law of nature.

In America, this dictum has never been challenged: our country remains faithful, for the most part, to Puritan and *petit bourgeois* traditions. In Freud's case, the commandment *zu lieben und arbeiten* must have had biblical roots: it echoes God's instructions to Noah (Genesis 9:1), "Be fruitful and multiply," and His wrathful decree to Adam (Genesis 3:19), "In the sweat of thy face shalt thou eat bread." Of course, most people have no choice in the matter—they must indeed labor for subsistence. But the point of view attributed to Freud did not address this self-evident necessity; his aphorism implies that it is unhealthy not to work, even if there is enough bread in one's freezer to last a lifetime.

It might be well to pause here to consider what kind of activity constitutes "work." Most people would agree, I suspect, that many essential tasks, even if they are oppressive, do not qualify as work.

133

Brushing one's teeth may be a boring annoyance, but, like all other efforts to safeguard one's health, it is subsumed under the rubric of biological necessity. Doing for ourselves with respect to eating, sleeping, reproduction, excretion, and temperature control actually takes up most of our lives, especially if these activities are defined broadly. (Shopping, food preparation, doing the dishes, disposing of garbage can all be classified as self-care with regard to alimentation.) It is only when doing these things on behalf of others (probably not including one's children) that it makes sense to regard them as "work." Family life necessitates some kind of understanding about sharing and dividing these unavoidable chores. Present-day feminists are therefore quite correct in refusing to accept that being stuck with more than one's share of household drudgery constitutes an acceptable fate.

Consequently, although in retirement I am as busy as ever with the innumerable aspects of self-care, I am "not working." It could be argued that composing an essay for this volume still constitutes work, but it is utterly different from seeing patients ("clinical work") because it is done *solely* for pleasure (including narcissistic gratifications, of course) and because it entails no responsibility (the project can be dropped at any time without untoward effects). Thus, a creative endeavor of this kind is closer to play than to work—a point that may be convincing if we recall that the adepts of most games play with the utmost concentration and seriousness and tend to be highly rewarded if successful. When I am asked, nowadays, what I "do," I am tempted to reply that I am a dilettante or a *rentier* (of course, I know better than actually to say such a shocking thing).

Around the turn of the century, when Joseph Conrad was asked to describe himself, he said he was "a Pole, a Catholic, and a gentleman." Conrad was neither a Puritan nor a *petit bourgeois*; he certainly had to labor for bread, first as a sailor, later as a literary man—but he did not characterize himself in terms of what he "did." Rather, he described who he *was*. I do not primarily cite his example to suggest that Freud's viewpoint about the need to work is excessively careerist; I merely wish to point out that, beyond careers, there are other, equally legitimate ways to look upon these matters. Feminists are clearly right to decline the depreciated role of "housewife," but they may be entering a dangerous trap in thinking of respectable opportunities exclusively in terms of careers; *a fortiori*, psychoanalysts should not speak *ex cathedra* about work constituting a requirement of mental health.

Of course, for Puritans raised in *petit bourgeois* homes, work may come to assume the very core of identity and the central aim of personality organization. Such rigid adherence to the notion that idleness leads to mischief is not pathological *per se*, but it may cause pathology if, for reasons beyond the person's control, the opportunity to keep on working is interrupted. Everyone is familiar with people who cannot tolerate retirement, or even become clinically depressed when deprived of their work. (The syndrome is common enough among psychoanalysts!) In cases of that kind, the lack of alternative means to maintain a modicum of self-esteem constitutes the illness; the Nazis' cynical inscription on the gates of concentration camps, *"Arbeit macht frei"* parallels the illegitimate claims of many psychoanalysts that not to work is to be impaired. It is not work that makes one free—the free person may choose to work or not to work, depending on the range of current possibilities for personal fulfillment.

Some years ago, TIAA, an organization that administers pension funds for college professors, published a survey about the retirement of its clients. Its most surprising current findings were that, on the average, these successful professionals voluntarily choose to stop work earlier than ever before—and that, for the most part, they are satisfied with retirement. Although a significant minority has launched a second career (often the option abandoned in favor of the professoriate in the first place), a substantial majority devotes itself principally to the cultivation of inner resources. These data give eloquent testimony to the value of higher education in enriching the lives it has touched; at the same time, the survey provides empirical evidence that disproves the contention that work is a necessary buttress of mental well-being.

I have often discussed these issues with colleagues (many of whom seem provoked by my decision to retire, as if it depreciated psychoanalysis as an activity); several have told me that my circumstances are exceptional because I have derived more satisfaction than most from the scholarly aspects of the profession—and presumably the same holds true for the retired academicians in the TIAA survey. I cannot deny that I have always enjoyed reading and writing more than battling disease; I submit, however, that this was true precisely because clinical responsibilities constitute work, whereas scholarship, however challenging and difficult it may be, amounts to the playful cultivation of one's intellectual faculties. The name of the game is to pick a challenge that one has a reasonable chance to overcome; then it is as much fun as playing golf or a good evening of bridge!

More cogent than the foregoing argument for the necessity to work is the claim that retirement is only enjoyable for those who derive sufficient self-esteem from their past vocational accomplishments. (It is no doubt bitter to be dissatisfied with oneself in the vocational sphere, but this is no less true if one perseveres with work than if one retires—there is not much prospect of reversing the verdict of history through some geriatric triumph.) At any rate, one must turn to the history of societies that produced a "leisure class" to find evidence that excellent adaptation does not require any record of work accomplishment. In industrialized communities, until relatively recently, only upper-class and upper-middle-class married women retained the privilege of never having to work. It is both pathetic and comical that most people now believe that the lives of these women would have been improved had they joined the ratrace of the working classes. Readers of 19th century fiction will recall that the characters of Jane Austen or Stendhal or Turgenev, both male and female, work only if they run out of money.

On some occasions, our clinical practice permits us to meet a rare individual who represents a throwback to the social conditions of such a leisure class; attention to the attitudes toward work of these anachronistic survivals of a bygone era is very illuminating about the actual role of work in human psychic life. I plan to present these matters as they emerged in the analyses of two young people, a man and a woman, who, in my experience, came closest in their circumstances to those of the pre-modern upper class. Ladies first:

THE QUEEN OF CHICAGO

I encountered this young woman shortly after she completed college and, as a result of a series of followup consultations over the years, observed her progress in life for about two decades. She was a member of the city's social and financial upper crust, that exclusive circle of families who have reigned in this area for at least five generations—since before the Great Fire of 1871. The unusual circumstances that led such a person to consult a psychoanalyst are neither pertinent to the topic of this book nor publishable without risking a breach of confidentiality. Suffice it to say that her upbringing had been so unreliable as to tempt her to repudiate her family's way of life by embarking on a career in child care in another city—a project interrupted by a physical injury that necessitated extended treatment and a return to her parents' home. Under the circumstances, she decided to take graduate training in her field because her psychoanalysis made it difficult to adhere to the schedule of any child care facility.

Far from being regal, this Vietnam era youngster was trying hard to impersonate an ordinary member of her generation. Of course, this was no easy matter, starting with her *name*, which is a household word in this area. Because of her wish to repudiate her actual status, she kept herself ignorant of her true financial situation, although it was impossible to disavow her family's extraordinary affluence. But money kept pouring into her personal accounts—so much more than she had managed to spend that the surplus in this "petty cash" drawer now exceeded a million! It was difficult to build a social life divorced from her parents' circle, because young people from middle-class backgrounds became intimidated, envious, or exploitative when they learned who she was: whether she liked it or not, she was treated like the future Queen of Chicago.

It was equally difficult, alas, to be an ordinary graduate student or an ordinary worker. A dean of the program she attended asked her to intervene with her father to favor the school with a donation—a serious ethical lapse that permanently destroyed her sense that her work could be evaluated on its merits. (But pity the poor administrator: the entire metropolitan area is blanketed with buildings donated by this girl's family!) When she began working part-time in a child care facility, that institution ran into a financial crisis and asked her to salvage it by taking it over as a private venture. The only place she found, except for the analysis, where she was seen as an individual rather than a representative member of a royal family was a church near her new apartment, where the clergy responded with evident sincerity to her profound religiousness.

She spent much time in the analysis worrying about her future. She soon realized that if she wanted to have a family, her children (who would be even wealthier than she, barring a national economic catastrophe) would need a father better able to cope with great wealth and prestige than she—in other words, there was no escape for her from the world of her parents. In that world, the men are responsible for safeguarding capital for their grandchildren, and women have to promote the family's social prestige. It is not impossible to have a vocation, but it must have at least as much status as engaging in major philanthropy, leading society functions, or triumphing through glamour and fashion. (When this girl eventually married, she chose a man whose mother had around two million dollars' worth of clothing in her closets.) It is simply too jarring to be in an ordinary job, where one takes care of children, only to dress formally for dinner when one gets home. Moreover, such a choice would be looked upon as bizarre in the relevant social circles.

Unfortunately, it was too late for the patient to embark on any career that might have made sense in the only social context available to her, nor was she truly *interested* in any prestigious occupation. After a few years of analysis, she discovered that her highest priority was marriage and having her own children. When she found a successful man of upper-class background to marry, the first period of treatment came to a close, and she decided to devote the next several years to establishing her family and giving her children a more reliable early environment than the one she had been provided.

Analysis was resumed when this woman was in her early 30's, in large measure because she could not cope with the hostility of her intrusive father as well as that of her husband. (From the sidelines, I got the impression that these attacks were stimulated by the envy both men felt about the devoted care she was giving her children.) One form of their campaigns against her was to depreciate her as a parasite who lived off the fat of the land. She was unable to defend herself against these insinuations, although she was actually extremely busy running a baronial establishment, taking personal care of children, husband, and a number of infirm relatives, and promoting her husband's business through her unmatched social contacts. She had become notably elegant and blossomed into quite a beauty. One result of the first analysis was a capacity for empathy and a sweetness of disposition that made her a favorite with dowagers of the old school who did not approve of the prevalent attitudes of the younger generation.

Although she was firm in her conviction that she was living in the only way that made possible discharging her family responsibilities, the patient also expressed some envy of women friends who had a profession, like medicine or academic life. Her own intellectual interests had expanded: she was more involved than ever with her religion, and (probably in identification with me and my wife, an art historian somewhat visible on the local scene) she had begun seriously to collect works of art. However, she took no pride in these activities, precisely because they did not constitute "work." She got more self-esteem from participating in the governance of a number of local cultural institutions, in the tradition of several generations of women in her family. The fact that she was more generous in supporting these organizations than either her husband or her father was, in a way, her response to their attacks on her. "I may not be a captain of industry," she seemed to be saying *sotto voce*, "but I am dedicated to the highest values."

The issue of values turned out to be pivotal during the second period of analysis. Gradually, she realized that her family (as well as that of her husband) idealized money and its acquisition, that their triumphs in business were empty exercises in narcissism and greed, and that their way of life was lacking not just in spiritual content, but even in personal decency. Eventually, her husband's unwillingness to change led to the breakup of this marriage, some time after the termination of the analysis. She consulted me during the separation because of her well-founded concern about the effects of her decision on the psychological welfare of her husband and children; I was able to refer the man to a colleague for appropriate help.

In parallel with the foregoing disillusionment with acquisitiveness as the supreme good, the patient's view of her own activities underwent a radical change. She began to value her own commitment to human decency and helpfulness, to the welfare of her children (and those of others!), and to the ambition to become a *good* person. She became more introspective, both in the analytic situation and elsewhere, and less ambitious in terms of commonly accepted criteria of success. She was no longer bothered about not having professional accomplishments, but derived self-esteem from such activities as her connoisseurship in collecting, her esthetic response to music, and the communion she experienced with God. I last heard from her after her remarriage, when she was around 40; the way of life she then arranged for herself was designed to promote these same goals.

Before I comment on the implications of these observations, let me present the second case I wish to describe.

A PRINCE OF BYZANTIUM

This man did not possess aristocratic antecedents; he merely dreamt of imperial honors befitting an Eastern potentate. However, his self-made tycoon of a father certainly had wealth enough to make any concern about finances irrelevant for the analysand. He sought treatment because in no respect was he able to organize an endurable life for himself; this paralysis of will defeated him in a series of educational ventures, despite his outstanding native endowments. When the analysis started, at his family's insistence he was attending an elite law school: at the age of 28, he was expected to justify the subsidies he received by engaging in constructive activities of some kind.

The patient's response to such pressure was a surface compliance that veiled a rageful negativism: he did no work in school, barely getting by on the basis of attendance at lectures. For the sake of safeguarding the analysis (which the parents would not have paid for if he had once again dropped out of school), he forced himself to do enough to graduate and obtained a job in a decent law firm, largely because of the reputation of the law school. In the tough world of big-city practice, his recalcitrance proved to be totally unacceptable, and he was fired before the end of his first year on the job. By that time, certain funds of his own that were previously tied up in a family partnership had become available to him, so that his parents no longer had financial leverage over him. He therefore declared that he had no intention ever again to seek employment.

To be sure, he was quite unhappy with the idleness that then supervened; he was particularly embarrassed about being unable to answer the recurrent query, "What do you do?" Although he was able to handle his capital in a responsible manner, he did not feel justified to call himself a "private investor." Because he was just as unable to organize enjoyable leisure activities as he was to commit himself to any vocation, I was ultimately able to convince him that his chronic state of disorganization constituted an illness—that, on the whole, what he had best do was work with me to repair this disarray. In other words, the relevant question was not what he *did*, but what he wanted to be if and when he got well; for the moment, he was (alas!) an invalid.

The only fantasy he had ever had, beyond princely splendor, was that of writing the great American novel—an ambition that could be sustained with confidence only through indefinite postponement of any test of its actual feasibility. Reading great literature filled him with more envy than he cared to tolerate, so that he remained surprisingly ignorant of the models all beginners need as they embark on artistic activities. He relieved the monotony of his existence by pursuing women who were easy marks for a Don Juan, and participating in certain groups for wealthy supporters of some cultural organizations. Very gradually, these contacts evolved into something of a social network that relieved his previous isolation. Ultimately, it became clear that he was not incapable of loving: he cautiously avoided emotional entanglements because of his propensity to invite abuse from sadistic women.

Although analytic progress was excruciatingly slow, the patient's idealization of wealth, power, and status was gradually overcome, so that he became motivated to obtain self-esteem on the basis of real accomplishments. He gave up chasing women he despised and became a more serious consumer of high culture. Through certain newly acquired friends, he got the opportunity to write reviews for several literary periodicals. These assignments hardly paid enough to cover his out-of-pocket expenses, but they organized his life to a great extent because of the ancillary research he needed to do to prepare him to assess the books he had agreed to write about. He did not feel he was "working"—he was now spending a respectable portion of his life in belatedly obtaining the education he had rebelliously sabotaged when he was in school.

In the process of these literary activities, the patient came across stories about people whose lives had resembled his current life. The most admirable of these exemplars of the contemplative life was the inventor of the essay, Michel de Montaigne. In the light of such a precedent, he did not feel humiliated by spending his time in challenging himself intellectually. He derived similar lessons from some of the characters in Jane Austen's fiction, especially the heroine of *Mansfield Park*, whose life is devoted to the pursuit of moral excellence. The psychoanalytic effort thus fit comfortably with a way of life focused not on work but on self-creation. (This complex person and his treatment are discussed in greater detail in Gedo and Gehrie, 1993, Chapter 2.)

DISCUSSION

My own experience since retirement has been congruent with those of the two young people I have described: self-esteem and joyful participation in life do not depend on *earning* a living or making a *working* contribution to society. It *is* essential to live up to one's ideals. For many people that means engaging in productive work. For others, however, it involves not productivity, but doing one's best, if only in private endeavors like raising children, reaching out for the deity, playing golf, or reading Tolstoy. At a certain stage of existence, it should be sufficient to maintain one's dignity during the process of biological dissolution.

It is certainly true that it is very satisfying to receive public appreciation for one's private accomplishments (as one generally does when working), but that is merely a bonus; it is not to be counted on. A religious commitment cannot be made in order to earn a reputation for piety, in the manner of Molière's Tartuffe—nor do sane people engage in healthful physical exercise to gain public approval. Students in literature courses may look upon the assigned readings as work, but in all other circumstances one reads literature for the pleasure it provides—and the narcissistic satisfaction of being regarded as a cultivated person is generally insufficient to get one through a 700-page Victorian novel. It is even less likely that one would write psychoanalytic articles in the expectation of positive feedback—they almost always disappear without a ripple. In other words, the principal motivation for human activities must be the private satisfaction to be derived from them. It is just as satisfying finally to master a foreign language as to make a scientific discovery, to climb a mountain, or to pick the winner of the Super Bowl. Even to do a good job at work!

The vast majority of mankind is condemned to hard labor and must squeeze its satisfactions out of prevailing through endurance and ingenuity. The "work ethic" beloved by Puritans amounts to the defensive idealization of these bitter necessities, in humble submission to a deity conceived *a priori* as benign and merciful. Only a small, privileged minority has ever had the opportunity to experience that it is actually preferable to have the freedom not to work, and the envious masses have always condemned such "cavaliers" as immoral. Freud's version of this condemnation, like most of the value system implicit in psychoanalysis (see Ramzy, 1965), was encoded in the vocabulary of a "health morality": unemployment is dangerous to your health. Those who think so should speak only for themselves.

REFERENCES

Gedo, J. & Gehrie, M., Eds. (1993), *Impasse and Innovation in Psychoanalysis*. Hillsdale, NJ: Analytic Press.

Ramzy, I. (1965), The place of values in psychoanalysis. *Internat. J. Psycho-Anal.*, 64:97–106.

9

MEN AT WORK: WORK, EGO AND IDENTITY IN THE ANALYSIS OF ADULT MEN

HOWARD B. LEVINE, M.D.

When "asked what he thought a normal person should be able to do well . . . Freud said simply, '*Lieben und arbeiten*' (to love and to work)" (Erikson, 1959, p. 96). This statement, which to my knowledge has never been corroborated and may even be apocryphal,[1] has nonetheless become an analytic truism and a staple of psychoanalytic lore. Given that Freud's reply elevates work to a place coequal to that of love, it is striking that in contrast to love, with a few notable exceptions (e.g., Menninger, 1942; Hendricks, 1943; Lantos, 1952; Jaques, 1960; Holmes, 1965; Applegarth, 1976; Kramer, 1977), the subject of work has received little specific attention in the psychoanalytic literature.

I shall explore the origins and meanings of work, with particular emphasis on the relationship between work, identity, and self-esteem. My discussion will inevitably touch on the ubiquity of work symptoms—i.e., the inhibitions in and conflicts related to work and the work place with which so many of our patients suffer—as well as the many descriptions of work-related issues that appear in their associations as defenses against and screens for the elucidation of more "internal," core conflictual issues—e.g., as the displacement for or avoidance of the transference. In addition, I shall examine the dynamic function of work in relation to its role in the definition of self and the regulation of self-esteem. In so doing, I shall be developing a line of reasoning

---

[1] Harold P. Blum, Director of the Freud Archives, suggested in a personal communication that this story may have derived from a passage in the *Introductory Lectures on Psychoanalysis*, where Freud (1916–1917) said, "The distinction between nervous health and neurosis is thus reduced to a practical question and is decided by the outcome—by whether the subject is left with a sufficient amount of capacity for enjoyment and of efficiency" (p. 457).

implicitly suggested by Freud (1930), in *Civilization and Its Discontents*, who wrote of work: "No other technique for the conduct of life attaches the individual so firmly to reality . . . for his work at least gives him a secure place in a portion of reality, in the human community. [*Work is*] *indispensable to the preservation and justification of existence in society*" (p. 80n; italics added).

The data that underlie my thoughts are derived in large part from my analytic work with male patients whom I have treated. Although I believe that work and its remuneration hold especially important meanings for men in our society, the fact that I have chosen to discuss these phenomena based on my experiences with male patients is purely coincidental. The fact that I shall explore work in a context that rests heavily upon the theoretical contributions of Erikson is not, for as I hope to demonstrate, insofar as work offers the ego a vital setting for the exercise of its activity in regard to the definition of a sense of self and the regulation of self-esteem, Erikson's (1950) concept of *ego identity* remains a seminal construct for the understanding of the psychological meanings and function of work.

THE MEANINGS OF WORK

The concept of work lies at the intersection of the social and psychological realms. As a term, work can refer to a place of employment, an occupation, an expenditure of effort, the product of one's labor, or the internal processes engaged in the creation of that product. Insofar as work may require an adjustment of the individual worker to the demands and strictures of a group or organization, work is also a social phenomenon. The various meanings and connotations of work have obvious connections, both conscious and unconscious, with "making" and "producing" and the products so made. In this sense, the personal psychological meanings of work can be seen to reach back into infantile experience and the growing child's fantasies, curiosity, and understanding about the contents, products, and functions of his body.

Adult attitudes toward work, whether realistic or fantastic, conscious or unconscious, also reflect the vicissitudes of the internalization of parental, family, and cultural values, both espoused and lived out, in regard to work and working. Hence, Holmes (1965) notes that:

> If the child perceives conflict in parental values and psychic investment in work, it becomes difficult for the child to relate the self to reality. . . . If, on the other hand, the child's family environment is such that he can introject clearly defined value concepts, . . . if the family recognizes, accepts and adheres to a certain set of [work] values and norms as a basis for the determination of status, success, or growth and if these

values or norms involve reality-based criteria which can be met during growth, the child will accept, and in fantasy elaborate on and develop through, these valued activities. . . . In terms of both actual practice and ideological tradition, work is a most important reality area for evaluation of the self and for the transmission of cultural values [p. 389].

In adult analyses, work furnishes the surface content for much that is spoken of in clinical hours. It can be an aspect of their lives that patients—notably, but not exclusively, adult male patients—talk a good deal about. This may be especially true in the early and mid-phases of treatment, before the transference neurosis has become consolidated and the patient's conscious affective interest comes to rest upon the vicissitudes of the analytic relationship. Prior to this phase of consolidation, work can offer patients a repository for all kinds of externalizations of aspects of their inner worlds. Thus, work may be seen as a playground (*tummelplatz*) for the transference of internal conflicts, wishes, prohibitions, fantasies, object relations, and so forth. It furnishes a never-ending supply of actors and opportunities for the actualization and enactment of the dramas of the inner world. It is, perhaps, partly for this reason that the subject of work, being most readily viewed as a screen for the projection of deeper conflicts, has previously eluded more specific and thoroughgoing psychoanalytic focus.

Mr. S. was a married graduate student with three small children, who entered treatment because of his dissatisfaction and anger with his graduate school program. He was uncomfortable with his newly resumed student status, bitter about frustrating obstacles that had befallen him and about his lot in life in general. He hated the fact that he had had to move his family to Boston to pursue his studies. His concerns about his work performance in his graduate program were foremost among the issues with which he began his analysis.

Very quickly, it became clear that Mr. S. was experiencing a high degree of performance anxiety, straining against a view of himself as a failure and loser. This view was connected to his fear that his idealized, unconventional father would approve of and accept him only if he were perfect. Elements of this feeling were connected in turn with a defensive need to identify with father's superior sense of himself and thereby avoid being categorized and devalued along with the "ordinary" workers, those who commuted to work each day in long traffic jams and routinely submitted to what father scoffed at as the humiliations of organizational hierarchies and nine-to-five jobs.

The patient's identification with his perception of father's grandiose and devaluing attitudes, coupled with a style of defensive avoidance needed to protect a fragile narcissism, combined to alienate and isolate Mr. S. from his peers and professors. Thus, as much as he feared and complained about graduate school and his performance there, Mr. S. also relied heavily on it as a longed-for source of approval, social contact, and structure for his still unfinished sense of identity.

In the initial phase of treatment, Mr. S.'s transference was one of great gratitude and relief that the analyst, whom he greatly respected, would be interested and invested in him. Here would be the father figure that Mr. S. hoped to have, one he could at last feel able to talk to about his problems. Within a few short months, however, internal pressures to demonstrate perfection in his work, and anxieties about the possibility of failure in his graduate program and in the analysis led to a shift in the transference from reverential gratitude to increasing pressure to perform and ultimately to angry opposition. Just as with his teachers and thesis adviser in the present and with his own father in the past, Mr. S. began to feel about his performance in the work of the analysis that only perfection would be acceptable to the analyst. This led to complaints that there was not enough time to do both the work of graduate school and the work of treatment, hypochondriacal preoccupations, and a strong desire to curtail the treatment.

Exploration and interpretation of these developments, with an emphasis on how they appeared in and affected the analytic relationship, helped relieve Mr. S.'s distress and allowed him to recognize the possibility that rather than becoming another work burden and source or possibility of failure, the work of the analysis could be used to help him overcome his work fears, work inhibitions, and the unconscious defensive maneuvers that kept him so isolated and unhappy.

WORK, WORK IDENTITY, AND SELF-ESTEEM

To the extent that work provides the personae and occasions for the dramatization of the patient's inner world, it may have been previously neglected by psychoanalytic theorists as a necessary surface that is far less interesting than what might lie behind it. In this sense, work may be regarded by some analysts as analogous to the day residue of the dream: a mere starting point, from which more interesting and rewarding explorations will begin. Some descriptions of the patient's work life within the analytic hour may be serendipitous, others unconsciously and conflictedly selectively reported or even created. When viewed as compromise formations, the analysand's reports of the vicissitudes of his or her work life may appear to function as a metaphorical or symbolic means through which the patient indirectly expresses a "deeper," more core conflictual set of problems or, alternatively, as a manifest surface clung to in avoidance of more emotionally charged conflicts.

Insofar as work and the work place do serve as repositories for the displacement of various conflicts, they can be the immediate location of the symptomatic discomforts that alert the patient to the need for treatment. Thus, for example, one patient may be seeking help for difficulties in his relationship with bosses, another with a doctoral dissertation he is unable to finish, a third with a generalized vagueness and lack of focus in his work life. For the most part, when analysts have paid attention to work as a distinct conceptual entity within the analytic clinical setting, it is this set of meanings and their associated disturbances in the capacity to work that have tended to engage their interest (see, e.g., Fast, 1975; Applegarth, 1976; Kramer, 1977; Lerner, 1987; Stark, 1989).

Seen from another perspective, however, the capacity for work and one's identity as a worker—what might be termed one's "work identity"—is an expression of and vehicle for the consolidation of an individual's *ego identity* (Erikson, 1950). To some extent, the degree to which this is true may be culture-bound. In contemporary Western society, it may be particularly true that the activities that define adulthood and masculinity—i.e., who one *is* as a man—are closely tied to the work one does, how one does it, how it is valued and remunerated. It is for these reasons that, in addition to the social and economic consequences, the psychological effects of prolonged unemployment are often felt to be so devastating (see, e.g., Ginsburg, 1942).

Taken in this sense, work is much more than a manifest content or surface phenomenon. As implied in the remarks of Freud (1930), Holmes (1965) and Erikson (1959), work furnishes the individual with an important proving ground for self-cohesion, self-definition and adaptive competency. It is a rich and vital meeting place for the intersection and creative integration of inner and outer reality. How one works reflects and contributes to the fundamental ego activities of adaptation and synthesis. Work is a mainstay and measure of self-esteem and an integral component of the processes that influence the definition and creation of the self.

As noted above, Erikson's concept of ego identity is a powerful contribution to psychoanalytic discourse, one that is crucial for our understanding of the positive role work plays in relation to self-definition and the maintenance of self-esteem. Of particular relevance to Erikson's view of ego identity is the connotation of the ego as active rather than passive, competent in relation to the drives and the superego, and interactively involved with its immediate environment in a creative attempt to fulfill the individual's needs and desires and to realize ideals, goals, and ambitions.

That the ego possesses the capacity to synthesize and integrate basic drives, developmental potentials, and opportunities for growth across many stages of early development, and to implement the product of that synthesis in meaningful activity that is consonant with and valued by the individual's culture, is crucial to understanding the intimate connection among ego, work, and self-esteem. In large measure, the process of maintaining a positive sense of self-esteem requires a feedback loop that begins with real action in the world, which is perceived by the self and others and assessed to be competent, valued, and consistent within one's social, cultural, and historical context. Thus, in most instances, self-esteem is maintained only to the extent that one's efforts at engagement with and mastery of the world are met with a "wholehearted and consistent recognition of real accomplishment" (Erikson, 1959, p. 90) by emotionally significant objects and/or their symbolic successors. This remains as true for the adult worker as it does for the child. Respect and approval of bosses and co-workers, promotions, publications, perks, raises, may all function as tangible signs of success and contribute to a positive sense of identity as a worker and therefore to a competent and esteemed sense of oneself as an adult.

Although the capacity to increasingly evaluate and regulate self-esteem in relation to an internalized set of ideals and standards is considered by many to be a measure of emotional maturity, it has been my observation that it is a rare individual, indeed, who possesses the inner strength to withstand the general condemnation or disapproval of family, friends, and community and who can measure self-worth solely in relation to inner ideals and convictions. Most patients—and, indeed, most of us—remain quite susceptible to the coercive pressures of those to whom we habitually turn for support and approval. Ibsen's play, *An Enemy of the People*, is an illustrative dramatization of the life crisis that follows when the scientific ideals and personal integrity of the main character, Dr. Stockmann, lead him into conflict with the venal, bourgeois community on whose good opinion his previous self-esteem, support for his sense of identity, and economic well-being had rested.

Stockmann's crisis of integrity mirrors that of Ibsen, himself, who was deeply hurt and angered when the liberal press that had previously championed his works bitterly attacked the presentation of his play, *Ghosts* (Le Gallienne, 1957). *An Enemy of the People* was Ibsen's response to his critics. His ability to continue to work productively in such circumstances reflected his possession of the unusual capacity to maintain his self-confidence and self-esteem in the face of external opposition and the withdrawal of previously held support.

In contrast to Ibsen, for most of us, the internalization of the capacity to regulate self-esteem is relative at best. Its origins lie in the emotional regard with which the significant objects of infancy and childhood meet the child's attempts at mastery of his or her self and environment. Even when achieved, it remains vulnerable to regressive alterations under emotional duress. As a result, the mechanisms for self-esteem regulation oscillate between varying degrees of relative autonomy from and dependence on a continuing need for external approval. In some of the men I have treated, work revealed itself to be a central arena in which conflicts and struggles over the measure and maintenance of self-esteem were played out.

Mr. W. was a lonely man in his late twenties, who came into analysis feeling devastated by the breakup of his marriage. Among his past and current difficulties were long-standing feelings of worthlessness, inadequacy, and failure. These were traceable in part to an identification with what he felt to be a devalued father and older brother, a childhood history of school failure due to dyslexia, feelings of being rejected by his father in favor of the older brother, and a generalized sense within the family that their fortunes had fallen forever when the prominent business of the patient's paternal grandfather was wiped out by the stock market crash of 1929.

As a result of his dyslexia, Mr. W. spent his latency years in a program for learning disabled and emotionally disturbed children, which he called "the dummy class." Later on in school, his considerable oedipal conflicts and elements of success neurosis prevented him from completing his college education. Partly as a result of his poor performance in school, Mr. W. viewed himself as inadequate and ineffective. This carried over into his work, social, and love life.

When Mr. W. began analysis, his negative identity as unfavored, unloved, a member of the "dummy class," influenced and was reflected in his character, conflicts and poor self-esteem and had deeply affected his sense of himself as a worker. In his job, he lived out his view of himself as despised, debased, and inadequate by playing the clown and the simpleton and performing poorly as a low-level accounting clerk. He day-dreamed of proving himself by making a killing in the business world and restoring the tarnished grandeur of his family name.

While many issues were explored in the course of a long and complicated analysis, the unfolding of Mr. W.'s work life, the analysis of the conflicts and identifications that affected his performance and the exploration and ultimate strengthening of his work identity represented major areas of psychoanalytic focus. Mr. W.'s initial presentation of himself as a buffoon, a toady, and an incompetent soon proved to be a reflection of both the narcissistic scars of his childhood school experience—the enactment of his identification with his uneducated, blue-collar father and the identity of being a worthless member of the "dummy class"—and a defensive reaction to his oedipal strivings, his enormous ambition, and the castration fears with which they were associated.

As these conflicts began to be elucidated and then resolved in the treatment, Mr. W. began to feel better about himself and to function far more competently. He completed his bachelor's degree and went on to obtain an MBA. He changed jobs, conducted himself in a more confident and professional manner, and slowly began to rise in the hierarchy of the business world. Where his previous efforts were met with ridicule and disdain, he now found himself responded to with promotions, and increases in salary and executive responsibilities.

Through the analysis of the narcissistic conflicts and success phobia that affected his work life, Mr. W. came to see himself as capable of aggressive, assertive, successful functioning. This change in his self-image bore fruit in the form of improved self-esteem, more competent performance in the work world, and positive changes in his work identity. The cycle of conflict, failure, and poor self-esteem was halted. Instead, reduced and resolved conflicts allowed for more successful performance, which garnered realistic approval and praise. This, in turn, led to a further enhancement of Mr. W.'s confidence and self-esteem, which positively influenced his subsequent work life and helped him to achieve still more successes at work, pay raises, approval of colleagues and employers, which yielded still further positive self-regard.

Although the cycle of negative work and self-identity and poor self-esteem was mitigated by this analytic work, certain major difficulties in Mr. W.'s love relations remained relatively untouched. For example, he continued to feel anxious and unworthy when faced with the prospect of getting close to any woman whom he truly valued, and he continued to suffer from difficulties in sexual functioning. Many of these problems, the causes of which are far too complex to consider here, would not be solved until Mr. W. undertook a subsequent course of treatment. What I wish to emphasize for now, however, is that much good was done in the sphere of this patient's self-esteem, work identity, and work life and that the analysis of the latter encompassed more than just the use of work as a screen through which his oedipal and narcissistic conflicts were revealed. While the analysis of these conflicts was inevitably tied to Mr. W.'s work conflicts and performance, the analytic focus on his work life had a salutary impact in its own right on his identity, character, and overall ego capacities; was intimately tied to the restructuring of his self-esteem, and led to a reorganization and positive reconsolidation of his work identity.

THE ORIGINS AND DEVELOPMENT OF WORK

Developmentally speaking, the origins of the adult capacity to work are closely linked to the achievements of latency, when learning and mastery of the world of toys, school, peers, and the intellect assume a central significance for the child. Erikson (1950, 1959) notes the latency child's investment and interest in the pleasure and prestige gained through mastery, the recognition for making things, for being competent and useful, and the opportunity for positive identifications with those who *know* things and know how to *do* things. He characterizes this time of life as the *stage of industry*.

The accomplishments of the stage of industry succeed and are built upon the achievements of still earlier stages of development. Of particular relevance to the ultimate consolidation of a capacity to work effectively are the mastery of one's body (e.g., sphincters, motility, sleep, eating, and other regulatory functions) acquired during the oral and anal stages, and the development of a guilt-free capacity for assertion and initiative, which begins in infancy and is consolidated as a product of the successful negotiation of the phallic-oedipal stage.

The child's mastery of the tasks of latency add a socially related dimension to ego development and work capacity that will be intrinsic and essential to the subsequent consolidation of ego identity during adolescence.

> [At] elementary-school age . . . the child is taught the prerequisites for participation in the particular technology of his culture and is given the opportunity and the life task of developing a sense of workmanship and work participation. The school age significantly follows the oedipal stage: the accomplishment of real (and not only playful) steps toward a place in the economic structure of society permits the child to reidentify with parents as workers and tradition bearers rather than as sexual and familial beings, thus nurturing at least one concrete and more "neutral" possibility of becoming like them. . . . *Work goals, then, by no means only support or exploit the suppression of infantile instinctual aims; they also enhance the functioning of the ego, in that they offer a constructive activity with actual tools and materials in a communal reality. The ego's tendency to turn passivity into activity here thus acquires a new field of manifestation, in many ways superior to the mere turning of passive into active in infantile fantasy and play; for now the inner need for activity, practice, and work completion is ready to meet the corresponding demands and opportunities in social reality* [Erikson, 1959, p. 128; italics added].

In the stages of adolescence and young adulthood that follow latency, "ego identity" is consolidated and begins to exert its influence on how the individual experiences and lives his or her life. Successful identity integration involves an alignment and synthesis of drive, endowment, and opportunity, and the exercise of the resulting ego capacities in action in the world. Pleasure in the accumulation of skills and the associated approval and prestige gained through mastery help to support and consolidate:

> ... self-esteem [which] grows to be a conviction that one is learning effective steps toward a tangible future, that one is developing a defined personality within a social reality which one understands.... Accruing ego identity gains real strength only from wholehearted and consistent recognition of real accomplishment, that is, achievement that has meaning in [one's] culture [Erikson, 1959, pp. 89–90].

From this stage on, in our society, work, especially but not exclusively for men, offers one such crucial means of solidifying identity, enhancing the ego, and bringing the self-recognition and coherence within the context of our culture.

CREATIVITY AND THE CAPACITY TO WORK

"All work is creative in principle ... [in that] it requires the continuous play of thought, imagination, judgment and decision-making" (Jaques, 1990, p. vii). Although not readily obvious, this is as true of repetitive physical tasks (such as work on an assembly line) as it is of abstract, intellectual or aesthetic tasks (such as writing, painting, or arguing a case in court). The problems of the potential alienation and boredom of workers when they are placed in a situation of routinized, mechanistic functioning rather than one of artisanship and control over the entire finished product of their labor are at least as old as the industrial revolution. In the early nineteenth century, for example, the Scottish historian and social critic, Thomas Carlyle, offered a number of what are now considered to be classic critiques of the consequences inherent in the worker's loss of connection with the work product. However, Carlyle's criticism notwithstanding, even segmented and repetitive jobs have the potential to take place within an inner context of pride in accomplishment, satisfaction in living up to various ideals (e.g., being a good worker, pleasing one's superior, supporting one's family) and the symbolic acknowledgment of work skills and work capacity that are inherent in tangible rewards for work well done, such as remuneration and promotions.

To a significant degree, the internal conditions for successful and creative work are based on the capacity to relate to one's work and work product either as a significant object or in the context of one or more unconscious object relationships. The analogy may be drawn here between the capacity to work and the capacity to be alone. In regard to the latter, Winnicott (1958) noted, "The basis of the capacity to be alone is the experience of being alone in the presence of someone. . . . Gradually, the ego-supportive environment is introjected and built into the individual's personality, so that there comes about a capacity to be alone. Even so, theoretically, there is always someone present who is equated ultimately and unconsciously with the mother" (p. 36). The same is true for work, where what is at issue is the extent to which individuals have the capacity to feel accompanied and/or sustained by a loving and accepting object as they face the task at hand. (In regard to the work of the analyst in the analytic setting, Skolnikoff [1988] has described the phenomena of the internalized others that are our constant companions as "silent observers.")

Alternatively, the work task itself may function psychologically as the object or at least may place individuals into better and more loving contact with their internal objects and/or their external representatives. In either case, a positive relationship to one's work task mitigates the loneliness of creation through the unconscious sense of contact and well-being with one's internal objects that can emerge from the work process. Failures to achieve this sense of relatedness, goodness, or connection through one's work may contribute to work inhibition and conflict. This may underlie such phenomena as "the tyranny of the blank page" that authors describe in instances of writer's block, as well as more ordinary work difficulties that come from continuing tension with internal objects around the choice or level of work.

Mr. J. was a fifty-three-year-old unemployed corporate executive, who sought treatment for depression, dissatisfaction with his work life, and uncertainty as to what direction in his career he wished to pursue next. He had promising managerial positions in the past, but they often ended badly, when his struggles with his bosses, whom he perceived as arbitrary and tyrannical, led to his rebellion against or obstruction of their aims. Mr. J. recognized the anger he felt toward colleagues and bosses, but saw his responses as necessary attempts to preserve his autonomy and demonstrate that he would not be forced to submit to their devious or bullying tactics.

Unemployment—and his entrance into analysis—brought forth many conflicts around wishes to prove himself and win the love of his father, an academic, who the patient felt had always looked down upon businessmen. As with any choice of career, Mr. J.'s was multiply determined. A natural fit existed between the technical, computer-oriented aspects of his managerial functions and the innate, hands-on engineering style with which he engaged his world and tended to solve problems. Of even greater relevance to our understanding of work, however, was his description of the complex financial systems he designed, implemented, and managed as "the conscience of the business world." It was his job to monitor and manage the rules that regulated avarice in exchange and that ordered and defined the proper way in which things were to be done.

The particular significance—one might say the irony—of Mr. J.'s position was that internally and throughout his life, he had struggled against powerful acquisitive impulses and sexual desires. These had a strong oral cast and were connected to early infantile experiences of maternal unavailability and a later ongoing sense of mother as emotionally removed. As a child, Mr. J. was sexually precocious and hungry for love. In his analysis and in his life, he lived out and described in detail a poignant longing for human contact, warmth, and touch. To this was added a painfully repetitive sense that his intellectual and aesthetic-minded father did not value or approve of his childhood and adolescent interests in cars, guns, or sex—or look favorably upon his choice of career in the business world.

As an adolescent, Mr. J. had not only struggled with powerful sexual urges, but with impulses toward socially delinquent behavior. The latter often led him into minor scrapes and difficulties with the authorities in his life. Thus, his career unconsciously represented his search for, defiance of, and identification with the external representatives of the superego controls, which he felt were weak or absent. At another level, being on the side of the financial overseers and regulators placed him in a potential connection and positive relationship with the superego aspects of his father. That he was in business, however, an activity he felt father neither appreciated nor understood, continued to symbolize his rebellion against homosexual submission and his angry defiance in the face of a love and approval that he felt he could never win.

In the face of these conflicts, Mr. J.'s transference evolved in a most surprising and salutary direction. My analytic curiosity about his inner experience and the details of his work life, coupled with my respect for his autonomy, combined to offer Mr. J. a tacit sense of support and approval for his work functioning and identity as a businessman. While there were the expectable moments of negative father transference, where he felt I was disapproving or being critical of him or trying to force him to submit to my will, the transference stayed predominantly positive, especially in regard to his efforts at work. It was as if he had found in me the approving father figure he had longed for and needed.

While this positive transference development had its drawbacks in other areas of his personality—e.g., the longings for closeness generated by our positive relationship led at times to fears of homosexual closeness or loss of individuality—in regard to his work life, his sense of my feeling respect and approval for his career seemed to allow him to unconsciously relate to his work as valued and a source of positive esteem, rather than as just another disappointment or delinquent defiance. In addition to reducing the conflicts with bosses and colleagues that stemmed from oedipal, homosexual, and autonomy conflicts, Mr. J.'s analysis also transformed his relation to his work from one with a symbolically deficient or defiant object to one with an object of value that had the approval of and that stood for his positive relationship with the analyst.

Storr (1988), in his treatise on *Solitude*, adds still another dimension to the intrapsychic meanings of work, when he notes the many authors who have linked creativity with reparation and compensation for early losses or later difficulties in interaction with others. In what may arguably be a too narrow understanding of all that Kohut meant by the term, "selfobject," Storr also suggests that work can represent or substitute for internal objects. "Work, especially of a creative kind which changes, progresses, and deepens over the years, can . . . provide the integrating factor within the personality, which Kohut assumes comes only from, or chiefly from, the positive reflecting responses of other people" (p. 151).

That individuals can use their work, rather than or in addition to interpersonal relationships, in the service of self-cohesion, or as a primary source of self-esteem and personal fulfillment can make for some interesting life opportunities and clinical dilemmas. To some extent, work and the work object are more easily controlled than are the behaviors and responses of other people. In some instances, authoritarian chains of command in the work place can reinforce the sense of omnipotent control of subordinates. If one possesses the capacity to work and the external conditions for the completion of work tasks are ripe, then productive work can effectively go forward in a state of narcissistic self-sufficiency and unconscious omnipotent control. In many patients, therapeutic resolution of their work difficulties may proceed as narcissistic conflicts are analyzed and narcissistic tensions are relieved. However, as in the case of Mr. W. presented above, concomitant progress in the far more unpredictable area of intimate personal relations may neither keep pace nor accompany such therapeutic gains.

CONCLUSION

I have tried to explore the origins and meanings of work, with an emphasis on the intimate relationship that exists between work, identity and self-esteem. I have examined work both as a manifest content in analytic material—i.e., as a screen for the displacement and display of core intrapsychic conflicts—and as a vital arena for the ego's activity in the regulation of self-esteem and the expression of ego synthesis and ego identity—i.e., as an integral component in the definition of self.

Any consideration of work must extend beyond the realm of the psychological and touch on issues that are social, cultural, and historical, as well. For this reason, and for its particular relevance to any understanding of self-esteem regulation, my conceptualization of work owes much to the work of Erikson and his views of ego activity and ego identity. This debt is further reflected in my formulation of the concept, "work identity," and in my brief description of the developmental origins of the capacity for work, which I have presented within an Eriksonian frame.

Since the clinical data on which these observations are based derive from the treatment of men, I am loath to extend my conclusions to women. Given the large numbers of women now in the work place and the important role that work performance and accomplishment plays in their self-definition and self-esteem, however, I suspect that much that I have described will be relevant for either sex. I have not attempted to present a treatise that should in any way be considered exhaustive. Rather, given the paucity of writings on this subject, I have attempted to both call attention to work and provide an opening statement in what I hope will become a productive and ongoing subject for analytic dialogue and investigation.

REFERENCES

Applegarth, A. (1976), Some observations on work inhibitions in women. *J. Amer. Psychoanal. Assn.*, 24:251–268.
Erikson, E. H. (1950), *Childhood and Society.* New York: Norton.
——— (1959), *Identity and the Life Cycle. Psychological Issues*, Monogr. 1. New York: International Universities Press.
Fast, I. (1975), Aspects of work style and work difficulty in borderline personalities. *Internat. J. Psycho-Anal.*, 56:397–404.
Freud, S. (1916–1917), Introductory lectures on psycho-analysis. *Standard Edition*, 15 & 16. London: Hogarth Press, 1963.
——— (1930). Civilization and its Discontents. *Standard Edition*, 21:59–145.
Ginsburg, S. W. (1942), What unemployment does to people. *Amer. J. Psychiat.*, 99:439–446.
Hendricks, I. (1943), Work: Thoughts on the pleasure principle. *Psychoanal. Q.*, 12:311–329.
Holmes, D. (1965), A contribution to a psychoanalytic theory of work. *The Psychoanalytic Study of the Child*, 20:384–393.
Jaques, E. (1960), Disturbances in the capacity to work. *Internat. J. Psycho-Anal.*, 41:357–367.
——— (1990), *Creativity and Work.* Madison, CT: International Universities Press.
Kramer, Y. (1977), Work compulsion—a psychoanalytic study. *Psychoanal. Q.*, 46:361–385.

Lantos, B. (1952), Metapsychological considerations on the concept of work. *Internat. J. Psycho-Anal.*, 43:439–443.

Le Gallienne, E. (1957), Introduction. In: *Six Plays by Hendrik Ibsen.* New York: Modern Library, 1957, pp. vii–xxx.

Lerner, H. G. (1987), Work and success inhibitions in women. *Bull. Menninger Clin.*, 51:338–360.

Menninger, K. (1942), Work as a sublimation. *Bull. Menninger Clin.*, 6:170–182.

Skolnikoff, A. (1988), The silent observer. Presented at Fall Meeting, American Psychoanalytic Association, New York.

Stark, M. (1989), Work inhibition: A self-psychological perspective. *Contemp. Psychoanal.*, 25:135–158.

Storr, A. (1988), *Solitude.* New York: Free Press.

Winnicott, D. W. (1958), The capacity to be alone. In: *The Maturational Processes and the Facilitating Environment.* New York: International Universities Press, 1965, pp. 29–36.

10

WORK AND ITS INHIBITIONS AS SEEN IN CHILDREN AND ADOLESCENTS

SELMA KRAMER, M.D.

The "work" of children and adolescents is *learning*. During my long experience as an analyst of children and adolescents, I have encountered a great many patients who for a variety of emotional reasons were not able to learn.

Anna Freud (1965) mapped the path infants and toddlers must take as they proceed from their earliest interest in play with their own bodies, to play with the bodies of their mothers, to play with toys. She demonstrated how the early random activity becomes increasingly organized; development and maturation lead to task completion and problem-solving, requisites for successful learning. Developmental progress from play to work requires a shift from primary- to secondary process thinking, the ability to tolerate frustration, and a far-advanced neutralization of energy. We are charmed to observe the excited pleasure of the child in his "work" of learning. But all children are not so fortunate. Some children have such great conflicts about learning that they fail to accomplish their work. For some other children, learning is inhibited by two contradictory patterns—they remember too much and forget too much.

EMOTIONAL CAUSES FOR LEARNING PROBLEMS

There are many emotional causes for inhibitions of learning in children. They include: (1) family secrets; (2) the plight of some children whose neuroses and learning problems arise because of their superior intelligence (Keiser, 1969); (3) residues of incest.

159

FAMILY SECRETS

I am convinced that *there are no true family secrets*. Parents may not
want their children to know realities about the family history that are
at the very least, unpleasant; at most, they may be concerned with
illegal activities, sadistic behavior, alcoholism, or even incarceration
or mental illness of a close relative. But the children know something,
and they know they are not supposed to know. What starts as an
intrafamilial conflict gives rise to intrapsychic conflicts about knowing
and hence about learning.

Ralph S. was referred at eleven and a half because of serious learning
problems in spite of good intelligence (IQ 128) and cleverness (he
outwitted his younger siblings, often extracting their allowances from
them). He could not study; if pushed to do so, he became belligerent
or depressed. He could not organize his homework, could not recite
in school, and failed easy as well as difficult tests.

The parents were an unusual couple, not typical parents who bring
children to analysis. Mr. S. was overly stylish and spoke as if he
were a character in a Damon Runyon play. He said that he was an
"entrepreneur," without disclosing his field of interest. His wife was
also stylishly dressed and elegantly coiffed; she had been a secretary
before marriage, and complained that the S.'s had few friends, mostly
because Mr. S. wanted it that way. (I was to get more than an inkling
of Mr. S.'s line of work when he paid me from a large wad of cash
and advised me that I need not maintain records of the financial transac-
tion. When I declined to accept his advice about not keeping records,
he looked at me with pity and disdain.)

Ralph was a tense, polite, unusually well-dressed prepubescent
youngster who wondered how I could help him with his learning problems. His first play in the office concerned "puzzle games." He used
toy characters whose affect and demeanor were obvious, or so I
thought. Ralph tested me repeatedly to see if I could guess their moods,
and accused me of not knowing anything. I confronted him with his
ambivalence, i.e., his conflicts about my knowing things; in part he
wanted me to be dumb and not know anything, but yet he knew that
I had to be somewhat bright if I were to help him. When Ralph persisted in making me "dumb," I told him he was attributing to me
worries that plagued him—whether he could solve puzzles, even
whether he could acknowledge that he knew what he observed. He
had to pretend to himself and to the world that he did not know what
he knew. I added that he could not let himself learn what he felt he
should not know.

This led to an increasingly pressured interchange which culmi-
nated in his asking me where my family's guns were kept. I made

running comments about the theme of recent hours, finally confronting Ralph with the fact that our talk about learning conflicts had led him to think about guns and to wonder whether I had guns. Ralph said that he was at least eight years old, visiting a school friend, when he realized that not every family answered the doorbell after dark with raised revolvers as did his family. He finally admitted that he had long suspected that his father was an "entrepreneur" in illegal dealings, but he and his siblings were not supposed to know.

Ralph said that he had long feared that his father could shoot him because he masturbated with lurid fantasies. His father bragged about his own premarital escapades and implied that some day he would introduce Ralph to a "clean whore." Ralph gradually began to function better in school. Toward the end of the analysis, he said wryly, "I finally asked my father why he wants me to go to college and law school when he didn't even finish high school. He answered, 'You're not man enough to go into my kind of work. But anyway, our family needs a lawyer to keep us out of jail, and you're the best one in the family for that.' "

NEUROSES AND SUPERIOR INTELLIGENCE

Keiser's (1969) paper on neurosogenesis in children with superior intelligence helped me understand some difficult cases involving problems with learning. His summary explicates his premises very well:

> Superior intellectual endowment had an adverse effect on the psychological development of several patients. In childhood, they regarded themselves as "exceptions" and they were so regarded by their environment. Precocious intelligence gave them access to information and understanding beyond their chronological age. The impact of their insights overwhelmed their immature egos, thus releasing libidinal and aggressive fantasies. This imposed further burdens on their developing egos. . . . The functioning of their intelligence was constricted. The greater sensitivity to stimuli required stronger methods to master the resultant excitation. It is suggested that for some patients markedly superior intelligence facilitates traumatic experiences which then lead to a neurosis [p. 472].

Shirley came to treatment at eleven because of a school phobia and learning problems in spite of very superior intelligence. It was hard for her to separate from her mother; after some weeks Shirley said, "I should not learn things [in treatment] that my mother doesn't know." In contrast to the insistence on privacy about analytic material in the usual eleven-year old, Shirley reported to her mother the content of every session. When I connected her early statement, "I should not learn things . . ." with her verbatim reports to her mother, Shirley flushed and said, "It doesn't pay to know more. No one likes it."

Shirley told me of how she had been admired, but later exploited because she was an "early developer." (The "exploitation" was her parents' making her "entertain" visitors by reading books at age four, solving puzzles for them, singing and dancing, all of which she had mastered early.) However, when she was just a little older, her precosity infuriated her parents; now they felt that she was a "smart aleck." Her mother said, "soon you'll be too smart for us"; Shirley fantasied not that she would abandon her family, but that her parents, her mother in particular, would abandon her. It was after that comment by her mother that Shirley's school phobia reached high proportions. Things she experienced or learned in school caused her to be scolded by her parents, and their earlier pleasant relationship ended.

She was disillusioned when her parents could not understand the material she had learned; they behaved as if they were offended by her mature thinking. When she was fourteen, she heard her parents plan to picket a local business because the owners were not supporting a political candidate of her parents' choice. Shirley told her parents that every citizen was entitled to back his own candidate. Her parents accused her of being fresh, and said that she knew too much for her own good. Shirley felt put down, was depressed, and found herself unable to master social studies, and finally all of the humanities. She could do well in mathematics because "no feelings are connected with math."

Slowly she revealed her only partly expressed awareness that she was smarter than either parent. She recalled an interaction that had occurred when she was as young as six or seven years old, which had upset her so much that she "forgot" the episode until she was well into treatment. She told her parents upon her return from school one day that she was chosen to be Snow White in a school play, adding that the handsomest boy in her class was to be Prince Charming. She felt he was such a good actor because when he was asked a question, he looked pensive and scratched his head. Both parents shouted, "Don't go near him, he has head lice!" Shirley was demoralized and depressed over her parents' unthinking reply. She felt as if her home had weak walls and a shaky foundation, and she blamed herself, her intelligence, for the fact that she felt so unsupported.

Incest, Learning Problems, and Somatic Memories

Until recently psychoanalytic articles on incest have been infrequent. Following the paper by Ferenczi in 1933, there was a dearth of published material until Shengold (1967, 1974, 1979, 1980) introduced the important concept, "soul murder"; Kramer (1974, 1980, 1983, 1987) wrote about maternal incest and its significance; Silber (1979) and Dewald (1989) wrote on the effects of parental seduction; Margolis (1977, 1984) reported consummated incest in an adolescent male; and Steele (1994) reported on child sexual abuse.

I focus on long-term consequences of incest by examining two phenomena I believe to be residues of parental sexual abuse. The first includes the varieties of physical sensation and disturbances in sexual functioning which, I feel, result from "somatic" memories. The somatic memories reveal that *the body does not forget even if the mind does*. The second pertains to the general and specific learning problems in patients who experienced incest by their parents.

Incest is particularly disruptive when committed by a parent, for in such instances the child easily loses the capacity to trust authority figures. In addition, a sense of guilt and responsibility for the act, which many parents impose on their children, is reinforced by other factors. Because the child is sensitive to the parent's role as judge of right and wrong, the child is very susceptible to remarks or behavior of the abusing parents intended to induce or reinforce a sense of guilt in the child. (Of particular relevance here is the process by which abusing parents displace their own sense of guilt onto the child, as was first described by Ferenczi in 1933.) Other factors promoting guilt include the bodily excitement arising from the sexual act, which occurs with an object still tinged with unresolved oedipal feelings and hence particularly forbidden, and sensual pleasure felt by the child when the genitals are stimulated. Victims of incest must face three questions: (1) Did it occur? (2) Did I let it occur? (3) Did I enjoy the experience? The victims wish they could answer "no" to all three. But to succeed in treatment, incest victims must face the guilt-provoking knowledge that there was pleasure in being stimulated, that is, treatment should enable the patient to learn the "unlearnable."

Within the range of general response to parental incest are important differences that depend on whether the incestuous parent is the mother or the father. It has been my experience that mothers who engage in incest with their children have more serious psychopathology than do fathers who commit incest. It appears that two factors exist in the mother-child relationship for maternal incest to occur: first, the child is unwanted, unrewarding to the mother, not satisfying to her narcissism, even from birth (Browning and Boatman, 1977). In addition, since the mother-child symbiosis is parasitic and is not resolved, the mother is unable to permit the child to individuate. Litin et al. (1956) and Brandt F. Steele (personal communication) verify a tight, unresolved symbiosis between the child and the mother who performs the incestuous act. This mother could not separate from her own mother and also had sexual conflicts that interfered with her marriage. Steele says, "It is the adult using the unwitting, obedient child to solve maternal needs, and exploitation and distortation of the normal, mutual interaction."

I found that where there was more than one child, the mother sexually stimulated only the one child who was unwanted or was perceived by the mother as inferior, a disappointment, so imperfect as to be dehumanized. The mother showed contempt by expressing very hurtful verbal hostility and derision; she used the one child (Kramer, 1974) for her sexual pleasure. Maternal sexual abuse started early as an outgrowth of the mothers' too zealous attention to the hygiene of their children's perineal areas. The "cleansing" continued for much too long and was converted by the mothers into masturbation of their children (see Herman-Gibbons and Berson, 1989). Two of my patients, Donald (Kramer, 1974) and Casey (Kramer, 1980) stopped the abuse when they reached adolescence, fearful that their mothers' attentions would produce orgasm. The abuse of the third patient, Abby (Kramer, 1980), stopped only after the child had been brought to treatment. I have come to believe that because the abuse started so early and involved the mothers when they were at the center of their children's universe, before intrapsychic separation of self and object had been achieved, the consequences for these children were extensive and severe, leading to the particular disturbance in reality testing that underlies what I have termed "object-coercive doubting" (Kramer, 1983). The child could not think and certainly could not learn without verification from the mother. The child had to coerce the mother in order to verify whatever the child was thinking or felt obligated to learn. This was repeated in the transference, so that when Abby came in during a storm, soaked to the skin, she asked me whether it was raining. When I turned the question back to her, she became frantic and insisted that I must tell her.

In contrast to mothers' possible early abuse, fathers are seldom sexually abusive until the child is well into latency or adolescence. The latter onset means that the child's reality testing is usually much better established and will therefore be significantly less affected by the incest and its consequences than in those instances where the sexual abuser was the mother and the incest began much earlier. However, considerable problems in learning may result from paternal incest, too.

Somatic Memories and Learning

A residue I found in patients of both sexes who were incestuously involved with one or both parents is part of a constellation I refer to as "somantic memories" of incest. These are bodily sensations that occur well into adulthood and are most often accompanied by great displeasure, aversion, or physical pain during foreplay, intromission, or coitus. Occasionally, in contrast to hyperesthesia, these patients reported reacting to touch in the opposite way, with muted feelings, frigidity, and anorgasmia. Some patients reported feeling fury during lovemaking, a fury that was at first incomprehensible, especially since they themselves have either initiated or consented to the sexual overtures. Reliving incestuous phenomena in the transference caused these patients to experience and complain of hyperacusis, hyperosmia, and sensitivity to touch (e.g., my couch was "scratchy"). One patient was panicked by male strangers whom she saw on the way to my office, afraid that I would allow them to touch her body.

Steele (personal communication) agreed that somatic sensitivity and other sexual problems in adults may derive from childhood sexual abuse. Steele's views are consonant with those of Katan (1973). Often, interrelated with the somatic memories are problems in learning, in retaining what had been learned, and in "showing what one knows," for example, by reciting in school, doing well on tests, and the like. These patients may also demonstrate muting of their affects, as well as problems in perceiving affects in themselves or in others. At times, this muting of affects may progress to a picture not unlike that of a clinical depression.

No patient initially told me incest had occurred; most did not remember. In fact, one patient had amnesia for the first eight years of her life. As treatment progressed and memories of the incest emerged, they were defended against by means of intermittent denial, disavowal, or splitting. Reconstruction was necessary in each case to present to the patient the story he or she had told me but could not really perceive or accept. Reconstruction also verified the patient's reality, in contrast to the parental denial of the incest. The somatic memories represent, as I stated earlier, that the body remembers what the mind cannot tolerate remembering.

INCEST, PROBLEMS IN LEARNING, AND INTERFERENCE WITH EMOTIONAL DEVELOPMENT

Casey came to analysis at age twenty because she "did not know where to go in life." She had trained for ballet, but now, although she had been told she had a successful career ahead of her, she found it impossible to become a professional dancer. She "froze up" on the stage and could not tolerate being touched or, especially, lifted by her partner. She also feared performing in public, would become confused and forget her routine. The analysis revealed that she also feared that being successful would mean leaving home, and separating from her mother.

Casey was the younger of two sisters; there was also a brother ten years younger. Her mother had not wanted to be pregnant with Casey, but when the pregnancy was accepted, the mother wished for a boy. Instead, she gave birth to a girl with a minor birth defect. Casey and her mother had been overly close, "enmeshed" at times, yet her mother demeaned her, most often in public.

She hated school and did badly in spite of good intelligence. Casey manifested splitting of the self and maternal object representations, which allowed her to retain a "good" representation of her mother, while relegating "badness" to teachers, onto whom all evil was placed. The self was "good," nonhostile, noncompetitive, nonsexy; her peers, whom she envied but could not relate to, were "bad." They did exciting things she wished to do but could not let herself do. Only after the two sides of self and object were fused could she remember what she had known but could not let herself acknowledge or tell me, namely that until Casey reached puberty, her mother had masturbated her. Casey revealed that her mother alternated between being overinvolved in handling her body, and coldly ignoring her. Her mother called Casey "my music box" and summoned her to bed saying "the lid is up." After masturbating herself and Casey, her mother would say "the lid is down, get out of bed." Even now Casey had to stop her mother from touching her clothed body, for she would stroke Casey in a sensual way. Casey's analysis was slow and, to her, distressing, for it meant that she had to see things in the relationship with her mother that were painful and embarrassing. She was reluctant to forego the security of allowing her mother to plan for her, to comfort her when Casey was troubled, to spend money on her. For a long time the analysis and the analyst were the intruders, threatening the sanctity of the distorted mother-child relationship. More than once Casey blurted out, "You want me to become independent, to give up what I count on!" At the same time she felt that I was as seductive as her mother had been, because I encouraged free association, which in Casey's mind was dirty and bad. Only when the actual seduction and its vicissitudes had been analyzed could Casey go through the development process necessary for her to be a separate and appropriately sexual individual, and able to study and to learn.

Casey had suffered a severe narcissistic injury as a result of her mother's use of Casey's genitals as a dehumanized part of herself, and also because of frequent rejection by her mother. This intrusion interfered greatly with Casey's early development and made her question the "ownership of her body" (Laufer, 1968, p. 115). Casey lacked a healthy sense of autonomy and self-worth. Mahler and McDevitt (1980) describe the toddler's glee in the growing autonomy of the practicing subphase, which is followed by the rapprochement subphase realization of separateness and vulnerability and threatened collapse of self-esteem. To obviate this threat, the mother must be emotionally available to the child and at the same time must provide the child with a gentle push toward independence. The analysis, not the mother, gave Casey the ''gentle push toward independence.''

There was more interference from the parents than in the usual analysis of a young adult. In addition, there was considerable resistance on Casey's part because she feared that exploring the maternal incest could mean that both she and her mother were homosexual.

Some months after she had begun to explore the sexual stimulation by her mother, Casey said plaintively, ''It's one thing to say 'She did it to me' and I can be angry and hate her, but it's another to say 'I wanted it and went out for it.' Did I feel I was to blame? I still feel guilty.'' Still later she said, ''She has a basic flaw, but if I give her up I won't have a mother.'' Casey had serious learning problems, for her conflicts over what she called ''worries about what I am allowed to know'' (about the relationship with her mother) intruded into most subjects, especially the humanities.

Casey's father was a successful professional tied to his career, glad that Casey's and her mother's preoccupation with each other made his wife less burdensome to him.

When Casey was in her mid-twenties, she had a number of sexual relationships with men whose appearance, intellect, or personality problems were such that certain aspects of Casey's relationship with her mother were replicated all too easily. Casey could not reach orgasm. At the same time, the continuing influence of the mother's masturbation of her was demonstrated when Casey complained that she could not tell whether her body and genitals were being stimulated by her mother or her lover. She said plaintively, ''Before, I could not get my mother out of my head. Now I can't get her out of my bed.'' Both foreplay and intromission caused anxiety because of this confusion. She said, ''His penis is no different from my mother's hand.''

She complained that her current lover, A., ''used'' her, seemed to ''turn on'' to her and then to ''turn off,'' much as her mother had. She had feared having an orgasm when masturbated by her mother, for doing so would show her mother and herself that she enjoyed their sexual encounters. She had no orgasm with A. For about six months, material about A. waned, presumably because Casey perceived that the relationship had no future. During this time there was a decided shift in the transference.

Casey now began to make demands of me in an entirely new way. Whereas earlier she had tried to coerce me to be a partner in the object-coercive doubting, her demands now were that I do what she wanted or that I not make her accede to what she felt was unfair. (These ''unfair'' demands were those that had been in operation

throughout Casey's treatment and dealt mainly with keeping appointments, payment, and such.) Now she broke appointments without notice and announced that she would not pay for them. At the same time,
she demanded extra appointments, telling me that she considered them
to be her privilege even if it meant inconveniencing another patient or
me. In contrast to the rather passive acquiescence she had displayed
through the earlier phases of treatment, now there was more definite-
ness, more aggression in her demands, and, I felt, more of a sense of
self. I found myself puzzled but not displeased by the change, and I
sensed some amusement, which I understand when I envisioned her
as a foot-stamping two-year-old, demanding with a sense of justification that I not leave the city for a week of meeting because "I won't
let you go away." "Why?" "Because I say so."

After some time, Casey again spoke of A., complaining that he
used her and then ignored her. In spite of her complaints, her affect
was such that I commented that she seemed not to want me to think
that anything in the relationship had been of value to her, or fun. Casey
retorted, "You're too snoopy. It's none of your business." Although
her voice was light, almost jesting, a quality she conveyed made me
think she was consciously withholding something.

She broke off with A. after a painful argument. After a few lonely
weeks, she met B., who was both more mature and more appropriate.
She told me that sex with him was different from sex with A. For
several months, during sex with A., she had had multiple orgasms
from the time of intromission. With B., she had one orgasm with each
intercourse, which they had many times a day.

I reviewed the recent material and commented that the "secrets"
about which Casey felt I was too snoopy had to do with her increased
sexual freedom and her ability to have orgasms. I also noted that there
had been a lessening and finally an absence of dreams about hairy
spiders or octopi (which the analysis had revealed to stem from the
sexual exploitation by her mother). Casey was pleased to be capable
of this sexual awakening and was especially delighted to have withheld
from me the secret of her sexual fulfillment.

I interpreted this as meaning that her brain, body, and her genitals
belonged to her, not to her mother or to me. And her teasing about
keeping the secret showed both of us that she had a mind of her
own. I could see that in the period in which she was negativistic and
demanding, and yet secretive about her increasing possession of her
genitals, she had made developmental strides. Whereas earlier Casey
could ask (seldom demand) that she be treated as an exception because
she had been sexually abused, she now conveyed, "I deserve; I am
entitled because I am separate, because I am I." She conveyed the
pleasure of achieving a feeling of secure separateness never sufficiently
experienced before. She now seemed to be fired by purpose and normal

striving, not by humiliation. That Casey could be teasing and secretive, but had a growing sense of purpose, signaled that she was now handling her aggression more appropriately. Rather than being turned against herself, the aggression, now mixed with libido, was modulated, directed outward, and useful in helping her to proclaim ownership of her mind and body. The better sense of self, of knowing what was hers, and of possessing her own genitals, was a sign of progress, although at times it caused resistance in the analysis. Is it normal for children to be demanding because they have a sense of self and are struggling to achieve autonomy; can we not consider the entitlement we see in some analyses to derive from the resumption of development?

Donald's analysis has been reported in detail elsewhere (Kramer, 1974). He had been referred at ten years of age because of his ''habits,'' that is, having to rise and sit down again a certain number of times in multiples of four. His parents requested an evaluation after he rose and sat sixty-four times in the midst of a raging summer storm; his mother worried what the neighbors might think! Donald was the only child born to parents who had married rather late. His mother was tied to her own mother; his father, to his own father. Donald's mother considered him strange-looking from birth and felt he was overly large, ugly, and too serious. His father spent a great deal of time with him, in part to protect him from the mother's carping.

When Donald refused to come for treatment, his parents complied with his wishes. Therefore, I did not see him until he was fifteen, when Donald and his parents were terrified by his mounting temper outbursts. He then came willingly, for he saw himself as a volcano that could erupt at any moment. He was extremely tall, cadaverously thin, and had severe pustular acne. He looked to the analyst as a place to get help with his temper, his separation fears, and his low self-esteem. Donald knew, but was afraid to acknowledge, that his mother was psychotic. In her interviews with me she revealed a paranoid psychosis. Donald complained about, but could not avoid, excessive closeness to and intrusion by both parents. His father was his protection and yet stimulated Donald when they wrestled. Donald and his father were certain that Donald could not pass his high school classes without tutoring by his father. His mother was ''crazy-clean,'' but she flitted into his room in ultrasheer nighties, always using an excuse to intrude on him. For a long time Donald had to have his mother test reality for him, even in areas she was ill-fitted for. Donald revealed that he had reached puberty early, having had his first nocturnal emission at nine and a half. He had been plagued by sexual excitement, by obvious bodily changes, by the acne that his mother said was caused by his doing ''bad things.''

The analysis enabled him to face his mother's psychosis, to separate both emotionally and physically from both parents, and to live much as does the average teenager. The analysis of the "object-coercive doubting" enabled him to do well in school without needing to involve his parents.

The "somatic memory" of maternal incest appeared during a period of severe regression near the end of his analysis when Donald expressed the delusion that I could see his nose and lips get bigger and smaller, that I was refusing to tell him what I knew, but was instead keeping it to myself, smiling sarcastically. Donald was in great psychic pain and pleaded with me to "tell him the truth." We had long before analyzed his mother's and his upward displacement from his genitals to his face; he had spoken of his anger at mother's perpetual, grimacelike smile, both sarcastic and seeming to "know" what others were thinking and were saying about her—one of her psychotic mechanisms. After months during which he was agonized, sure that I knew but would not tell him of my awareness of his upward-displaced tumescence and detumescence, I made a reconstruction in which I said that I felt something had, indeed, happened; someone had not only known, but had caused the size of a part of his body—his penis—to change; he was ashamed by that person's sarcasm. Donald responded, "I knew it all the time! My mother bathed me until I was past fourteen. She bathed me *all over*." Donald had found these baths to be emotionally painful, shameful, and exciting all at the same time. Since he reached puberty, at nine and a half, he would have an erection when, in her efforts to "clean" Donald, she rubbed his penis. We were able to pursue the sexual abuse in the transference: I might have evil and magical qualities that enabled me to read his mind; he was able to agree with my comment that he feared that I could cause him to have an erection when we talked of sexual matters as his mother had by touching him; finally he was able to acknowledge his pleasure in this fantasy as well as his exhibitionism when he implored me to look at him.

Late Emergence of Childhood Incest in Treatment of Adults with Childhood Learning Problems

Mr. S. entered treatment because of chronic dysthymia that was seldom relieved. He said that he felt like a cartoon character who was always under a dark cloud. He was the eldest of four children of a middle-class family. There had been considerable competitiveness with his brother, two years his junior, and relatively little interaction with his two sisters, four and seven years younger. He felt he had been favored by both parents, yet he began to feel uncomfortable with each parent in mid-latency.

Early in the analysis Mr. S. described his low self-esteem in terms of his lack of real achievement in school, saying, "Here you see someone who never achieved his potential." He had been an excellent student in the early grades; he even skipped third grade. But by fifth grade his pleasure in learning dropped off. He was no longer enthusiastic or excited about learning, and he lacked his early curiosity. He felt he was the least able student in his class, the only one not to attend college. He faithfully attended every high school reunion, "As if," he said "to rub my nose in it. They are so educated. I am not." The reality that his schooling had ended after high school when his father's serious illness required him to work in the family business did not lessen his conviction of inferiority. He felt noble in giving up college, yet he was guilty to feel the victor over his father when he proved himself to be the better businessman. He married young. His first-born was a son with whom he was always dissatisfied; two years later there was a daughter from whom he was aloof and distant; even when she was quite young he had been squeamish about cuddling her. When I asked whether he had felt the same way with his son, he was visibly upset, saying, "that would be absolutely wrong." He could not persist along this vein, yet he knew that as a small child he himself had been treated with affection by both parents, and had liked it.

After a year in analysis, Mr. S. told me about certain business strategies which had him constantly on tenterhooks. He walked a fine line between compliance with the law and "cutting corners." He paid off governmental authorities and inspectors and then feared that they would report him; he did the same thing with the union, skirting around regulations that dictated employee benefits and safety regulations. In a transference reenactment, he suggested a "deal." If I charged him less, he would not report my fee as a medical expense on his tax form. When I commented that he was checking in order to see whether I would cut corners, he was strangely relieved and at the same time afraid that I would criticize him for wanting to play "tax games" with me. The recognition of the conflict in the transference relieved his uneasiness only a little. (Lest the reader think that many patients have tried to "play money games" with me, let me say that Mr. S. and Ralph's father were the only ones to do so.)

Mr. S. continued to be preoccupied with his wish and fear that I would join him in cheating I.R.S., and some months later said, "I had a strange thought . . . if I had something on you, you couldn't tell anyone what I did." The fantasy that he and I would break the law continued as a recurrent transference theme after oedipal themes and themes of sex play with his peers had surfaced in the analysis.

Mr. S. now said that he felt much better than when the analysis started. He wanted to end treatment; in fact, it was urgent for him to do so because a planned expansion of his business needed his presence. I told him that I felt termination was not timely. I also recognized in myself some relief, for the material had become repetitious with increased resistance. I pointed out that his decision to end analysis followed upon the "deal" he had proposed in which both of us would break the law, and that he had fantasies about "squealing on each other" that had left him uneasy. When he insisted that he had to move out of state I told him that our work was not over and that I felt we should resume in the future.

He returned after a five-year hiatus. He said he was in Philadelphia again (I was to discover later that he had been back for two to three years), and wished to see me because of dreams he could not understand and a recurrence of the "dark cloud" feeling. Only now, in the sixth year of the analysis, for the first time, material surfaced about a wayward uncle. He had vague memories of knowing a family secret about his father's brother who had fallen in with criminals and had been sent to prison. Later, he remembered that his parents, alone of all the relatives, had offered his uncle temporary shelter after his release from prison. This memory was followed by upsetting dreams of a dark room in which there was a giant rocking horse monster. He had "somatic memories," feeling smothered and rocked at the same time.

His business machinations recurred after having been absent for about two years. Mr. S. felt endangered, for he knew that he was asking for trouble. One day he said that a thought popped into his head—"You never know what will happen nor who will do it to you." When I confronted him with the fact that he was again tempting fate by breaking the law at the same time he was remembering his uncle, he said "It must have been after he got out of jail. But he didn't sleep in my room. My father wouldn't let him." He was puzzled about his statements: "You never know. . . ," or "He didn't sleep in my room. . . ." He said those thoughts just came to mind. Slowly and painfully he remembered what had happened. He had been sent to awaken his uncle who on waking said he had missed Mr. S. so much. "He hugged me and rocked me, rubbing me against him. My pants got wet. I thought I had wet myself. I changed, but I didn't tell anyone. Next time I didn't want to wake him up but sort of did. I went back, and there is something vague about stealing money from his room when he was out. He must have known. Maybe he wanted us to have something on each other. . . ." His uncle's use of Mr. S.'s body to masturbate continued for about a year. It ended when Mr. S.'s father told the uncle to leave; Mr. S. was afraid his father had found out.

The emergence and working through of the effects of incest when Mr. S. was between eight and nine years of age took place quite late in the analysis. Until then there had been no mention of his uncle, and possibly there had been no recollection of him. The patient's repeated need to endanger himself by failing to adhere to the letter of the law, in spite of his constant worry about punishment, had been the subject of the analysis over a considerable period of time. At first, his delinquency was approached in the analysis as a masochistic need to be punished for anal-sadistic and oedipal fantasies, both of which were there in abundance, but he had never completely stopped his "cat-and-mouse" game, nor was the low self-esteem alleviated until the "uncle incest" had been analyzed.

LEARNING PROBLEMS AND INCEST

There are many degrees and types of learning problems that arise in patients who did not experience incest. I have not, however, analyzed any case of incest that does not manifest some sort of learning difficulty. Several theoretical formulations are useful to explain this phenomenon.

The very title of Frank's (1969) paper on primal repression, "The Unrememberable and the Unforgettable," connotes the intrapsychic residues of early severe traumas. Frank says that even after secondary-process mentation has been firmly established, physiological, environmental, and emotional traumas may overwhelm the higher ego functions and, by promoting repression, may create conditions suitable for passive primal repression. Although Frank's clinical material does not include incest, it involves late (adult) residues of profound infantile trauma. Frank demonstrated that reconstruction enabled the patient to "know," to "show that he knew," by questioning his parents about his having come close to freezing to death because of parental neglect. Frank feels that passive primal repression encompasses a developmental, rather than a defensive vicissitude, and that a common feature of passive primal repression is the absence of preconscious representation, which results from, among other causes, mental overstimulation. I am convinced that both physical and mental overstimulation may result in amnesia and in problems in learning. Just as in the case Frank cited, I feel that memories of incest may be retrieved with the aid of reconstruction in psychoanalysis.

Woodbury (1966) describes defenses against intrusion by the incestuous parent, which appears as a shell against both feelings and knowledge. He describes altered body-ego experiences, similar to Donald's insistence that I knew what his body was experiencing (penile tumescence and detumescence displaced upward to his lips and nose).

Shengold (1967) reports a patient's use of massive isolation to "keep the overstimulation and rage in check." He adds an important caveat, *namely*, that a special need for denial should alert the analyst to the likelihood that "he is dealing with one of the [people] who have lived through too much" (p. 414). Shengold (1974, 1979) also refers to "vertical splitting," a defense that makes "the good mother preserv- able only at the *expense of the compromise of reality testing by denial*" (1974, pp. 107–108; italics added).

Repression may be partial, as in a case reported by Finkelhor (1979), whose patient did not forget that her father masturbated her on her chest and later took her to the bathroom and had her soap his penis and masturbate him. She did not forget or deny the stimulation, but instead repressed her fury. However, when her fiancé rubbed her breast, she slapped him (pp. 185–214). She could acknowledge that her father's manual stimulation felt good, but that admission made her feel even worse, at the mercy of the adult and out of control of her own body and emotions.

Others report on the interference with thinking and learning in children who have been victims of incest. Ferenczi (1933) is very clear in his description of the child's inability both to know and to learn. He also alludes to the introjection of the *guilt feelings* of the adult. In describing patients with problems of doubting similar to those of my patients who had suffered maternal incest, he states:

> I obtained new corroborative evidence for my supposition that the trauma, especially the sexual trauma, as the pathogenic factor cannot be valued highly enough. Even children of very respectable, sincerely puritanical families, fall victim to real violence or rape much more often than one had dared to suppose. It is the parents who try to find a substitute gratification in this pathological way for their frustration, or it is people thought to be trustworthy who misuse the ignorance and innocence of the child [p. 161].

He describes interferences with the child's thinking and reality testing, as well as with his autonomy, and alludes to the formation of pathologi- cal defenses: "These children feel physically and morally helpless, their personalities are not sufficiently consolidated in order to be able to protest, *even if only in* thought, for the overpowering force and authority of the adult *makes them dumb and can rob them of their senses*" (p. 162; italics added). Ferenczi describes identification with the sexual aggressor and goes on to say:

> The most important change, produced in the mind of the child by the anxiety-fear-ridden identification with the adult parent, is the introjec- tion of the guilt feelings of the adult which makes hitherto harmless

play appear as a punishable offense. When the child recovers from such an attack *he feels enormously confused*, in fact, split—innocent and culpable at the same time—*and his confidence in the testimony of his own senses is broken.* Not infrequently the seducer becomes over-moralistic [pp. 162–163; italics added].

The mental mechanisms used against remembering, knowing, and revealing what they have experienced rule incest victims' lives and color their object relations. The victims have low self-esteem, are self-critical, and have myriad doubts about themselves. It is for this reason that I feel (as does Shengold) that it is important that the analyst verify the incest experience as it emerges in treatment. I, for one, have never encountered an adult who has fabricated a story of incest. Most of them have had to repress, deny, isolate, or otherwise defend against knowing, for psychic survival or for survival within the family. The learning problems in maternal incest are unique.

As mentioned above, my patients abused by the mother as infants had an unusual constellation in their object relations. The patients coerced the maternal object or her substitute to argue one of the opposing sides of the child's intrapsychic conflict (or its derivative). The lack of adequate selfobject differentiation or the persistence of the selfobject (Kernberg, 1976), caused this type of doubting to be considerably different from the doubting of the obsessive-compulsive individual who has separated and individuated, who is troubled by conflict between components of his own psychic structure. My patients used the incompletely differentiated self and object to express and to argue the conflict, a conflict that was usually, but not always, about knowing something; but there was almost never any closure to the conflict. The inability to learn was balanced by a dogged insistence that the object must tell them what she knew really had happened. A teacher of one of my "maternal incest" patients said she had never before encountered a child with such pressured questioning to whom no answer was ever satisfactory.

In addition, my patients were strongly conflicted about physical separation from their parents. In the course of their analyses it became obvious that they controlled their parents' freedom by their supposed need for help with homework and by their separation problems. The parents were extremely compliant in response to their children's control. Later, when their children resumed development and began to take steps toward independence and autonomy, some parents protested, even complaining to me that analysis was changing their relationship with the child. However, these patients' most profound attempts to control were evident in the object-coercive doubting. I speculate that its origin was in the child's uncertainty about what was happening to his or her body and how it was taking place when, at the time of incomplete differentiation, the child's genitals were repeatedly stimulated. The child struggled against his or her intrapsychic resistance against knowing, the latter accentuated by the denial of reality by the mother.

Although colleagues have told me of similar doubting in patients who had experienced paternal incest, I myself have not seen object-coercive doubting except where the mother has sexually overstimulated the child from a time before the differentiation process normally evolved. I have seen in paternal incest patients considerable rumination about "did it occur," but the quality of his self-doubting process is different from that in object-coercive doubting. I keep an open mind about this, however, and remain interested in material that might corroborate object-coercive doubting in paternal incest victims. Although paternal incest is more common than maternal incest, I find it interesting that I encountered a large number of paternal incest cases only after the analysis of the first two maternal incest cases had been completed. While it would be easy to say that it is happenstance, I really have no explanation for this phenomenon in my practice. I do not rule out a countertransference reaction that could have prevented me from responding to subtle paternal incest cues. My patients' material about maternal incest was not at all subtle.

CONCLUSIONS

I have described two important residues of incest: (1) "somatic memories" and (2) problems in learning each related to the other. In regard to the former, I feel it is significant that incidents and affects that are otherwise repressed or denied persist in somatic form.

The learning problems I have described are a function, in part, of powerful resistances to remembering the events and feelings connected with the incest. Other contributing factors, especially in the young child, include identification with the abusing parent's distortion of reality and obeying the parental admonition to not know or tell what has happened between them. In the older child, shame, guilt, and the need to deny sexual pleasure help to reinforce the not knowing. In children of any age, what begins as a defense against specific memories and their related feelings can become generalized into a cognitive style.

As a component of their learning problems, many incest victims demonstrate an inability to trust themselves to know or to trust others to be honest. This distrust has important technical implications for the analyst in helping these patients to test reality and therefore verify the actuality of the incest (see Shengold, 1967, for a related view).

Sachs (1967) offers a relevant perspective when discussing the role of the analyst in helping patients to distinguish between fantasy and reality and their influences on conflicts, conflict resolution, and the behavioral residues of acting out. His description of what may happen when the patient is told by the analyst that some kind of trauma has, indeed, occurred is a poignant reminder of how meaningful psychoanalytic treatment can be for adult patients who were sexually abused as children. "There occurs . . . a release from obsessional self-doubt which has affected some aspects of reality testing [and a strengthening of] the distinction of fantasy from actual events after their occurrence. The belief and acceptance of the memory results in an exhilarating feeling of relief . . . at least someone believes me" (p. 422).

Why is it that relatively few psychoanalysts have written about incest? Do *we* have problems in knowing and reporting what we know about incest? I have noted that antipathy to recognizing and working with derivatives of incest is especially great in cases of maternal incest (children who had been masturbated by their mothers from infancy, often until adolescence). Such countertransference-based reluctance can often lead to superficial treatment or to the patient's dropping out of treatment altogether. If patients leave treatment in which incest is unrecognized and with continuing personality problems and unresolved intrapsychic conflicts, they often seek another therapist to relieve their continuing intrapsychic pain and to help them minimize their tendencies to act out. Of seven "incest" patients in treatment with me in recent years, four had been in prior treatment with a total of seven prior therapists.

In conclusion, I feel that there are many reasons for children to manifest inhibitions in their "work"—the child's appropriate work, which is learning. I have proposed multiple causes for these inhibitions, and I feel that psychoanalysis or psychoanalytic psychotherapy are extremely useful in treating patients handicapped by an inability to know, or to show what they know.

References

Blin, B. (1985), Psychobiology and treatment of anniversary reaction. *Psychosomat.*, 26(6):505–520.

Brenner, I. (1988), Multisensory bridges in response to object loss during the Holocaust. *Psychol. Rev.*, 75:573–587.

Browning, D. & Boatman, B. (1977), Incest: Children at risk. *Amer. J. Psychiat.*, 134:69–72.

Dewald, P. (1989), The effects on an adult of incest in childhood: A case report. *J. Amer. Psychoanal. Assn.*, 37:997–1014.

Ferenczi, S. (1933), *Confusion of Tongues Between the Adult and the Child: Final Contribution to Problems and Methods of Psychoanalysis.* London: Hogarth Press, 1955.

Finkelhor, D. (1979), *Sexually Victimized Children*. New York: Free Press.

Frank, A. (1969), The unrememberable and unforgettable. *The Psychoanalytic Study of the Child*, 24:68–77. New York: International Universities Press.

Freud, A. (1965), *Normality and Pathology in Childhood. Writings*, Vol. 6. New York: International Universities Press.

Freud, S. (1916), Some character types met in psycho-analytic work. *Standard Edition*, 14:311–331. London: Hogarth Press, 1957.

———— (1918), From the history of an infantile neurosis. *Standard Edition*, 17:3–122. London: Hogarth Press, 1955.

Herman-Gibbons, M. & Berson, N. (1989), Harmful genital care practices in childhood: A type of child abuse. *J. Amer. Med. Assn.*, 261:577–579.

Katan, A. (1973), Children who were raped. *The Psychoanalytic Study of the Child*, 28:208–224. New Haven, CT: Yale University Press.

Keiser, S. (1969), Superior intelligence: Contributions to neurosogenesis. *J. Amer. Psychoanal. Assn.*, 17:452–573.

Kernberg, O. F. (1976), Technical considerations about borderline personality organization. *J. Amer. Psychoanal. Assn.*, 24:795–829.

Kramer, S. (1974), Episodes of severe ego regression in the course of an adolescent analysis. In: *The Analyst and the Adolescent at Work*, ed. M. Harley. New York: Quadrangle, pp. 190–231.

———— (1980), Residues of split-object and split-self dichotomies in adolescence. In *Rapproachement: The Critical Sub-phase of Separation-Individuation*, ed. R. Lax, S. Bach & J. A. Burland. New York: Aronson, pp. 417–438.

———— (1983), Object-coercive doubting: A pathological defensive response to maternal incest. In: *Defense and Resistance*, ed. H. P. Blum. New York: International Universities Press, pp. 325–351.

———— (1987), A contribution to the concept "the exception" as a developmental phenomenon. *Child Abuse and Neglect*, 11:367–370.

Laufer, M. (1968), The body image, the function of masturbation, and adolescence: Problems of ownership of the body. *The Psychoanalytic Study of the Child*, 23:114–125.

Litin, E., Griffin, M. & Johnson, A. M. (1956), Parental influence on sexual behavior in children. *Psychoanal. Q.*, 25:37–55.

Mahler, M. S. & McDevitt, J. B. (1980), The separation-individuation process and identity formation. In: *The Course of Life*, Vol. 2., ed. S. I. Greenspan & G. H. Pollock. Madison, CT: International Universities Press, 1989, pp. 19–35.

Margolis, M. (1977), A preliminary report of a case of consummated mother-son incest. *Annual Psychoanal.*, 5:267–293. New York: International Universities Press.

———— (1984), A case of mother-adolescent son incest. *Psychoanal. Q.*, 53:355–385.

Sachs, O. (1967), Distinction between fantasy and reality elements in memory and reconstruction. *Internat. J. Psycho-Anal.*, 48:416–423.

Shengold, L. (1967), Effect of overstimulation: Rat people. *Internat. J. Psycho-Anal.*, 48:403–415.

—— (1974), The metaphor of the mirror. *J. Amer. Psychoanal. Assn.*, 22:97–115.

—— (1979), Child abuse and deprivation: Soul murder. *J. Amer. Psychoanal. Assn.*, 27:533–557.

—— (1980), Some reflection on a case of mother-adolescent son incest. *Internat. J. Psycho-Anal.*, 61:461–476.

Silber, A. (1979), Childhood seduction, parental pathology and hysterical symptoms. *Internat. J. Psycho-Anal.*, 60:109–116.

Steele, B. F. (1994), Psychoanalysis and the maltreatment of children. *J. Amer. Psychoanal. Assn.*, 42:1001–1025.

Williams, M. (1987), Aftereffect of early seduction. *J. Amer. Psychoanal. Assn.*, 35:145–165.

Woodbury, M. (1966), Altered body ego experiences. *J. Amer. Psychoanal. Assn.*, 14:273–303.

II. CLINICAL CONSIDERATIONS

11

ON WRITER'S BLOCK: FOR WHOM DOES ONE WRITE OR NOT WRITE?

STANLEY L. OLINICK, M.D.

Writer's block exists in varying degrees, probably with common developmental and psychodynamic origins. The term designates specific instances of work inhibition; these are temporary, recurrent, or enduring, anguishing in varying intensities, and denote the inability of the writer to find thoughts and words with which to communicate his potential fictive and conceptual creativity, whether handwritten, typewritten, word-processed, or even dictated. Competition and envy are evident. Often, shame is felt, and to acknowledge the disability publicly is prohibited. The victim may be reluctant to recognize the block as a psychological problem. There may be a sense of guardedness, of concern about invaded privacy. Dissatisfaction in the area of oral dependence is a recurring theme, as is the accompanying theme of anxiety about aggression consequent on frustrated dependent-narcissistic needs.

We know from professional writers that their work is often painful, though with joy of accomplishment. Anecdotal examples of avoidance of the act of writing are numerous. Many writers joke about sharpening pencils to postpone the ordeal of starting work, of blemishing the pristine page. The story is told of Ernest Hemingway who, asked how he went about doing his work, replied, ''First I defrost the refrigerator.'' This was an apt metaphor of putting off his work in order to thaw something frozen and inaccessible. Inevitably, sexual symbols come into focus. The oral, kitchen reference may have indicated an internalized feminine, probably maternal, influence which required denial or screening with humor. That Hemingway's persona was aggressively masculine and depreciatory of women places the

183

metaphor into an ambiguous setting. Was there not a conflict here? By whom or by what influences were he and so many others inhibited or delayed in getting to work? For whom or despite whom do writers write or not write?

The novelist, short story writer, and essayist Joyce Carol Oates (1993) has said, "Most writing is engendered out of a feeling of loss and nostalgia, a desire to memorialize what we have experienced and where we have lived." This is a statement attested to independently by many knowledgeable and sensitive professional writers. I would add that nostalgia is a notoriously deceptive experience and concept, wherein the presence of grievances, disappointment, and anger tends to be overlooked in favor of the familiar bittersweet screen of home-sickness (Olinick, 1992). Loss in this context suggests not only bereavement in the usual sense, but also disappointment and disillu-sionment.

One writes to make sense of one's experiences, imaginatively, fictively, or even scientifically. The fiction writer will produce work that is subtly and profoundly transformed or reinvented from actual experience. The scientific, psychoanalytic writer works from the tem-plate of clear, objective observation of his subjective and intersubjec-tive data. Here, too, the personal element enters: as Goethe said, "Everything I write is a fragment of a great confession," a valid generalization for most writers. One also writes to be confirmed, to be attended to, to enter into a special dialogue. As universally expressed in Hamlet's final words to Horatio, a person who has suffered loss, grievance, and conflict wishes his story to evoke a sympathetic under-standing and acceptance. Creativity in the arts is used to affirm the sense of the artist's worth as a person. In a television interview, the actor Laurence Olivier responded to a question thus: "What does an actor want? I'll tell you: LOOKATME!!! Lookatmelookatmelook-atme!!!"

The factors that enter into the understanding of the psychology of the writer and specifically of the inhibition or facilitation of his writing can be brought together under a single heading, although not into a unitary theory. A previous publication (Olinick and Tracy, 1987) discussed the hypothesis that stories are devised for and told to an imagined and projected transference imago. For instance, John Updike (1993) writes of Edith Wharton, ". . . holding herself to the exacting standards of what she called 'that dispassionate and ironic critic who dwells within the breast.' " During many years, I was at times periph-erally aware of writing for a vaguely defined, taciturn, critical colleague in some distant city. It was necessary for me to keep that fantasy figure satisfied with the quality and nature of my output. This was, like Wharton's, a projection of superego and ego-ideal processes repre-senting a variety of attitudes and control over my self-esteem, with a readiness at times to give begrudging commendation.

One writes or withholds writing, then, not in strictest solitude, but in the presence of and to control one's transference imago, for purposes of approval and esteem or from fear of being diminished or depreciated—also to turn passivity into activity or vice versa, to compensate for loss. There may be grandiose expectations with anticipated hurt and anger, suggestive of the pattern of expectations in some instances of sexual impotence, as when psychogenic impotence dissembles aspirations to hyperpotency.

I consider the writer's transference imago to be a probably ubiquitous phenomenon. Writing can thereby offer a conduit for undoing loss and for expressing aggression. The writer must deal with his own aggression and his own concern about the aggression and loss of his reader, especially of the transference imago reader, whose superego origins, it must be remembered, are partly in aggression. He is dependent on that reader and this dependence can be a notable precursor to displaced resentment, conflictual anxiety, and paralysis or blocking.

An analogy to writer's block lies in the "choking" familiar to sports enthusiasts. In tennis, omitting the effects of fatigue and loss of concentration, competitive pressure may at critical moments evoke fear of aggression and of narcissistic hurt ("This guy could win!" or "Am I entitled to win?"), with a temporarily uncontrollable and saddening surrender of skill. This is an overdetermined happening, sometimes occurring only across the net from a particular opponent. With the player's tension, a transference imago is projected: a forbidding or indomitable adversary is embodied in the idiosyncratic meanings of tournament and opponent.

There are familiar instances of psychoanalytic candidates who mystifyingly and unendingly delay writing their case reports or such case reviews as are required for graduation. Some of these same colleagues spend hours laboriously writing defensive daily notes of all their patients, intending thus to protect themselves from possible malpractice suits. Not always are projected transference images so persecutory and defeating; they may be supportive and confirmatory.

Inhibition of envy and competitiveness, of curiosity and scopophilia, enter these phenomena in varying degrees. Reading block and inability to recall and narrate jokes and dreams are perhaps cognate and analogous, but are beyond the scope of this essay. While it may seem that all such instances are ultimately consequences of an inhibiting depression or phobia, these are not sufficiently explicit explanations.

Other than content of the writing, with aggression explicit or disguised, the process of writing may itself become subject to conflictual anxiety over aggression. Both the act of writing and the syntactical process of writing can become expressive of affect. A ready example is the genre of satire, with its special blending of disguised anger, motive, style, allusion, metaphor, irony, etc. Literary style, as Alter (1989) observes, is "the instrument of an attitudinally defined act of communication" (p. 84). Not only esthetics, but emotions enter into the automatic, preconscious choice of syntax, vocabulary, and other expressions of meaning, including authorial control of the reader, whether that reader can be an actuality or a transference imago. Such control may be benevolent or hostile.

I should add that in the historic progression of the act of writing from quill pen to word processor, there have been writers who have resisted each advance in technology. Can poetry be written on a machine? The regressive pull of the familiar and habitual and the fear of the unknown are conducive to displacing, symbolizing, or metaphorizing of writing; the affective connections are for some writers with the physical act, for others with content, or with the transformations of the inner inspiration to the actual page in syntactical variations. A person who must rely on the unfamiliar in himself and in his writing instrument, who must depend on the benevolence of an unknown reader—unconsciously the writer's own transference imago—and who may be developmentally conditioned to expect rejection, hurt, and disappointment, delimits and protects himself with anger and anxious conflict from the intimacy of sharing his imagination and thoughts.

Henry Roth, author of the innovative novel *Call It Sleep* (1934), presents a famous instance of devastating writer's block. He has been emotionally and physically disabled for decades, virtually unable to write and to build upon his successful first novel. Two volumes of a six-volume autobiographical novel have at long-last been published (1994, 1995). Roth speculated to a recent interviewer (Michaels, 1993) that his inability to have dealt with unconscious incestuous feelings in his novel was responsible for his later difficulties in writing a successor to that admired work. He also emphasized a continuing "alienation," referring to such uprooting experiences as his family's move from the Jewish Lower East Side to "heterogeneous Harlem" (p. 19), and his further move at age twenty-one from his family and Jewish roots to the Greenwich Village apartment of Eda Lou Walton, a non-Jewish professor, writer, and poet, one of the central figures of a literary salon, and twelve years older than he. It was to her that he dedicated his novel. Roth had found a new love object, less incestuous, less threatening, and less secret. She supported him and encouraged his writing; one surmises she slept with him, and she collusively lent weight to his infantilizing dependency.

I assume that by "alienation," Roth meant that the assimilation to America he sought was at a heavy price: he lost his conflicted personal roots to his family, religion, and ethnicity. He was left without a stable sense of identity. Much later, at the time of the 1967 Arab-Israeli War, with his sense of "reunion" with Judaism and Zionism resulting from Israel's victorious triumph, he found temporary renewed interest in writing (Harris, 1988; Michaels, 1993). This was an effect of ethnic identification with an effectively aggressive Jewry, releasing for a time his own repressed aggressive energies.

He has said it was a "source of great chagrin" (Michaels, 1993, p. 20) that, when his novel was published, critics of the Left attacked it, while those of the Right praised it. Roth says ruefully, "I thought I was writing a proletarian novel." For a sensitive idealist, this criticism was mortifying to his already unstable self-esteem. Narcissistic rage must have been generated, but held in repression until the 1967 War. Sympathetic to Communism as Roth had been, these conflicts between his artistic endeavors and his politics further inhibited his work, miring it in humiliation, disappointment, and anger. Roth was, I venture, also frustrated by his awareness that European Communist writers did not take their affiliation as a form of personal mission and redemption as did he and other American writers. These failed redemptions, or alienations, including his separation from family and ethnoreligious affiliations, afflicted him with a sense of helplessness, a surrender to infantilizing, repression of aggression, and writer's block.

To extrapolate from an author's fiction to his actual life, or vice versa, is usually impermissible and imprecise. Still, the creative transformations of *Call It Sleep*, with its detailed interior monologues by the latency and prepubescent child, and with vivid depictions of the child's confusion and conflict during scenes of or references to sexual seductions and violent aggression, do imply something more than creative imagination alone—rather, to an intimate personal sense on the part of the author. Through such depiction, I infer that the writer is refinding and reorganizing his own feelings and identity. The child of *Call It Sleep* was infantilized by his doting, seductive, and fiercely protective mother and terrified by his distant and often savage father, who jealously protested the closeness of mother with son. The child was depicted as timorous and often made anxious by his own curiosity and latent aggression. The indirect and direct evidence suggests that Roth's writer's block was a consequence of his writing having become invested with anxiously conflicted sexuality and aggression, engendered in part out of the originality and innovativeness of his first novel. That is, originality became a source of discomfort when it symbolically served his conflicted oedipal triumph and ethnic rebellion. His transference imago was persecutory and inhibiting, presumably as he had experienced his father.

Perhaps one can apply to Roth as writer, T. S. Eliot's words about the complete artist—that the more complete the artist, the more separate will be the suffering man and the creative mind (Donoghue, 1993 cited, p. 35). Roth's sadly and painfully unfulfilled life as a writer was a consequence of his creativity becoming overwhelmed by his suffering—a suffering caused by cumulative effects of multiple developmental, epigenetic conflicts, structured into superego processes and transference imago.

Roth went on in subsequent years to a supportive marriage with a talented young composer and pianist who gave up her career for what seems to have been a martyred life as housewife, schoolteacher, and mother. He worked for much of this time at manual labor, struggling against his block.

There are suggestive contrasts to Roth's history in that of the sculptor Jacob Epstein (1880–1959), a man who ruthlessly and determinedly followed his own assertive inclinations. When his parents moved uptown from lower Manhattan, Epstein defiantly remained behind, later moving to England where he was, still later, knighted. Throughout, he opposed bourgeois conformity in a life of loyalty to his artistic modes, for instance committing adultery with a number of his lover models who bore his children, who in turn were raised by his fiercely loyal wife. He has been represented as self-centered, boastful, bestial, and ungrateful (Stannard, 1993). Hardly a paragon of mental health, he was a vivid instance of successful rebellion and thereby may serve as a foil to Roth. He braved criticism without adversely affecting his work, in fact, perhaps as prerequisite to successful work and despite his tormented life.

The eminent literary critic and essayist Lionel Trilling aspired to be a novelist and envied the lifestyle and literary success of Ernest Hemingway. The latter's "violently impulsive life" confirmed Trilling's sense "that wickedness—or is it my notion of courage—is essential for creation." He is further quoted, "I defeated myself long ago when I rejected the way of chutzpah and *mishegass* in favor of reason and diffidence" (Hulbert, 1993, p. 9).

We may assume that the transference imago, or superego processes, that controlled Trilling's writing was in part a projection of internalized family and ethnic expectations and requirements, including those represented by his wife and her editorial, intellectual, and literary standards. We know from Diana Trilling's memoir (Trilling, 1993) that she carefully edited Lionel Trilling's writings and that this was in keeping with his wishes. From the same source, we know that Lionel was raised in strict conformity to family and ethnic standards, that his "rejection of chutzpah and *mishegass*" stemmed from these, whatever were his own internally structured needs and fears. There was no room for a Hemingway literary persona in this ménage.

The sources of Henry Roth's transference imago were more seriously conflicted, or should we say that his capacity for compromise and concession with his conflicts, for synthesizing creatively the raging conflicts with which he was beset, were less effective than were Trilling's. That he dedicated his one novel to Eda Lou Walton suggests that she was a factor in his imago. We know that his political and literary ideals and ideologies were in strong opposition with each other and that his ethnic, religious, and familial ideals were at unresolvable variance with communism and standards of the Greenwich Village with which he identified for a time. So disparate were the elements that entered into his transference imago, so riddled with anxious conflicts, that any efforts to appease his projected conscience were doomed to failure.

CONCLUSIONS

There has been more illustration than scientific proof of my theses; this has been a meditative essay, based on years of pondering behind the analytic couch or behind the pages of books and journals. Because of concern about confidentiality, invaluable transference and clinical process data are regrettably absent. I have instead resorted to scanty, but relevant, biographical material, chiefly concerning that brilliant, but curtailed writer, Henry Roth. Understanding his misfortune may help us in the treatment of other cases of writer's block. I have found bibliographic sources to be meager and not very helpful. That great fount of psychoanalytic information (even now after a half-century!), Fenichel's *The Psychoanalytic Theory of Neurosis* (1945) offers nothing beyond a reference to "writer's cramp"—probably what we now know as carpal tunnel syndrome and another example of the invasion of a formerly psychic or psychogenic domain by the advances of physical medicine. Clinical experience of writer's block seems not to be extensive.

The person with writer's block is likely to have been narcissistically vulnerable to either frustration or indulgence of dependent, including sexually dependent, needs, the indulgence leading possibly to infantilizing, the frustration perhaps to mobilizing the anxiety of narcissistic injury. Either outcome may lead into a sense of being victimized, with attendant problems of rage, hate, and consequent inhibition and repression. The act of writing, sexualized and aggressivized, entails the evoking of paralyzing anxieties and other affects. This is in a conjunction of writing intended for a transference imago manipulated in accordance with the subject's narcissistically vulnerable, dependent, aggressive needs, i.e., with anxiety about shame and lack of satisfaction.

The writer who cannot write feels relatively worthless and irrelevant. His impaired personal integrity and entitlement renders him unable to win the approval and support of the transference imago. He is left with anxious conflict between effective assertion and frustrated dependence. He must "defrost the refrigerator." His anguished inner cry is "Notice me! Tell me I'm worthy!" The expectation against which he was defended was that he would be diminished and humiliated. In such a situation, he dare not write. His self-fulfilling passive-aggressive expectations are thus confirmed.

REFERENCES

Alter, R. (1989), *The Pleasures of Reading in an Ideological Age*. New York: Simon & Schuster.
Donoghue, D. (1993), Joyce's many lives. *N.Y. Rev. Books*, 40(17):28–35.
Fenichel, O. (1945), *The Psychoanalytic Theory of the Neuroses*. New York: Norton.
Harris, L. (1988), A critic at large: In the shadow of the golden mountains. *New Yorker*, June 27, pp. 84–92.
Hulbert, A. (1993), Review of *The Beginning of the Journey: The Marriage of Diana and Lionel Trilling*, by Diana Trilling. *N.Y. Times Book Rev.*, October 24, pp. 7 & 9.
Michaels, L. (1993), The long comeback of Henry Roth: Call it miraculous. *N.Y. Times Book Rev.*, August 15, pp. 3, 19 et seq.
Oates, J. C. (1993), Sidebar in *N.Y. Times Book Rev.*, August 15, p. 6.
Olinick, S. (1992), Nostalgia and transference. *Contemp. Psychoanal.*, 28:195–198.
——— & Tracy, L. (1987), Psychoanalytic perspectives of story telling. *Psychoanal. Rev.*, 74:319–331.
Roth, H. (1934), *Call It Sleep*. New York: Avon Books, 1964.
——— (1994, 1995), *Mercy of a Rude Stream*, Vols. 1 & 2. New York: St. Martin's Press.
Stannard, M. (1993), Review of *Epstein: Artist Against the Establishment*, by Stephen Gardiner. *N.Y. Times Book Rev.*, August 22, p. 3.
Trilling, D. (1993), *The Beginning of the Journey*. New York: Harcourt Brace.
Updike, J. (1993), Reworking Wharton. *New Yorker*, October 4, p. 198.

12

CREATIVE WORK, WORK INHIBITIONS AND THEIR RELATION TO INTERNAL OBJECTS

Maria V. Bergmann

> Between the conception
> And the creation
> Between the emotion
> And the response
> Falls the Shadow
> —T. S. Eliot (1925)

This essay explores the relationships of patients engaged in creative endeavors with their internalized objects. A parental object will be internalized as love-giving if a "libidinal dialogue" with a "good enough" object is possible, so that creative work is safeguarded from within, and narcissistically valued by its creator.

The intrapsychic interaction that concerns us is characteristic of the relationship of the self and its objects in the internal world (Sandler and Rosenblatt, 1962, pp. 132–133). Such interaction results in an internal structure "... [replicating] in the intrapsychic world both real and fantasied relationships with significant others" (Kernberg, in press). In the external world artists create things that people use. However, from an intrapsychic point of view, creative work can be conceptualized as an unconscious communication addressed to an internalized object. Such communication is a psychic reality "... not a fantasy that is taken for the real truth, for an actual event, but the 'real' recollection of a psychic event with its mixture of fact and fantasy" (Arlow, 1969, p. 43).

This chapter is an adaptation of a paper by the same title (Bergmann, 1994).

At times certain events emanating from psychic conflict impair the creative process and lead to work inhibition. As internalization becomes structured and internalized self- and object relations appear in the interaction between ego and superego, permanent inhibition of creativity may result. Accessibility of internalized objects varies from patient to patient and also between neurotic and borderline pathology. Conflict may be deeply repressed in neurotic pathology, but is more easily accessible in borderline cases, when object relations have not readily yielded to the formation of intrapsychic structures. In neurotic patients, inter- and intrapsychic conflicts usually have been superseded by object relations that have been repressed, so that at first only intra-psychic conflicts seem apparent. As analysis proceeds and regression takes place, one uncovers object relationship conflicts within psychic structures. In borderline cases, internalized object relations have not lost their voices.

I propose that disavowed hostile aspects of internalized relation-ships with parental objects will lead to inhibition or even paralysis of the creative function. I shall deal only with cases who come to the analyst's attention because their creativity was hampered by internal conflicts. In these patients a predominance of hostility toward and from internalized objects has been experienced. A feeling of lack of appreciation of the creative process or product by parental objects toward their creator is apparent.

Oremland (1989, p. 28) characterizes creativity as a form of object relatedness that occurs early on and continues throughout life. The creator's relationship to the created product is symbol-forming and communicative. Although artists are symbol creators, they may none-theless need major encouragement to preserve their product: their sym-bolizing capacity tends to break down under excessive pressure of hostile affect toward their internalized objects.

Psychoanalytic writers have drawn attention to the hostile feelings artists sometimes have toward their creative products. As a rule, the artistic product is a symbolic object, but the symbolic function may be lost in severe pathology. An example is given by Gross and Rubin (1973) who report that Edward Munch, after a psychotic break, treated his paintings like [internal] objects "stacking them upright on the grounds surrounding his house and claiming their exposure to every kind of weather was a 'horse doctor's cure' which would do them good" (1973, p. 351). De Tolnay (1960, p. 16) describes how a day after Michelangelo's death "... an inventory of Michelangelo's be-longings was taken ... February 19 [1564] by the notary of the Gover-nor of Rome. ... Much less was found in the house of Michelangelo than had been thought. The artist had had many of his drawings burned. As for works of art, [there were] ... three unfinished marble stat-ues ... one of them ... identified as the Pieta Rondanini. ..." It was "obvious" and confirmed by Vasari, that Michelangelo had created this Pieta for his own grave. Liebert (1983, p. 398) stresses that the Pieta Rondanini is unique in that it is the only work Michelangelo actually tried to destroy and then abandoned: "After years of work he mutilated the group. . . ." Liebert believes that a psychoanalytic inquiry into Michelangelo's destruction of the Pieta needs to focus first on why the mutilation occurred at that time, and on how to regard Michelangelo's own explanation for the destruction, "that he was so vexed by Urbino's nagging that he attempted to destroy a group for his own tomb" (p. 402).

Liebert quotes Steinberg's explanation that "the slung leg was to be recognized as an "unmistakable symbol of sexual aggression or compliance." Steinberg believes that Michelangelo "destroyed it in despair" when he found that he had pushed ". . . the rhetoric of carnal gesture beyond the limit of acceptable expression . . ." (p. 399).

The analyst treating a creative patient may be called upon to protect the product from its creator's fury. Destructive impulses may be only periodic. In the examples that follow, work inhibition reproduced conflictual relationships to internal objects. To overcome the resulting creative impasses my patients had to be helped to realize that they wanted me to protect their artistic product from their own aggression. Failure to do so resulted in a negative therapeutic reaction and difficulty in differentiating the analyst from the internalized object toward whom hostility was unconsciously directed. In the wish to destroy what had been created, this hostility was externalized. Such episodes give analyst and patient a chance to arrive at a more dynamic understanding of the creative process *per se* and of its inhibition.

Creative impairment can be experienced both as total incapacity to work and as inability to work at the highest potential. Inhibited patients feel a sense of urgency about incomplete work. This creates anxiety, but may not be recognized as a subject of analytic inquiry. Initially patients may not be motivated to explore their intrapsychic conflicts. They hunger unconsciously for a new object who can be trusted to remain libidinally invested and support their creative efforts until the work is completed. In Oremland's experience, the artist demands that the analyst relate to the artistic product as both part and not part of the patient's self. In my experience, this interrelatedness creates a triple-faceted, unique transference situation in which the analyst is expected to relate not only to the patient's intrapsychic problems, but also to the ongoing work process and product as an *external* event. During periods of positive transference the patient believes that the analyst furthers creative capacity, accepts the creative product as valuable, and agrees that its completion is a primary life goal. A therapeutic alliance is facilitated when the analyst is differentiated from ambivalently cathected internalized imagoes. The therapeutic alliance has a crucial role in helping the patient form a bridge of communication with the creative aspects of the self, liberating the forces of creative self-expression. Interpretations may enable the patient to gain distance from a conflict-laden dialogue with internalized parental imagoes. Intrapsychic separation leads to a decrease of creative inhibition and may be the first breakthrough of an autonomous creative experience on the part of the patient.

A complex correlation exists between psychic disturbance and creative inhibition. There are severely disturbed people who may be highly productive, whereas others may use their creativity as a way of managing intrapsychic conflicts. Many pathological solutions are beyond the scope of this paper, which examines cases where analysis facilitated productivity in greatly inhibited patients by attempting to illuminate how internalized pathological object relations contributed to creative inhibition.

Laura, a sculptor in her forties, came to analysis because she was "stuck." Her artistic work required more than a single burst of energy to complete. Unable to do this, she was compelled to disassemble the new sculpture and return it into already existing shapes. She then became anxious that she would never be able to make her sculpture whole again. She frequently needed to bring these incomplete attempts to her sessions, and upon associating to her work would find it easier to complete.

When Laura first came to see me she was overweight, a chain smoker, and a heavy coffee drinker. She frequently consumed alcohol to the point of stupor. She was easily aroused sexually, but after marriage did not experience orgasm. She had a disturbed sense of self. She would "forget to work," but pretended to others that she had completed a work of art. In states of greater reality-testing capacity she wondered: "Where have I been all this time?" It appeared that Laura's forgetting to work occurred in fuguelike states.

In childhood Laura took care of a cranky brother three years her junior, whom mother could not handle. She recalled never being thanked for her efforts, even though they restored peace in the family. When Laura was between nine and ten years old she had major surgery requiring general anesthesia. During her prolonged hospitalization her mother stayed in an adjoining room where she and Laura's father spent many hours behind closed doors. Her father visited Laura daily and brought her the funnies, but always remained in the doorway. He never entered her room to kiss or touch her, although she was not contagious. Laura thought he did not want to touch her because she was ugly and crippled, and maintained this self-image from then on. We reconstructed that her father had a germ phobia.

Following her recovery Laura began to masturbate compulsively. In fantasy she was spreading germs to everyone, particularly her phobic father. Germs were equated with semen and impregnation; she fantasized producing a defective baby with him. Masturbation and overeating made her feel whole again, undoing feelings of genital mutilation. The underlying fantasies contained death wishes toward the oedipal father, and revenge themes for having been rejected. Laura needed to fend off her cannibalistic wishes. She was physically attracted to her mother, who constantly offered overgratification and had devouring impulses. Laura felt drawn to mother's body; its layers of fat fascinated her. In recurring dreams, she wished her mother's fat would engulf and protect her. Both parents overgratified Laura with material things, but failed to make her feel lovable. When Laura was twenty-one, both parents died a short time apart, leaving her traumatized and desolate. She sometimes fantasized her mother was alive inside her, and at other times that she carried her as a dead anal baby inside her belly.

At a certain point in her analysis Laura wrote down her thoughts rather than save them for her analytic hour:

I begin every day with convictions and end in doubts—coffee, cigarettes, vodka and wastebaskets filled with the day's fresh start. These line up in my studio like sentinels of a beheading. Every day I murder a few hours before I start my work and then run from it in guilt, only to return the next day to retrieve what I had lost, thereupon doubling my losses. The third triples, the fourth quadruples, and so on into the following day's loss. What is strange is that like a true gambler, I return each time with a fresh hope that I have found some winning combination. My fantasy is that the work will arrive whole, magically, out of one sitting. It is a childish, passive fantasy.

Luck or nature or God or hired hands [the analyst] will do the work for me. . . . I feel I belong nowhere. . . . I cannot get to my destination, nor can I go back to where I started. I'm lost and my time is running out. . . . In my fantasies I think that success could kill me, a heart attack or cancer. Meanwhile I'm eating up my savings. Worse, I'm eating up my heart. Who wants to die like that? In my fantasy it's better to die with a little posthumous work and, if you'll forgive the pun, it could be inscribed on my tombstone, I met my last deadline. The biggest risk you take is that it may be said of you that your little operation was a success and wasn't it too bad the patient died?

Laura's ritualistic behavior involved symbolic actions designed to resurrect her parents and subsequently kill them again, underscoring the prominence of the murder theme in her written piece. At the beginning of her day Laura did chores her late mother would have done for her, then proceeded to "make herself beautiful" or "hide her ugliness" from her father. After these ritualistic restitutional reenactments she felt ready to start working, but usually the day was nearly over.

These rituals also served to protect her creative work from wishes to hurt her fantasized bad internalized objects. She manifested separation anxiety related to completing her work, as unconsciously this would amount to triple murder—parents and little brother. Her work inhibition was "an act of kindness." A fear of revenge by parents or sibling made oedipal victory a threatening prospect, comparable to Loewald's (1980) concept of parricide.

Laura was frightened when she felt close to me or had homosexual dreams in which she was nursing or making love. She feared finishing her sculptures because she expected to be faced with an ugly baby her parents would hate, created either by us or by her and her father. This fantasy sometimes had the status of a genuine belief.

Laura's inhibition of creativity was overdetermined. Conflicts over her gender identity and her feminine genital castration anxiety were prominent. She was enraged that her parents subjected her to surgery as a child. She fantasized that it had left her ugly and deformed. In her art work she repeatedly recreated a crippled body, a fantasy image connected to her surgery. Her traumatized body image also expressed itself in disassembling her sculpture and fearing she would never be able to make it whole again. Her tendency to self-denigration made her doubt her work was good enough to keep. At other times Laura successfully completed artistic efforts. This gave her a sense of autonomy from parents and siblings and was followed by a marked decrease in hostility. She often mentioned that in her innermost soul she was really working for her father's enthusiastic response and approving smile. These paternal gestures would signify she was whole as a female and did not have to feel ugly.

When in a state of narcissistic self-denigration Laura could not sustain object love, placing her work in danger of destruction. At a particularly difficult juncture in a project she wished to flee; she could not rely on creativity to sustain her. The analytic gain of lengthening her creative attention span from twenty minutes to several hours corresponded to her ability to form an internal self-image as a creative artist.

Laura remained dependent on the outside world for reaffirming her self-esteem. The traumatic impact of Laura's body image confusion following surgery had coalesced into a fantasy that to be successful she would have to be male like her brother, or beautifully feminine like her mother. This fantasy continued into adulthood and impeded her work as a sculptor. Narcissistic and oedipally competitive fantasies retained a sense of "actuality" sustained by projective identification whenever hostility or depression temporarily got the upper hand. After Laura's omnipotent fantasies and murderous wishes were analyzed, she became a happier and more creative person capable of executing projects she could finish without first disassembling them. These artistic successes gave her satisfaction, pride, and greater stability in the real world.

Ellen came to treatment in her twenties, deeply depressed. Her husband had died. The marriage had been loveless. Ellen came from a poor farm family in the dustbowl. As a child she had been close to her father, a revered but isolated professional in a small town. Ellen felt ambivalent toward her mother who she thought preferred her little brother. She fantasized her mother only loved her because she performed endless, hated household chores. Ellen always worked. She put herself through college and then haphazardly embarked on an acting career. Her family discouraged emotional freedom, leaving her unable to trust her abilities as an actress.

In her first play Ellen had a small character part in which she appeared totally disguised; I would not have recognized her. She fantasized that revealing herself on stage might disclose her hostile fantasies about her mother and brother; she felt intensely jealous of their relationship. Ellen had noticed early in life that she could conceal her real feelings and pretend other emotions; she could "act" and get away with it. Initially we worked on differentiating her own hostile conflicts about family members from those of the characters she portrayed.

Early in analysis she got her first prominent acting part, but experienced such a crisis animating certain lines that she was in danger of losing the role. When prolonged analysis did not reveal the cause of her increasing inhibition, she became frantic, deeply depressed, and less and less verbal. Finally she asked whether I would "go and see" her try to rehearse the lines that paralyzed her.

When I slipped into a rehearsal I could immediately recognize that her affect became flat and unconvincing when she had to express the hostility of an evil and powerful female character. Ellen failed as an actress when her lines expressed themes related to her own sadomasochistic and murderous fantasies about her mother, which her strict superego would not permit her to acknowledge.

Sandler (1990) discusses underlying internal obstacles in a psychic constellation similar to those that accounted for Ellen's behavior:

> . . . if one *identified* with some aspect of the parent, then one would duplicate that perceived aspect in oneself and become more like that parent. If one *introjected* the parent, then the introject would not modify one's self-representation but would become an internal companion, a

sort of back-seat driver. Of course one can . . . identify with the introject just as we might identify with an object perceived in the external world [p. 865].

In Ellen's case the introjected mother was not sufficiently differentiated from the real mother, and neither was sufficiently differentiated from the character Ellen was portraying. The introjected mother thus served as Sandler's "back-seat driver" when Ellen was on stage, forbidding the vocalization of hostility.

After I saw Ellen rehearse, subsequent verbalization became possible. We could now explore her hostile introjections. It was only by seeing a rehearsal that I could help her articulate that expressing hostile wishes on stage was prohibited by the maternal introject. My participation helped form a boundary between herself, her mother, and the character she was creating.

Aided by a liberated verbal capacity, Ellen became able to analyze conflicts related to her internal objects. This further enhanced her creativity. Subsequently, she drew on her creative capacities to externalize bad objects, including the analyst in the negative transference. She used her treatment to transpose affects based on libidinal and hostile fantasies to create the characters *she* was playing. When she became able to dip freely and without anxiety into her personal experiences, she created a leading role where she combined the excessive punctiliousness and cleanliness of her mother with her love of "beautiful objects" she saw in my office. This enabled her to sublimate hostile themes in an exquisitely integrated characterization of a woman who cared more about things than about people.

It was fortunate that Ellen was able to become creative and unencumbered in her work before she discovered I was pregnant, as this evoked her hostility toward mother and brother with renewed ferociousness. Ellen had a masturbation fantasy in which she visualized a woman [the analyst] looking like Diana of Ephesus with many ever-lactating breasts. The woman permitted Ellen to nurse forever, like a mother who never left. These libidinal fantasies did not disappear, even after oedipal wishes became prominent.

After I gave birth she sent me flowers and a note that said "I forgive you." Her own feminine wishes emerged subsequently. Ellen remarried and had several children. A few years after ending her treatment, she once brought them for a visit. In her work, she became famous.

Emma came to analysis at the age of thirty-one. She was a designer and, while in analysis, became an artistic fashion photographer. She was tall with very short plantinum-dyed hair and heavily made-up eyes. She wore slacks or very short skirts; and had a collection of androgynous-looking watches which were her only jewelry. At first glance it was hard to tell from her attire of personally designed T-shirts depicting skulls of clean-shaven male heads, the prominence of her boots, blazers, and knapsack, whether she was male or female. Unexpectedly, her appearance was quite elegant. Emma had been bulimic and anorexic since age thirteen and frequently suffered from anxiety attacks accompanied by light-headedness, tachycardia, and a fear of dying. She was prone to get rashes, which worsened when she would pick at her face, "trying to rid it of impurities." Emma's symptoms were related to gender conflicts, lack of self-constancy, and developmental deficits.

Overeating felt comforting when she was lonely or angry, but as soon as she was excessively full, she had to rid herself of that feeling by vomiting. Subsequently, she felt cleansed and restored, as if the entire episode had never happened. Emma stated that she wished her body would look neither feminine nor masculine, but "in between." She did not want her breasts to protrude. She enjoyed oral, anal, or vaginal intercourse equally, and in her masturbation fantasies three men pleasured her at her three orifices simultaneously.

Emma was an only child. Her father was a professional man; her mother never worked. When she was between four and five, her parents built a home on barren land outside a village, where the villagers disliked "foreign invasion." Emma felt an outsider with the village children. She played mostly with boys. A feeling that she did not belong never left her. The family had their main meal at noon. Emma's mother left snacks in the refrigerator for Emma's evening meal before Emma's parents went out for the evening. Emma ate alone and put herself to sleep. This happened frequently from the time she was four years old. She was allowed to call a neighbor "when something was wrong," but she never did. Sometimes there were noises or storms outside and she became frightened when the shades rattled. She could not fall asleep. In analysis, she still had occasional insomnia and anxiety attacks at night.

Emma's mother spent the first three years of her life in an orphanage and was adopted by Emma's grandmother, whom Emma loved. Emma described her father as artistic and with a sense of humor. She adored him. He played with Emma, threw her up in the air, and did acrobatic feats with her from the time she was little. He insisted the world was rational and that nobody needed treatment. He was both paternal and maternal and always cheerful.

Emma experienced her mother as lifeless and her father as ebullient. Since Emma's father provided an affective antidote to the deadness of her mother, Emma was unable to relate to him as an erotic oedipal object. She identified with him and feared being like her mother, who never represented a genuine rival for his affections. Emma talked about her mother's lack of motherliness, her own loneliness and depression as a child. At home, her mother was often withdrawn, and a remote presence. Emma treated her toys and books as she felt treated by her mother. She did not learn to play and felt lost. The failure of Emma's mother to play with her and participate in Emma's activities as a companion created passivity and boredom and led to Emma's work inhibition. There was "something missing" between Emma and her mother. Her mother seemed distant and very sad. Emma remembers pushing in the eyes of her dolls. She was interested in building things, like her father who was an architect. But no one showed her how to play or build. Sometimes she played boys' games with a neighbor. They played in the mud and played cards. There were many little girls who played housewife. They had clothes with ruffles. She never liked to look like "little women," and wore bluejeans instead of dresses. They never got dirty; they tried to be attractive. Emma felt alienated from them, as her own mother had rejected the maternal role. Although she loved her mother, she could not identify with her. She was told she was like her father and looked like him. She remembers being put into the bathtub with an older boy where they played with each other's genitals. He was her closest friend. She did not have girlfriends until she was ten. She had her first circle of friends in high school.

At twenty-two Emma had her ovaries severed; her mother was "progressive" about it and her father "neither supported nor devalued her," but let her make her own decisions. Freud (1931) thought that women wanted to acquire the man's penis in intercourse to feel feminine, and to have a child to feel maternal. He thought femininity and motherhood went hand in hand. For Emma there was a conflict between femininity and motherhood. It was clear that she rejected motherhood; when she was "freed" from it, she could enjoy sexuality as a woman. In her creative work she identified with her father and, at least overtly, she lost her fear of becoming like her mother. Unconsciously, her creative product was a substitute child, and her creativity a substitute for motherhood.

Home life was disturbed by the parents' violent fights which usually ended in mother's inconsolable crying. Sometimes her parents did not speak to each other for days. A frightening silence reigned. Emma was fearful her parents would separate, she would lose one of them, or her father would kill her mother.

When she was thirteen she was left with a visiting girlfriend while their parents took a trip together. As a protest, the two girls decided to diet; they each lost over ten pounds. When the parents returned they were shocked and thought the girls had been ill. After that Emma developed a secret pride in her figure. She began to overeat when she was alone, but immediately vomited when she felt too full. Afterward she felt purified and her depression lifted; she could start life anew. This was how her bulimia-anorexia cycle began.

When Emma was about twenty-five her mother confided that her father had a woman friend. Emma felt very sorry for her; she became more clinging the more independent Emma became. It became clear to Emma that she needed to move away.

In her analysis, Emma's relationship with both parents functioned as resistance. She had to be sure I would not be clinging like her mother or doctrinaire like her father. She had inordinate anxiety about expressing neediness, and it took her a long time to experience me as a new object. The eating disorder indicated her feelings of deprivation by her parents. At the end of some of our sessions, Emma left me "starving," with a wish for less silence and more contact, which she could not gratify. While her actual bulimia-anorexia ritual disappeared, its characterological problem remained until much later in treatment. At times her psychoanalytic "intake" was in jeopardy: Emma learned only gradually to internalize our work.

Emma unconsciously wanted to incorporate aspects of both parents and combine them into one. She feared disidentifying with either parent, lest she might lose one. This accounted for her lack of capacity to develop gender identity. Having both sexes within her meant keeping her parents together, and led to an androgynous self-representation. As she learned to differentiate herself from each parent, a process analogous to normal separation-individuation took place. It became possible to reconstruct long periods of her lonely childhood where food was her only companion. When Emma was alone she had felt disoriented. She lost contact with a part of herself which she recovered only via her bulimia-anorexia ritual.

We reconstructed that during her childhood Emma's mother made Emma feel desolate, perhaps creating a feeling state analogous to what mother had felt in the orphanage. In Emma's associations, this sometimes led to sudden breaks of communication with me when she would become anxious and relive her childhood loneliness and her fear of death. Emma suffered from a pervasive feeling of inner emptiness; being empty or full represented a double danger. Her difficulty in associating was a sign of inner emptiness. In analysis I had to "feed her something" before she could associate on her own. She spoke of her emptiness as a "contact problem."

As a photographer, Emma developed a special ability to recognize in a person the potential to become a mirror image of a famous personality from stage or screen, now dead. The doubles she created in photographs were so convincing that they were enthusiastically accepted for exhibitions. Emma acquired an impressive position in her new field. Her work became original, artistic, and her fashion photographs of both men and women appeared in top magazines.

With her fluctuating sense of identity, she freely used disguises and poses to impersonate unexpected personality types. A masquerading quality was apparent. For an album she made as a birthday present for her father, she appeared in a long green velvet gown, looking exquisitely feminine. One might say she wore a "femininity costume" for him. The impersonation of famous women represented an unconscious wish to transform her depressed mother into an alive, beautifully feminine woman with whom Emma could have identified.

In her work for fashion magazines, Emma had a sense for the dramatic and unusual. This manifested itself in the use of extraordinary color combinations and unexpected bodily poses. Her female figures frequently exhibited a phallic, regal stance, exemplified, for instance, by a very high hairdo which, on closer inspection, achieved its height and shape from being interwoven with a cactus.

Emma also worked for men's fashion magazines. Men were photographed in precarious acrobatic poses evoking her childhood games with her father. They exhibited a magical ability to perform great physical feats defying gravity. She knew how to appeal to the homosexual component in fashion-conscious heterosexual men, as well as to homosexual men: her bisexuality was used in the service of creativity and artistic self-expression.

Patients like Emma pose a special problem for analyzing sources of psychic conflict, particularly if these are also sources of creativity. It remains a challenge to find ways of aiding psychological maturation, liberating creativity, and analyzing conflict simultaneously.

Emma's creativity was a substitute for procreation. As she had turned her aggression against herself by having herself sterilized, the question arose to what extent her artistic work was a sublimation, or reaction formation, underscoring her fear of identifying with her mother.

Pregenital sexuality, bisexual wishes, and sadomasochistic tendencies were integrated in her pictures rather than expressed in her personal life. It is a question to what extent the deeper sources of conflict are available in treatment as long as they are successfully expressed in creative work. However, as Emma's work became liberated from her conflict-laden attachment to each parent, and as she solved her separation-individuation problems in analysis, her work blossomed. One could see that its originality represented a sublimation rather than a need to deal with conflict by representing it symbolically in her photographic work.

DISCUSSION

Many analysts who study the relation of creative persons to their products, are influenced by Winnicott (1953, 1965, 1971). According to

Winnicott (1971) artistic work takes place in the "transitional space" between mother and child and reorganizes that space. In this "transitional space" there may be communication with more than one object. Elements of love and aggression motivate efforts to facilitate communication with an idealizable mother who understands the message and therefore the child. The "other" or "not-me" may not be the mother, but may represent the transformation of the primary object for the sake of experimentation by the infant—and later the adult—in the environment with things outside the self, and without participation of the object. Endowing the transitional object with fantasy, the infant becomes progressively more individuated, finding his or her way in the external world, increasingly separated from the mother he or she internalizes as a safe object. The extent to which this development is relevant for the adult creator varies, but I believe there is always a need for personal space and empathic communication with an object related to the artistic process, and a need to express idealization and restitution of an internalized object representation. Achievement of autonomy suggests that pathological aspects of the dialogue with the internal object do not interfere with productivity anymore.

Rose (1987) points out that the creative function may be blocked at a very early developmental level. The capacity for the timing of work may be disrupted as well. Relatedness disrupted by a serious, sometimes traumatic break between object and growing child may lead to severe work inhibition.

When narcissistically invested primary objects fail to give sufficient recognition to the child's independent efforts that later lead to mature achievements, the child as an adult may have a tendency toward masochistic submission to work (Novick and Novick, 1991). Sexualized and sadomasochistic fantasies also contribute to work inhibition. Severe fluctuations in self-esteem may produce obsessive doubting about creative work capacity or lead to work paralysis. Gedo (1983) discusses creative paralysis and work inhibition related to trauma. Ambivalence or splitting, originally object-directed, may subsequently be displaced or projected onto the creative product, leading to work paralysis or destruction of the product.

All three patients manifested bisexual wishes and sadomasochistic impulses endangering the self or the creative product. Emma and Laura experienced conflicts related to early traumatization by premature separation from their primary objects. This influenced libidinal and psychosexual development, which in turn led to problems of body image formation. All three patients had been put in the position of being caregivers of their mothers, early in life (Bergmann, 1985). The creative process gave impetus to their desire to free themselves from this role.

In the cases discussed, masturbation fantasies served as compromise formations; they simultaneously expressed a need for the object and a denial of that need. Fantasies also expressed a sadomasochistic bond with internal objects and the narcissistic wounds inflicted by them. Analysis of masturbation fantasies frequently released creativity.

As a result of analysis, internal objects became less threatening, superego conflicts more benign, and lasting gains in creativity were achieved. Laura's creations centered on a restitutional narcissistic fantasy designed to alleviate psychic pain. Although analysis enabled her to give up her addictions, increase her attention span, sleep undisturbed, and form successful relationships, it was unable to release her creative capabilities to the extent it helped the other two patients.

The creatively inhibited patient is usually unable to invest creative work with an adequate amount of healthy narcissism. To the extent the patient's narcissistic fantasy is rooted in an unrealistic appraisal of his or her ability, it is destined to interfere with creative activity in pathological ways. Some creative patients surrender personal narcissism in favor of their product in the service of an aspect of their ego ideal: they will sacrifice momentary gains for the sake of creative work. What they produce may tyrannize them until they become satisfied with their product, which becomes a triumph of creative self-expression.

Patients with creative disorders, such as Laura, Ellen, and Emma, need the therapeutic support of an analyst against forces that threaten to destroy the creative process or the creative product. In these three instances I found that my activity, albeit minimal, created a previously unexperienced communication and new awareness about the value of the creative product via a transference object, the analyst.

Freud's analysis of Hilda Doolittle, as described by Richards (1992), resulted in undoing her inhibited creativity. His technique provided understanding of her narcissistic injuries from early childhood, her bisexuality in her personal life and its role in her creativity. He demonstrated ". . . the capacity to understand fantasy as unreal while at the same time treating it and experiencing it as real and crucial" (p. 26). Doolittle thus was able to use this liberating communication with Freud to identify with him, leading to new compromise formations which rescued and enhanced her creativity. As Freud provided Doolittle with a capacity to identify with him as a new internalized object, her creative inhibition disappeared.

My "extraanalytic" activities involved either *seeing or hearing something concrete* that was in "creative trouble," or crisis. Meeting the need of seeing or hearing within the working frame of analysis protected the artistic products from destruction and overcame the work inhibition. One is tempted to speculate that, just as the earliest dialogue between mother and child relates to recognizing her face and hearing her voice, so my active intervention may have constituted an important affective experience crucial for creativity that was either absent during early development or needed affirmation anew because of internal deficits.

Neubauer (1987) reports several cases in which he was able to correlate disturbances in perception and memory with difficulties in object-relatedness and the capacity for internalization. He asks, "Is visual perception necessary for 'knowing' about the object, that is, for the object-self differentiation and internalization?" (p. 345). He asks whether such a "representational fault" interferes with autonomous ego development and reality relationships. Neubauer's patients needed to use the analyst's presence to enhance the ego functions of perception and memory. In my cases of work inhibition, where my "hearing or seeing something" alleviated the work crisis and promoted internalization, I felt I was augmenting early primitive affect and perception of a product related to a self-representation not yet fully formed.

At the time of my "concrete" activities, the creative products were cathected by the patients and myself in a precariously shared "narcissistic alliance," which I felt I needed to support the patient against destructive, regressive rages. I was being tested as to whether I was different from the parent in my ability to accept, symbolically, anal or urethral products or vomit. Equal in importance to early psychosexual reliving was the surfacing of narcissistic injuries related to body products, body image, and a conflicted sexual identity. Paranoidally tinged anxiety and fantasies emerged that hostile internal objects would demand death as punishment for success.

My activity helped my patients improve the "dialogue" with their internal objects from whom positive feelings had previously been withdrawn. Internalization was a result of this process.

An analysis can be looked upon as mutually creative between patient and analyst. These particular patients sought help because they could not finish a piece of work or an artistic creation. However, while seeking the analyst's help, patients do not want to share their creation with the analyst: it must be the patient's alone. In reliving childhood conflicts, the patient projects jealousy and hate onto transference, and the creative process becomes inhibited once more. The analyst must then demonstrate that in spite of these feelings the patient is permitted to be the sole creator of his or her creation without having to fear its destruction by a jealous parent. As children, the patients regarded the creation of products as jealously guarded by parents; they frequently experienced not having permission for free self-expression of their *own* creativity, while simultaneously being excluded by the parents from *their* creations. I refer to the primal scene, the oedipal experience, the creation of babies, to name but a few. Such exclusions are reexperienced in treatment; the patient does not feel entitled to have his or her "baby" without sharing it with the analyst.

Not until the analytic relationship is built on a sense of trust and the patient believes in his or her own autonomous capacities, can the patient acquire the ability to separate the actual creative product from a fantasized product in constant danger of reclamation by the parent. The creative product, proceeding from the patient's known creative self-expression, can, for the first time, belong to its creator alone.

REFERENCES

Arlow, J. A. (1969), Fantasy, memory, and reality testing. *Psychoanal. Q.*, 38:28–51.

Bergmann, M. V. (1985), The effect of role reversal on delayed marriage and maternity. *The Psychoanalytic Study of the Child*, 40:197–219. New Haven, CT: Yale University Press.

——— (1994), Creative work, work inhibitions, and their relation to internal objects. In: *The Spectrum of Psychoanalysis*, ed. A. K. Richards & A. D. Richards. Madison, CT: International Universities Press, pp. 353–371.

Chasseguet-Smirgel, J. (1991), Sadomasochism in the perversions: Some thoughts on the destruction of reality. *J. Amer. Psychoanal. Assn.*, 39:399–415.

Freud, S. (1920), Beyond the pleasure principle. *Standard Edition*, 18:3–64. London: Hogarth Press, 1955.

——— (1931), Female sexuality. *Standard Edition*, 21:221–246. London: Hogarth Press, 1961.

Gedo, J. E. (1983), *Portraits of the Artist*. New York: Guilford Press.

Gross, G. E. & Rubin, I. A. (1973), Sublimation: The study of an instinctual vicissitude. *The Psychoanalytic Study of the Child*, 27:334–359. New York: Quadrangle.

Kernberg, O. F. (in press), Psychoanalytic object relations theories. In: *Psychoanalysis: The Major Concepts*, ed. B. E. Moore. New Haven, CT: Yale University Press.

Liebert, R. S. (1983), *Michelangelo: A Psychoanalytic Study of His Life and Images*. New Haven, CT: Yale University Press.

Loewald, H. (1960), On the therapeutic action of psychoanalysis. *Internat. J. Psycho-Anal.*, 41:16–33.

——— (1980), The waning of the Oedipus complex. In: *Papers on Psychoanalysis*. New Haven, CT: Yale University Press, pp. 384–404.

Neubauer, P. (1987), Disturbances in object representation. *The Psychoanalytic Study of the Child*, 42:335–351. New Haven, CT: Yale University Press.

——— (1988), Alberto Giacommetti's fantasies and object representation. In: *Fantasy, Myth, and Reality*, ed. H. P. Blum et al. Madison, CT: International Universities Press, pp. 187–196.

Novick, J. & Novick, K. K. (1991), Some comments on masochism and the delusion of omnipotence from a developmental perspective. *J. Amer. Psychoanal. Assn.*, 39:307–331.

Oremland, J. (1989), *Michelangelo's Sistine Ceiling: A Psychoanalytic Study of Creativity.* Madison, CT: International Universities Press.

Richards, A. K. (1992), Hilda Doolittle and creativity: Freud's gift. *The Psychoanalytic Study of the Child*, 47:391–406. New Haven, CT: Yale University Press.

Rose, G. J. (1987), *Trauma and Mastery in Life and Art.* New Haven, CT: Yale University Press.

———— (1990), From ego defense to reality enhancement: Updating the analytic perspective on art. *Amer. Imago*, 47:69–79.

Sandler, J. (1990), On internal object relations. *J. Amer. Psychoanal. Assn.*, 38:859–880.

———— & Rosenblatt, B. (1962), The concept of the representational world. *The Psychoanalytic Study of the Child*, 17:128–145. New York: International Universities Press.

Tolnay, C. de (1960), *Michelangelo: Vol. 5, The Final Period.* Princeton, NJ: Princeton University Press.

Winnicott, D. W. (1953), Transitional objects and transitional phenomena. *Internat. J. Psycho-Anal.*, 24:89–97.

———— (1965), *The Maturational Processes and the Facilitating Environment.* New York: International Universities Press.

———— (1971), *Playing and Reality.* London: Tavistock.

13

THE VICISSITUDES OF SHAME IN STAGE FRIGHT

GLEN O. GABBARD, M.D.

In previous work on stage fright (Gabbard, 1979, 1983), I have stressed that the anxiety that occurs in front of an audience occurs on a continuum from "normal" concerns that one may not do the best job possible, to more severe inhibitions that interfere with careers in the arts. In this communication I shall narrow my focus to the latter category—stage fright as work inhibition. Even extraordinarily accomplished performers have become afflicted with performance anxiety of such intensity that they avoided public performances for many years.

The psychoanalytic literature on the subject suggests that stage fright is a highly overdetermined symptom that relates to a variety of intrapsychic conflicts that stem from developmental phenomena. Flugel (1938) noted that the demand the performer experiences to produce may be linked to conflicts associated with anal erotism. Bergler (1949) regarded infantile voyeuristic terror as being at the heart of stage fright. Oral fantasies of being devoured in retaliation for early voyeuristic pleasures seem to be common to many performers he had analyzed. Ferenczi (1950) connected stage fright with the performer's narcissistic intoxication, which precipitates a state of embarrassing self-observation. Castration anxiety linked to oedipal concerns and exhibitionism were observed by Fenichel (1954) as key psychodynamics of the stage fright experience.

In my own work (Gabbard, 1979) I noted several prominent themes in the stage fright experiences of performers I had treated. One involved shame related to the experience of genital inadequacy or loss of bowel or bladder control. I also noted the link between stage fright and unconscious aggressive impulses that produce a feeling of guilt that one is triumphing over oedipal and sibling rivals in the act of a successful performance. A third element I noted was the phenomenon of separation anxiety, which I linked to the rapprochement subphase of separation-individuation as described by Mahler et al. (1975).

In a subsequent discussion of the narcissistic issues in stage fright (Gabbard, 1983), I stressed how the needs of the self may be fulfilled in the act of performing. The fear that one will not receive the much-needed affirmation of the self by the audience may be pivotal in the stage fright experience. In Kohut's (1971, 1977) terms, the failure to receive a mirroring response may result in "disintegration anxiety." I also emphasized anxieties about greed inherent in performance. In this regard, a *successful* performance can be highly disconcerting to the performer who feels conflicted about having all the adulation and acclaim for himself. Moreover, being in the limelight carries with it the concern that envy will be stirred up in others so that the performer may be the target of envious attacks. Hence, both fear of failure and fear of success may be integral to the experience of stage fright.

In my continued work with patients who suffer from stage fright, particularly with those whose anxiety about performance is so intense that it undermines their professional success, I have been impressed with the pivotal role played by shame. Although each case reveals multiple determinants that converge to produce stage fright, a common thread of shame appears to underlie the major determinants that produce the symptom. In this report I shall explore five recurrent themes I have observed in severe cases of stage fright, all of which are related to the affect of shame.

Separation Anxiety

Shame may be regarded as a narcissistic disturbance that originates as the child attempts to separate and individuate in the face of parental messages that encourage the child to maintain symbiosis (Kinston, 1983). Mahler et al. (1975) observe a tendency, present even in healthy mothers, to feel hurt or rebuffed by their toddler's enthusiasm for autonomy. The researchers recorded frequent irritation by the mothers at their child's striving for separation that might be expressed as follows: "If you don't want anything to do with me, then I don't want anything to do with you either." This perception of maternal disapproval convinces the child that he or she has failed by striving to become a separate, autonomous person. Kinston (1983) has suggested that this sense of failure is the origin of the negative self-evaluation inherent in shame.

The child in the rapprochement subphase of separation-individuation is caught in a terrible dilemma between self-assertion and individuation, on the one hand, and a return to symbiosis encouraged by the

mother, on the other. The child is lured by the siren song of the symbiotic pull from mother, but recognizes at some level that succumbing
to the pull will mean self-destruction. Children who are individuating
want to be valued for their courage and mastery of independence but
feel exposed, vulnerable, and an intense sense of shame when that
affirmation is not forthcoming from the parents. As Kinston (1983)
notes, "The price of individuation is shame" (p. 219).

In the throes of this dilemma, the toddler becomes terrified that
maternal disapproval will lead to abandonment. Preoccupation with
the mother's whereabouts and a need to maintain eye contact with
her become all-consuming in this subphase of separation-individuation
(Mahler et al., 1975). An analogous state is often produced when a
performer is struck with stage fright. Actors and musicians, for example, often describe a horrible sense of aloneness and isolation when
they are performing (Gabbard, 1979). Some musicians find that they
can perform with a minimum of stage fright in ensembles or orchestras,
but are virtually paralyzed with fear if they are asked to perform solo.
The dread of abandonment may also take the form of a conviction that
members of the audience will get up and leave the theater during the
performance (Gabbard, 1979).

Even the most seasoned and accomplished performers may be
struck with this variant of stage fright at particular moments in their
careers. Such was the case with Laurence Olivier at the age of sixty.
After 45 years in the theater, he suddenly became afflicted with a
devastating case of stage fright. In a television interview (*60 Minutes*,
January 2, 1983), his description of his stage fright suggested that
separation anxiety was at the core of his experience. He had been
playing the title role in *Othello* with Frank Finlay as Iago. He began
to feel his throat constrict and felt that he could not breathe. Each night
before they went on together, he begged Finlay not to leave the stage.
Olivier even threatened that if Finlay did make his exit as planned, he
would run off the stage with him. Echoes of the rapprochement child
were seen in his request for Finlay to stay just off stage so that Olivier
could maintain eye contact with him. He felt so ashamed of his intense
concern about abandonment that he would try to turn away from the
audience. As Kinston (1983) observes, the action component of shame
is the wish to hide.

STAGE FRIGHT AS INDULGENCE IN FORBIDDEN PLEASURES

The sheer exhibitionistic thrill of performing in front of an audience
can bring on a profound sense of shame because the performer feels
a strong sense of indulging in forbidden pleasures. The following case
example will illustrate this theme.

Ms. A. was a twenty-six-year-old actress who was stricken with stage fright that had been refractory to a course of behavioral desensitization and hypnotherapy treatment. She came to analysis with a desperate wish to conquer her symptoms. As she walked from the door of my office to the couch, she was exquisitely conscious of my watching her, and was deeply concerned about how I might react to her body.

In the course of the analysis, a dream about performing led to a breakthrough in our understanding of the central themes of her stage fright. In the dream, Ms. A. was acting in a play, but felt that she did not have the right kind of clothes for the performance. She feared that she looked "sleazy." She could sense that everyone in the audience was whispering about her. As she attempted to walk across the stage, she fell flat on her face. People in the audience were saying, "God, are you disgusting! We can't stand you!" She felt a profound sense of shame and humiliation.

In her associations to the dream, Ms. A. remembered her brother's wedding. She felt her bridesmaid's dress was too revealing. It fell off her shoulder, revealing her breasts, and it was slit up the side, showing a great deal of leg. At a reception after the wedding, she remembered getting somewhat intoxicated and dancing wildly with a number of different male partners. She remembered one man watching her from the periphery shouting, "Take it off!" She felt like a stripper or a prostitute, and she hated to admit that she enjoyed being the center of attention.

She thought of the connection between a white wedding dress and virginity, and she associated to seeing the film *The Age of Innocence*. She described a sense of shame that she was not innocent because she had had an incestuous relationship with her brother (the groom at the wedding) when she was a little girl. She went on to say that she was convinced at the wedding that everyone knew of her incestuous background as they watched her dance. She also made a connection between falling in the dream and being a "fallen woman."

She recognized that when she acted, the exhilaration she felt was linked to a compelling sense that she was enjoying herself too much and deriving pleasure that was forbidden. She imagined that people in the audience would see her as the sleazy, fallen woman who had engaged in sexual activity with her own brother. The terror of being "found out" and regarded as disgusting made it extremely difficult for her to become absorbed in the performance. Instead, she was preoccupied with what the audience was thinking about her.

The incestuous aspect of the performance in Ms. A.'s case is particularly apposite because of the frequent association between performance anxiety and childhood sexual abuse. Kramer (1991) observed a characteristic cognitive impairment in sexually abused children so that they find it hard to "show what they know." Many of them could not make a classroom presentation because of anxieties about what they were showing. Ms. A.'s anxiety about what I would see as she walked from the door to the couch, or what the audience would see in her performance, was clearly linked to her fear that her incestuous past was visible. Kramer (1991) describes a similar case of a ballerina who froze up on stage.

Similar psychodynamic issues in the stage fright of a twenty-nine-year-old actor who terminated psychotherapy prematurely are described by Levinson et al. (1978). This patient's main symptom was performance anxiety, and he had sought treatment because of how the anxiety impinged on his career. He was an only child and had a highly seductive mother who created feelings of jealousy in his father. As a child, the patient had been a genital exhibitionist, and when he was acting on stage, he became consciously aware of a profound sense of dread that a successful performance would make women in the audience fall in love with him.

Although shame and guilt are variously defined, one way they can be differentiated involves the dimension of exposure. Whereas guilt is often connected with a secret transgression, shame is usually applied to situations in which a transgression is publicly exposed. The anxiety associated with performing before an audience is often linked to a feeling of shame that one's worst secrets (involving incestuous or otherwise forbidden indulgences) are visible for everyone to see.

THE DREAD OF SUCCESS

The literature regarding the connection between shame and failure is controversial. For example, M. Lewis (1991) defines shame as a combination of an evaluation of one's action, thought, or behavior as a failure and an associated generalization of that failure to a more global self-evaluation. He differentiates embarrassment from shame by pointing out how embarrassment can occur with a compliment, even though no self-evaluation of failure has occurred. In my view, this distinction is specious because it stays at the level of cognition but ignores the unconscious meaning of success.

Shame frequently accompanies success and the experience of receiving acclamation from an audience. Shame is connected with the *unconscious* assessment of the self as greedy, basking in the limelight. Paradoxically, success may be experienced as a *failure to be selfless*. There are often strong parental prohibitions about selfish strivings, and performers receiving acclaim may be ashamed that they are not living up to parental expectations of selflessness. Shame may also be associated with the feeling of having to see the audience and receiving undeserved adulation. This theme, of course, resonates with the fundamental dilemma of separation-individuation: success as an autonomous individual risks parental censure.

Mr. B. was a forty-year-old professional man who played the organ as a hobby, but was paralyzed with stage fright when he tried to perform in public. When a church organist was taken ill, he was asked to substitute at the last minute. The following day in his analysis, he reported that he had gotten through the pieces required by the church service, but he also said that he worried throughout his performance about the compliments he would receive after the service. He particularly dreaded everyone hugging him and congratulating him. He said to his analyst, "I dread the thought of people appreciating me."

His analyst asked him what made him so anxious about that experience. Mr. B. replied that "it feels like I've done something bad. By playing well, that is, I've done something bad. In many ways I think I'm a better organist than the woman who plays regularly. I was terribly afraid that people in the congregation would make comparisons and think that I'm better than she is. I guess you could say I'm afraid that I'm going to feel superior."

The analyst made an observation at this point: "Maybe you enjoy feeling superior and that's what upsets you." Mr. B. replied, "But it's not right for me to enjoy it. The ideal person I would like to be is a person who feels equal to everybody. That's the way I was brought up. I don't want to come across as superior or snobbish. I have no right to feel that way. I must remember my place. As I played yesterday, I found myself saying that, even though I was doing better than the regular organist, my life is still a mess. I kept telling myself not to get carried away."

Mr. B.'s frank disclosures about his thought processes during his performance reveal the link between his stage fright and feelings of shame about his success. The positive evaluation of the self in the act of performance clashes with his parental socialization, which was to view himself as equal to others. In addition to the shame, Mr. B. clearly was experiencing guilt feelings about the meaning of his performance as an act of killing off rivals, a theme that was traced back to intense sibling rivalry when he was a child. This aspect of Mr. B.'s stage fright relates to what Modell (1971) terms a "universal primal fantasy": to have something good means that somebody else will be deprived (Gabbard, 1983).

EXHIBITIONISM AND GENITAL INADEQUACY

In his explication of the shame-prone state, Mayman (1974) notes that side by side with the excitement and exhilaration of early childhood nudity is the anxiety that one's genitals will be regarded by others as laughably insufficient and pathetic. The sense of being exposed and vulnerable to ridicule from the audience is a common experience of most performers. Stage fright dreams often appear to be variations of this theme, as in the following case example.

Mr. C. was a twenty-nine-year-old actor who lived in terror of forgetting his lines on stage. He entered psychoanalytic psychotherapy to understand the basis of this terror. One particular dream he reported early in the process was useful in helping us identify the origins of his fears.

In Mr. C.'s dream, he was late for an entrance in the first act of a play. He was hurrying into his costume backstage and had no time for makeup. He could not find the hat he was supposed to wear. He could only find a woman's hat and was growing increasingly desperate because the actors on stage were running out of ad libs to cover the lateness of his entrance. He put on a tall, white, woman's hat and rushed onto the stage. However, after he was on the stage, he recognized that the white hat was dirtied by brown makeup. His performance was awful. He could not remember his lines, and he found himself terribly concerned about what impression he had made on a beautiful young woman in the front row of the theater.

I asked Mr. C. what came to mind about the dream, and he responded that he felt humiliated because he was unable to perform. The dream depicted his worse fear as an actor.

I asked Mr. C. if anything came to mind about the woman's white hat that he wore in the dream. He said that it reminded him a bit of a top hat like a magician wore. He then remembered seeing a magic act in which a stage magician had a collapsed top hat that sprung open when he slapped it against his hand. This memory led him to think about the process of an erection. He wondered if not being able to find his hat in the dream represented his fear that his penis was small and shriveled instead of erect. He then noted that when he dreamed of having intercourse, he often was unable to penetrate the woman's vagina.

As he continued to associate to the dream, he connected the brown-colored makeup on the white hat to fecal soiling. He wondered how homosexuals felt when they soiled their penises with feces during anal coitus. Mr. C. then associated to a performance artist in New York he had read about who defecated on the stage.

I interpreted to him that his fear of performing on stage seemed to parallel his concerns about his sexual performance. His wish to have his erect penis admired by the beautiful woman in the dream was transformed into a humiliating and shameful spectacle in which he lost bowel control.

Mr. C. speculated that he was being punished because the beautiful woman in the audience reminded him of a married woman he lusted after. If he succeeded in his performance in the dream, he would have stolen her from her husband, so he needed to make himself suffer.

Mr. C.'s dream reveals the extent to which performing was connected in his unconscious with phallic exhibitionism. Freud (1900) observes:

> It is only in our childhood that we are seen in inadequate clothing both by members of our family and by strangers—nurses, maid-servants, and visitors; and it is only then that we feel no shame at our nakedness. We can observe how undressing has an almost intoxicating effect on many children even in their later years, instead of making them feel ashamed. They laugh and jump about and slap themselves, while their mother, or whoever else may be there, reproves them and says: "Ugh! Shocking! You mustn't ever do that!" [p. 244].

For Mr. C., his performance revived that childhood wish to romp about in the buff. Shame was related to his conviction that the audience would respond with the same harsh reprimands he experienced from his parents as a little boy. Moreover, as indicated in the analysis of the dream, Mr. C. was concerned that the ridicule and humiliation would be connected with the inadequacy of his genital display.

Shame is also connected with fantasies of fecal soiling. Kinston (1983) comments that since bowel control and separation-individuation are concurrent developmental issues, negative valuations of the self are linked with filth and feces, and the associated object relations may be regarded as sordid and disgusting. Mayman (1974) emphasizes that shame stemming from phallic exhibitionistic issues often extends to potentially humiliating problems of bowel or bladder control.

Another feature of Mr. C.'s dream is that the audience appears indifferent to his genital display. This manifest content is typical of many stage fright dreams in which the performer is either naked or partially clothed. In a detailed analysis of such dreams, Myers (1989) discovered that these dreams may represent a repetition of painful and traumatic childhood experience. The indifference of the onlookers represents memories of parents and others who failed to notice the child's exhibitionistic display. No matter how much the child tried to attract the parents' attention, the child always experienced the parents as not noticing, which led to feelings of low self-esteem and rejection. In this regard the repetitive nature of such dreams may represent an unconscious effort to master actively the passively experienced trauma.

Looking, Showing, and the Primal Scene

Much of the stage fright experience revolves around issues of looking and showing. Voyeurism is, of course, the flip side of exhibitionism, and as Wurmser (1981) notes, shame punishes us as much for being caught in the act of looking as it does for exposing ourselves. Conflicts around seeing something forbidden may be activated in performance through identification with the audience. Over 70 years ago, Melanie Klein (1923) observed that watching a performance in a darkened auditorium (whether at theaters or concerts) frequently has the unconscious meaning of the primal scene. In this regard stage fright may set in with the awareness that the audience is observing a forbidden act on stage.

Ms. D. was a thirty-five-year-old concert pianist who had come to psychotherapy for reasons that were apparently unrelated to performance. Although she had mild anxiety at the beginning of a performance, she had never experienced stage fright at an intensity level that interfered with her ability to play piano. She was shocked, then, when she "froze" in the middle of a performance during her first pregnancy. She was playing the "Bravura" passage of a work by Chopin when she suddenly went blank. She had a visual image of a blue-eyed wolf staring at her from the audience, and her heart froze. (As far as I could ascertain, Ms. D. was completely unaware of Freud's "Wolf Man" and certainly never made a link in her own mind with that case.)

After being stuck for what seemed like an eternity, but probably was no more than a few seconds, she recovered and continued her concert. As she recounted the experience in the psychotherapy, she noted that in her mind's eye, the face of the wolf was transformed into her own face staring at her from a distance.

I asked her what was unique about the performance situation that led her to be paralyzed with stage fright when she had never been afflicted before. She recalled looking at the keyboard and noting how obviously pregnant she was (she was seven months pregnant at the time). She said, with a nervous laugh, that the audience clearly could see that she was a sexual person. She felt a deep sense of shame connected with this thought and wondered if the audience felt embarrassed at seeing her.

In this scenario, looking and showing are linked by the patient's identification with the audience. Ms. D.'s fantasy that she was watching her own performance is a common experience among musicians and other performing artists. Part of the stage fright reaction is depersonalization, in which an observing self is split off from a performing self so that performers may experience themselves as actually watching their own performance (Gabbard, 1979, 1983; Kaplan, 1969).

Ms. D. had conscious memories of primal scene experiences from her own childhood, and the combination of her pregnancy and the exhibitionism of performance led her to identify with the audience as observers of a primal-scene equivalent. In this case, however, the roles were reversed so that she was the one engaging in sexual gratification while the audience watched. Arlow (1961) discusses a particular form of a typical dream involving the act of defecating as a public spectacle. He states that such dreams portray a regressive representation of the primal scene, in which defecating has replaced intercourse. He also notes the importance of role reversal in such dreams. Whereas in the original primal scene, the child is the one who experiences the humiliation of being an uninvolved observer, the tables are turned in the adult dream, where others observe the dreamer in an act of instinctual gratification. Arlow observed that there is often a wish to avenge oneself on one's parents by this role reversal.

CONCLUDING COMMENTS

When stage fright is severe enough to be debilitating, shame is likely to be central to the experience. The affect of shame manifests itself in several variations, five of which are explored in this chapter: (1) anxiety about separation and abandonment, (2) fear of being seen as indulging oneself in forbidden pleasures, (3) fear of success, (4) exhibitionistic wishes associated with fears of genital inadequacy, and (5) derivatives of primal-scene experiences manifested by conflicts over looking and showing.

This overview of the shame dimension of stage fright reflects how the language of object relations may be more suited to shame than instinctual considerations (Kinston, 1983). As Wurmser (1981) stresses, a fear of unlovability is at the heart of shame, and this conviction leads to the terror of abandonment that accompanies stage fright. The combination of a negative evaluation of the self with a fantasy of how the "other" (represented by the audience) is reacting to one's display are irreducible features of the stage fright experience that firmly embeds it in an object-relations context. One of the paradoxes involved in performance is that the performing artist may deal with shame connected with the fundamental separation-individuation issues by attempting to garner public acclaim, only to feel ashamed when that acclaim is finally forthcoming. In that regard, some performers feel they "can't win" because shame is inevitable, no matter how the audience responds.

H. B. Lewis (1971) stresses the possibility of another relational perspective on shame. She states that shame may be an early affective state universal in infants that is designed to repair ruptures in the emotional bonds with important objects in the milieu. The experience of shame may produce an empathic response in significant persons in the environment, who then strive to heal the rupture.

The quest for lovability is an ongoing endeavor in the life of a performing artist. Each foray from the stage wings into the spotlight carries with it both the risk of humiliation and the hope of validation for the self as an autonomous and individuated agent. Shame serves as the great leveler. The old theatrical expression, "you're only as good as your last performance," is emblematic of the repetitive nature of the performer's task. Each performance is a new beginning where the self is on the line again. Mastery is never complete, and the impossible quest of the artist provides live performance with an electricity that can never be captured on tape.

REFERENCES

Arlow, J. A. (1961), A typical dream. *J. Hillside Hosp.*, 10:154–158.
Bergler, E. (1949), On acting and stage fright. *Psychiat. Q. Suppl.*, 23:313–319.
Fenichel, O. (1954), *The Psychoanalytic Theory of Neurosis.* New York: Norton.
Ferenczi, S. (1950), *Further Contributions to the Theory and Technique of Psychoanalysis.* New York: Basic Books.
Flugel, J. C. (1938), Stage fright and anal erotism. *Brit. J. Med. Psychol.*, 17:189–196.
Freud, S. (1900), The interpretation of dreams. *Standard Edition*, 4 & 5. London: Hogarth Press, 1953.
Gabbard, G. O. (1979), Stage fright. *Internat. J. Psycho-Anal.*, 60:383–392.
——— (1983), Further contributions to the understanding of stage fright: Narcissistic issues. *J. Amer. Psychoanal. Assn.*, 31:423–441.
Kaplan, D. (1969), On stage fright. *Drama Rev.*, 14:60–83.
Kinston, W. (1983), Theoretical context for shame. *Internat. J. Psycho-Anal.*, 64:213–226.
Klein, M. (1923), Infant analysis. In: *Contributions to Psychoanalysis: 1921–1945.* London: Hogarth Press, 1948, pp. 87–116.
Kohut, H. (1971), *The Analysis of the Self.* New York: International Universities Press.
——— (1977), *The Restoration of the Self.* New York: International Universities Press.
Kramer, S. (1991), Residues of incest. In: *Adult Analysis and Childhood Sexual Abuse*, ed. H. Levine. Hillsdale, NJ: Analytic Press, pp. 149–170.
Levinson, P., McMurray, L., Podell, P. & Weiner, H. (1978), Causes for the premature interruption of psychotherapy by private practice patients. *Amer. J. Psychiat.*, 135:826–830.

Lewis, H. B. (1971), *Shame and Guilt in Neurosis*. New York: International Universities Press.

Lewis, M. (1991), Self-conscious emotions and the development of self. *J. Amer. Psychoanal. Assn.*, 39(Suppl.):45–73.

Mahler, M., Pine, F. & Bergman, A. (1975), *The Psychological Birth of the Human Infant*. New York: Basic Books.

Mayman, M. (1974), The shame experience, the shame dynamic, and shame personalities in psychotherapy. Presented at George S. Klein Memorial Meeting, unpublished.

Modell, A. H. (1971), The origin of certain forms of preoedipal guilt and the implications for a psychoanalytic theory of affects. *Internat. J. Psycho-Anal.*, 52:337–346.

Myers, W. A. (1989), A transference resistance in male patients with inhibition of urination in public places. *Psychoanal. Q.*, 58:245–250.

Wurmser, L. (1981), *The Mask of Shame*. Baltimore, MD: Johns Hopkins University Press.

14

AGGRESSION, BODY IMAGE, AND WORK INHIBITION

Stavroula Beratis, M.D.

Inherent in the fundamental psychoanalytic concepts of primary narcissism (Freud, 1914), undifferentiated phase (Hartmann et al., 1946), and normal autistic and symbiotic states of mental development (Mahler and La Perriere, 1965) is the notion that initially the child cannot distinguish between his self and the world around him. Among the conditions that facilitate the differentiating process of self from object there is a cognitive perceptual input, mentioned by Freud (1915) as the beginning of reality ego, which operates through the reception of stimuli from close and distant receptors. Actually, the perceptual input from close tactile receptors, when the infant touches or sucks parts of his body, results in the registration of two simultaneous sensations, which constitute a unique experience, leading gradually to the distinction between the self and the nonself (Freud, 1923; Hoffer, 1950). On the other hand, vision offers a more comprehensive image of the body parts, leading gradually to the synthesis and integration of the assembled pieces.

In addition to the perceptual side of the child's cognitive apparatus, what is of central importance in the differentiating process between self and nonself is the sequence of partial deprivation and of gratification of needs as regulated by the maternal object. Because of the complete helplessness of the human infant, mother controls the provision of protection, care, and food. The child, in a state of partial deprivation, which includes expectation, longing for gratification, and a certain degree of frustration, realizes that someone from the outside has to intervene in order to feel satisfied.

The human infant is born unprepared to face the world on its own. The elementary ego of the young child has to be complemented and supported by the mother's ego. The mother has to protect the child from internal and external stimuli and provide a balance between gratification of needs and deprivation. The child, according to the pleasure principle, has to be protected from being overwhelmed and traumatized by the expression of libidinal and aggressive impulses (Freud, 1924; Hartmann, 1948; Hoffer, 1950). All this implies a libidinal investment of the infant's own body as well as of the outer world, and a discharge of the aggressive impulses, mainly through the muscular system, away from the self to the nonself. Libidinal investment of the self and object has to outweigh the aggressive investment.

All the above processes, the objective perception of reality, the balance between gratification of needs and partial deprivation, the predominance of the libidinal over the aggressive investment, and the interplay of impulses, are necessary conditions for a successful differentiation between the self and the nonself. And what is instrumental for the achievement of these conditions is the presence of a "good enough mother" (Winnicott, 1958) whose ministrations contribute to the successful initiation and evolution of the various developmental paths. The more flexibly adjustable the mother is to the infant's cues in achieving an optimal responsiveness, the better equipped the child becomes in differentiating successfully the mental representation of the self and the nonself.

The gradual creation of self and object mental representations is a laborious task, involving initially introjective and projective mechanisms, which gradually become elaborate identificatory processes under the dynamic influence of the child's ability of fantasying (Sandler and Nagera, 1963). The mental representation of the self includes the representation of the body image or the body self. It should be noted here that the notions of the body image and body self, rather than body ego, are meant in the way Hartmann (1950) and Jacobson (1964) described them, as the mental representation of one's own person, while the ego, in accordance with the structural model, is conceptualized as a highly organized mental structure having a variety of functions.

Safe and stable mental representation of the body image in normal development is characterized by a predominantly libidinal rather than aggressive investment of self and object, accomplished through the instrumental presence of the "good enough" mothering person, the internalization of satisfactory experiences with her, and the child's fantasies as they modify the internal objects and the interaction with them.

The psychological achievement of stable, libidinally invested self-object representations are considered among the important conditions that enable the individual to move smoothly along developmental lines, to preserve a balance in the fluctuations of his self-esteem, and through feeling loved and loving to complete successfully the tasks of adolescence so as to enter adulthood with the potential of being socially and professionally productive.

When, however, the process of separation-individuation takes place with a mother who is unpredictable, unresponsive to her infant's needs, unable to adjust flexibly to his cues, in short, when the mother-child relationship during that phase of development is inadequate, reality becomes a series of traumatic experiences for the infant. Under such circumstances, the infant is bound to resort to manifestations of aggression, experiencing helpless rage, a situation that leads to the development of mental representations of object and self that are characterized by defects caused by the destructive component of the aggressive drive, which dominates the libidinal component. Solnit (1982) describes these defects as equivalents of fractures. He believes that such fractures, if not repaired, may result in a permanent loss of function, in particular a loss in the capacity for basic trust and in a permanent impairment of the ability for object relations.

In what follows I shall describe clinical material derived from the case of a patient who presented with an inhibition in his academic work, an inhibition that seemed to be related to a defective body image. The damage, however, was not as excessive and permanent as that described in Solnit's cases. My hypothesis is that this patient was confronted with the burden of his own intense aggression not as early in his development as Solnit's cases. This spared him from a permanent impairment of function. In his subsequent development, however, an intense castration fear and castrated self-image developed, resulting in a serious work inhibition.

<h2 style="text-align:center">HISTORY</h2>

Mr. B., a twenty-five-year-old single man, sought psychoanalytic treatment because he found himself unable to continue his studies in medical school. He suffered from a work and learning inhibition of several years' duration.

The patient was an only child. While in elementary school, he thought of himself as a "bright boy," doing relatively well in academic subjects but very poorly in athletic activities. During adolescence, his school performance deteriorated, and he thought of himself as both physically and intellectually impaired. He had few friends; he was not very popular among his classmates.

Mr. B. described his father as a brilliant and knowledgeable person who was, however, never satisfied with his professional life. He wanted to be a physician, but was "just a chemist," complaining all his life about the misfortunes that had supposedly interfered with the realization of his ambitions. The patient described his mother as a competent, intelligent woman. She worked as a teacher and was constantly interfering in both his own and his father's life. It was difficult for Mr. B. to move away from her emotionally, their interaction being characterized by overstimulation and ambivalence. In his heterosexual relationships, the woman seemed to play the dominant role. Each of several relationships was characterized by a sequence of separations and reunions as he refused to satisfy the woman's wish for a marital commitment.

OEDIPAL CONFLICT AND DEFECTIVE SELF-IMAGE

During the course of the patient's analytic treatment the central themes were his feelings of inferiority with respect to his father, and his defective self-image. While he was very close to his mother, he considered his father, who was preoccupied with his work and spent little time with his son, as absent. Admiring his father for his intellectual gifts, he saw himself as very little in comparison to him. He found him antagonistic, with a derogatory attitude toward him. Mr. B. often felt angry, complaining that his father did not give him enough, was not sufficiently supportive and encouraging, and did not exercise with him to help him become a strong man.

The patient's defective self-image included intellectual and somatic elements. He saw himself as unable to remember well and slow in his ability to learn. He experienced his body as placid, lacking in strength, as being too narrow in the shoulders and too large in the hips. This defective self-image became clear in a dream reported early in the analysis. In it, there were several people with missing parts—limbs, parts of their trunk, and internal organs. Among these mutilated people, there was a physician with part of his brain missing who could not function adequately, being slow in his capacity to think and to express himself verbally. This person reminded him of a physician he knew who had deserted his wife and lived as a homosexual. In his associations, the patient brought up a retarded girl who had hydrocephalus and spina bifida, was brain-damaged and damaged in the lower part of her body so that she was unable to think well and walk properly. He insisted that as she could not function well, she would be better off dead. In subsequent weeks, Mr. B. worked on the theme of his defective self-image as it was represented by the brain-damaged homosexual physician and the retarded girl with the spina bifida.

He reported childhood memories related to a castrated, defective self-image. When the patient was four years old, his father became sick with poliomyelitis and was bedridden for a long time, unable to move or to speak. The patient recalled feeling very frightened, wondering if his father was ever going to regain his voice. He also had a vivid memory of a little boy, a close friend of his, who could not walk or speak properly, again because of poliomyelitis. At about the same time he remembered being frightened by a physician who approached him from behind, holding a huge syringe. He recalled that, when he was four or five years old, after he himself had recovered from an illness, he was running downhill toward his parents to show them how fast he was, and fell down. He hurt himself and thought he had been badly damaged. When he was eleven to twelve years old, he was hospitalized for meningitis, feeling weak and frightened. Soon after being discharged from the hospital he developed a persistent interest in building up a very complicated mechanical model. This interest had an obsessive quality. Every time he added a piece to the model, he would show it to his parents. At some point the model fell down and broke, which upset him deeply. He commented with sadness that even though his parents helped him to put it back together, the model was never again the same.

Mr. B. blamed his father for feeling defective. He complained that his father interfered with his physical and intellectual development, depriving him of activities that might have promoted his bodily strength and his intellectual growth. He repeatedly mentioned childhood scenes in which his father took away a toy car he loved, which used to move freely and whistle. He also recalled an incident where he himself had taken apart this emotionally invested toy without being able to stop himself. He subsequently managed to put it back together with the help of his mother, who intervened and controlled his destructive urge. He reported several incidents purporting to show how his father's stinginess deprived him of activities that might have promoted his physical and intellectual growth. At the same time, he recalled that as a child he used to steal money from his father's pocket, trying to take what his father refused to give him.

Preoedipal Conflicts

The patient often reported material indicating the effect of oral and anal aggression on his psychic life. He recalled that at times he had fantasies in which flying reptiles would attack his head, biting off pieces of his memory. Another fantasy of his was being a lethargic snake that would sometimes wake up and bite. He equated this action with efficient studying. In a repetitive childhood dream, he would fall off a platform to find himself in a scary world, where a female monster with big mouth and long tail ate raw fish and offered him some of her food.

Since his childhood years, Mr. B. had been involved in voyeuristic activities. He would watch his mother getting dressed or undressed and would stare at her pubic area, unable to take his eyes away from it. This behavior continued throughout his adolescence. As a child he had watched his parents having sexual intercourse. As an adolescent he watched through windows as women were getting undressed. During the same period, he abused his dog, trying to "break the dog's pride" by depriving him of food, locking him up alone, not taking him out to have a bowel movement and then punishing him for having a bowel movement inside his room.

DISCUSSION

The patient's castrated self-image was a central issue in his pathology. He experienced himself as missing parts of his body, especially his brain. This intense castration complex was reinforced by oral- and anal-sadistic fantasies corresponding to preoedipal fixations. It became obvious that aggressive impulses were not adequately fused with libido so as to be neutralized during the course of development (Freud, 1924; Hartmann, 1948; Solnit, 1972). The mother-child relationship was at the same time overstimulating and frustrating, not allowing for a smooth developmental process. The patient felt bewildered and angry, not knowing if the maternal object, like the monster in his fantasy, was going to devour him or offer him food. He had difficulties separating from the maternal object, apparently because of inadequate libidinization of his body and non-well established self- and object-constancy (Mahler and La Perriere, 1965). In order to deal with separation anxiety, he identified with his mother, incorporating female characteristics in his self-image, developing object relations in which dependency and helplessness predominated.

The patient entered the oedipal phase without having resolved adequately the task of separation-individuation and without having achieved stable object constancy and self-image representation. Conversely, derivatives of non-neutralized aggressive energy had a constant impact on various developmental tasks and processes, influencing his behavior and the formation of his psychic structure, including his body image. Aggressive fantasies related to oedipal conflicts were added to aggressive elements related to preoedipal issues, burdening his psychic apparatus. In this context his castration complex was especially aggravated by an admixture of oral- and anal-sadistic elements.

Various factors seem to have contributed to the displacement and localization of the effects of castration from the lower part of his body and genitals to the central nervous system and his intellectual functioning (Pearson, 1952; Buxbaum, 1964). Such factors were the early experiences of the effects of poliomyelitis on his father and his childhood boyfriend, as well as his own meningitis which temporarily affected his academic performance. In addition, throughout the patient's development, special emphasis was given to the intellectual capacities of his father, who was internalized as an "intellectual giant" impossible to compete with. In the patient's fantasies and their behavioral derivatives the elements of competition between his father and himself were always intellectual and work achievement.

The patient's aggressive fantasies, projected to this paternal mental representation, created a punitive, castrating internal father figure. This impressive paternal introject immobilized the patient's ego, inhibiting his capacity for work. He allowed himself to achieve up to a certain point, but then he had to inhibit and immobilize himself because he did not dare to destroy the "intellectual father-giant." His intellectual and work activities were equated internally with destroying the father. Instead, he turned his aggression against himself and saw himself as defective, as if parts of his body were missing. The work inhibition that plagued the patient was an extension and derivative of his defective, castrated self-image, serving moral masochistic needs and unconscious wishes for a female identification, allowing for the preservation in fantasy of the passive homosexual attachment to the father in the context of a negative Oedipus complex (Freud, 1940). The paternal introject, elevated to a special status and supplanting the parental authority (Sandler et al., 1963), remained the object of the patient's admiration as well as competition, attracting both passive homosexual wishes of penetration from behind, and aggressive fantasies in which he was the sadistic, active castrator, as manifested in his behavior toward the dog.

The patient's idealized self- and object representations were not modified and integrated into a stable structure of an approachable ego ideal that might facilitate the establishment of goals leading to ego activity and maturation. They functioned as constant reminders of the patients' deficiencies, reinforcing his feelings of inadequacy, his aggressive, competitive fantasies about his father, and his defense constellation in being dependent and castrated. The work inhibition, a result of the patient's aggression turned inward, revealed his castrated self-image, protecting the paternal mental representation from being destroyed and at the same time preserving the passive homosexual attachment and identification with the castrated maternal object, thus alleviating separation anxiety.

REFERENCES

Buxbaum, E. (1964), The parent's role in the etiology of learning disabilities. *The Psychoanalytic Study of the Child*, 19:421–477. New York: International Universities Press.

Freud, S. (1914), On narcissism: An introduction. *Standard Edition*, 14:67–102. London: Hogarth Press, 1957.

—— (1915), Instincts and their vicissitudes. *Standard Edition*, 14:109–140. London: Hogarth Press, 1957.

—— (1923), The ego and the id. *Standard Edition*, 19:3–66. London: Hogarth Press, 1961.

—— (1924), The economic problem of masochism. *Standard Edition*, 19:157–170. London: Hogarth Press, 1961.

—— (1940), An outline of psychoanalysis. *Standard Edition*, 23:141–207. London: Hogarth Press, 1964.

Hartmann, H. (1948), Comments on the psychoanalytic theory of instinctual drives. *Psychoanal. Q.*, 17:368–388.

—— (1950), Comments on the psychoanalytic theory of the ego. *The Psychoanalytic Study of the Child*, 5:74–96. New York: International Universities Press.

—— Kris, E. & Loewenstein, R. M. (1946), Comments on the formation of psychic structure. *The Psychoanalytic Study of the Child*, 2:11–38. New York: International Universities Press.

Hoffer, W. (1950), Development of the body ego. *The Psychoanalytic Study of the Child*, 5:18–23. New York: International Universities Press.

Jacobson, E. (1964), *The Self and the Object World*. New York: International Universities Press.

Mahler, M. S. & La Perriere, K. (1965), Mother-child interaction during separation-individuation. *Psychoanal. Q.*, 34:483–498.

Pearson, G. H. J. (1952), A survey of learning difficulties in children. *The Psychoanalytic Study of the Child*, 7:322–386. New York: International Universities Press.

Sandler, J., Holder, A. & Meers, D. (1963), The ego ideal and the ideal self. *The Psychoanalytic Study of the Child*, 18:139–158. New York: International Universities Press.

—— & Nagera, H. (1963), The metapsychology of fantasy. In: *From Safety to Superego*, ed. J. Sandler. New York: Guilford Press, 1987, pp. 90–120.

Solnit, A. J. (1972), Aggression: A view of theory building in psychoanalysis. *J. Amer. Psychoanal. Assn.*, 20:435–450.

—— (1982), Developmental perspectives of self and object constancy. *The Psychoanalytic Study of the Child*, 37:201–218. New Haven, CT: Yale University Press.

Winnicott, D. W. (1958), The capacity to be alone. *Internat. J. Psycho-Anal.*, 39:416–420.

15

GENITAL SELF-EXAMINATION: THE PRECURSOR OF EXAMINATION ANXIETY IN WOMEN

ELEANOR GALENSON, M.D.

As the number of women pursuing professional careers has increased during the past 20 years, more and more female patients present symptoms that reflect their conflicts over various aspects of performing as wives and mothers on the one hand, and as working professionals on the other. In my psychoanalytic practice, I began to notice some 15 years ago that many of my women patients complained of hitherto uncommon symptoms, which recurred periodically; this was particularly evident in a group of women who were doctoral candidates in various fields of study. They suffered from a variety of psychological problems that differed considerably from one another, and they were all intelligent and ambitious people who were eager to excel in their particular area of work.

It was after several years of analytic work during which various other symptoms had been explored, that this particular group of women seemed to develop a more specific group of symptoms in connection with university examinations, particularly when there was competition with men and when the examinations were oral. I began to realize that these symptom patterns were familiar to me, that I had encountered them before in an entirely different age group and in a different setting—namely, in the nineteen- to twenty-four-month-old infant girls whom Roiphe and I studied in the course of our research on the emergence of early genitality (Roiphe and Galenson, 1981). We were able to delineate a normal developmental sequence of early genital awareness which was followed by symptoms related to the three major anxieties—fear of object loss, fear of anal loss, and castration anxiety. This cluster of symptoms appeared to represent preoedipal castration reactions related to the awareness of genital differences. Although these reactions were different in girls than in boys, there were far-reaching consequences in both sexes.

I believe there is a connection between the preoedipal castration reactions of infant girls and the examination reactions of adult women in that both represent anxiety related to the female genital anatomical structure as contrasted to the male urinogenital conformation. Clinical material from the analytic treatment of two women patients illustrates the remarkable similarity between the symptom patterns during such widely separated eras of life and the dynamic connection between them.

THE ADULT CLINICAL SYNDROME

Ms. A., a twenty-six-year-old woman who had undertaken psychoanalytic treatment because of severe recurrent anxiety attacks, was the second of three children in an intellectually ambitious family. She had been encouraged to seek professional education, unlike her mother who had remained at home while her children were growing up. Ms. A. was an excellent student who had been socially adept from her early childhood, but her feelings of physical unattractiveness had persisted despite the considerable admiration she received from family and peers.

A brother was born when Ms. A. was fifteen months old. She seemed to have been convinced that this baby was hers, a fantasy that was encouraged by her parents and strengthened even more as her mother retreated into a postpartum depression. Her first severe anxiety attack occurred at age sixteen, during the summer before she was to go off to college. This attack was accompanied by mild feelings of depersonalization and fears that her parents would die. She sought psychiatric consultation during her first year in college after she had "blanked out" during an examination, received some help from psychotherapy during the next three college years, but undertook analytic treatment with me upon graduation since her symptoms persisted.

Ms. A. recalled that she had experienced anxiety before examinations in high school, yet she had been able to sustain her position at the head of her class academically. But when she was intellectually challenged in college where she had to compete with male students for the first time, Ms. A. began to study incessantly for fear that she might miss some minor point in the assignment. Yet the more she studied, the more confused she became in regard to the basic principles she was attempting to understand. Evenings became a continuous torture of gorging herself with food in order to be able to concentrate on her work and then loathing herself the next morning for these eating binges.

By the end of her first year in college, Ms. A. had developed a number of rituals, some of which she recalled having had to perform between her eighth and twelfth years. She also had to do a good deed every day: she had to telephone her mother to inquire about her health. These calls inevitably precipitated a quarrel between mother and daughter which ended with both of them in tears. Although the ambivalent nature of Ms. A.'s relationship with her mother was certainly not new, it had now reached a far greater intensity.

Ms. A. soon developed several additional rituals as her anxiety increased: hand washing, returning to her kitchen over and over to make sure the stove had been turned off; a number of bedtime rituals were necessary as well. A new symptom appeared toward the end of her first college year—a mounting hypochondriasis which was accompanied by sexual fears and preoccupations connected with a new relationship with a boyfriend. As she became obsessed with the flood of fantasies that seriously interfered with her ability to concentrate, Ms. A. finally sought psychoanalytic treatment when she graduated.

The major theme of her fantasies consisted of repeated exposure of her naked body to a group of men who would then laugh at her as she tried to cover her genitals. The fantasies reminded Ms. A. of the disgust she had felt when she had seen her mother's body as they undressed in a locker room during Ms. A.'s adolescence. She also recalled the "huge breasts and protruding abdomens" of the other women in the locker room, which reminded her of her mother's body as she thought it must have looked during her pregnancy with Ms. A.'s brother. With the return of these memories, Ms. A. developed an amenorrhea that persisted for four months during which Ms. A. was certain she was pregnant, although several pregnancy tests were negative.

After Ms. A. was graduated from college, she entered a graduate program in preparation for a professional career. She improved steadily until the final period of her graduate studies when her bulimia, hypochondriasis, menstrual irregularity, and dissatisfaction with her appearance all recurred as she anticipated each impending graduate school examination. These examinations appeared to represent a "showdown" during which Ms. A. thought her intellectual inadequacy would be exposed.

Her symptoms represented three types of anxiety: fear of separation, fear of anal loss, and anxiety over her genitals which Ms. A. regarded unconsciously as having been seriously damaged. While feelings of intellectual inadequacy were indeed equated with Ms. A.'s genital concerns, penis envy was by no means the only dynamic constellation underlying the preexamination symptoms that emerged.

Ms. A.'s eight-year analysis yielded a quite satisfactory analytic result in that she was able to complete her professional studies and establish a heterosexual relationship which eventuated in a successful marriage. However, she was never completely convinced that she could rely on her intellectual capacity. Periods of self-doubt and mild anxiety would occasionally return during the subsequent years while Ms. A. reared her children and was engaged in part-time professional work. Many years later, Ms. A. visited me to tell me about the deep contentment she felt with her first grandson who reminded her of her brother when he was first born. This memory seemed to give her a sense of satisfaction in her own life achievements, which she had never before experienced. It seemed to me that Ms. A. had finally acquired the phallus she had missed so intensely as a young toddler.

Ms. B., the thirty-two-year-old mother of three children, sought analysis because of severe insomnia which was often accompanied by acute anxiety states. Four years of psychotherapy during her early twenties had modified these symptoms, but they began to recur as her children became increasingly independent of her and as she planned to reenter professional work from which she had retired during her early twenties to rear her children. Ms. B. had not been able to pursue her educational ambitions during her adolescence because of family circumstances, but had been forced to work at a well-paying job which was far below her intellectual potential. As her children entered adolescence, Ms. B. began to take courses to qualify for an advanced degree in the profession she had been practicing on a part-time basis and without full credentials. She was extremely anxious as to whether she could ever "cross the border" into the professional territory which she considered primarily to be a "man's world." It was in contemplation of entering this higher level of professional work that Ms. B.'s prior symptoms of insomnia and anxiety states returned, along with a new feature. She could not concentrate on intellectual work unless a family member was in the room with her. Ms. B. sought analytic treatment as these symptoms became overwhelming.

The patient was the third of four children in a religiously conservative family. Her parents had condemned sexuality verbally, although they appeared to condone it by their own actions. Ms. B. recalled having been severely reprimanded by her parents when she began to masturbate at about three years of age, a prohibition later reinforced by her religious teachers. The struggle against masturbation was somehow connected with feelings of intense jealousy of her next younger sibling, a brother 18 months her junior. She felt that her mother had always favored him, and she had developed a persistent sleep disturbance and temper tantrums between her third and fifth years, symptoms she thought were related to her mother's relative indifference to her needs.

Another feature of Ms. B.'s early development was her special acrobatic talent which had been recognized and applauded by her parents as early as her fourth year. Her acrobatic performances before her father and his friends continued well into her early latency years and were an important source of exhibitionistic pleasure for her. But they were brought to a close rather suddenly between her eighth and ninth year when she began to recognize the sexually tinged interest in her body which her father and his friends conveyed as they watched her. Her acrobatic performances were then replaced by an intense devotion to her schoolwork; she became an excellent student, soon establishing herself as a leader among her peers, partly because of her sense of humor and her capacity for verbal expression which continued to characterize her even during the troubled periods of her life. However, both her family life and her school life were altered abruptly during Ms. B.'s midadolescence by a change in the family's circumstances.

Instead of continuing her academic studies, Ms. B. undertook training for a professional career in which she had only a marginal interest. She married during her early twenties, reared her children, and had a part-time job until her early thirties. Then she was once again able to return to academic studies, finally achieving advanced status in her field. But now she was brought into competition with men for the first time; she needed constant reassurance and validation of her opinions, whereas she had been a very self-confident student during her younger years. In addition, she developed a group of symptoms in relation to examinations. In preparing for them, she felt she had to recall *all* the material in order to maintain control, and even when she had achieved excellent marks on an examination, it was an empty triumph since she felt she had been an imposter, only pretending to know the material and having hoodwinked her examiners. In discussing these feelings with her women friends, she found they were quite sympathetic with her anxieties, whereas her husband told her to simply shape up and pass. She worried constantly about the impression she had made on the examiners, and even when she had been assured that she had done well, she felt it was a fluke and that she would never again be able to repeat the performance.

As Ms. B. described her feelings about performing "in public" during one of her analytic sessions, she recalled the acrobatic triumphs of her childhood, which she now connected with trying to compete with her mother for her father's attention. Furthermore, she knew she had always done better in private than in public appearances, and began to compare herself unfavorably with me because of my public achievements. She thought I possessed something special beneath my calm exterior, a thought she had often had about her mother. She hoped to get something valuable from me through the analysis that would solve her doubts about her capacity for intellectual work. Then she added, in a depressed tone, that no matter how hard she tried, she probably would not get what she wanted. To my question, "What is it that you think you want?" she replied, "I suppose a penis. That's what they all say, but I don't think that that's where it is. However, I did have the fleeting thought that this examination business has something to do with whether I can or cannot perform like a man."

In her sexual life with her husband, Ms. B. had always preferred clitoral masturbation to vaginal intercourse, fearing that she would lose urinary control during intercourse. During her previous psychotherapeutic work, she had connected this fear with memories of humiliating episodes of loss of urinary control as a child, a memory that led to her awareness of her fear of humiliation in connection with the school examinations; she was afraid her mind would not function clearly and that she could not get to the point. She felt she could not compete with men intellectually because they could stand alone on their own two feet while she needed the comfort and support of her friends and family.

In the quotation that follows, Ms. B. mused about her problem of committing herself to a "real" career and its implication of working as a man does:

> I wonder if I really would like that. Many women approach working more like a game—it has a termination point—marriage, a trip, a pregnancy. But someone who invests so much energy in work hasn't enough left over for the rest of life. Men don't let up—they focus and concentrate on what they're doing. Maybe it's like their sex, or more like masturbation is for me. I can control that, get it over with, like a shot of insulin—almost devoid of human quality. Working stimulates sexual tension. So you need that kind of outlet. With men, sex doesn't interfere with the rest of their lives, while women wallow around in that pool. Men pop into the pool, but they don't get stuck in it like women do. Women are accessible for men to gloop a little semen into; then they run on to their next appointment in the office when she is wallowing in the same pool and waiting for the next opportunity.

My patient then wondered whether there might be a happy medium for her—an integrated life with commitments like a man but also some opportunities for creative outlets.

By the time her analysis was terminated, Ms. B. was able to commit herself to her new career and had made peace with her husband as to the changes this decision brought about in their relationship, although she had a return of anxiety from time to time when called upon to address a large audience.

THE GENERAL CLINICAL PICTURE OF PREOEDIPAL
CASTRATION ANXIETY IN ADULT WOMEN

These women and others whom I have treated present a clinical picture characterized by intellectual performance anxiety of an intense nature. Although they differed from one another in character structure and in many other aspects of their psychology and psychopathology, the women were strikingly similar in their devaluation of their own intellectual functioning, a devaluation that gave rise to marked anxiety when they were faced with intellectual competition, particularly if this involved competition with men in relation to preparation for a career, "work." The pending examinations precipitated in each woman a cluster of regressive symptoms that were striking in their similarity, particularly as they recurred at regular intervals throughout the academic year.

It is relevant that most of these patients had either selected a woman therapist themselves or had been referred to me by a male colleague who thought the patient's problem indicated the choice of a female as therapist. While I do not believe that the sex of the therapist is, in most cases, an important determinant of the outcome of treatment, particularly when this judgment is made at the beginning of treatment, it is significant that most of these women eventually stated that they had decided before they consulted me that I might serve them as a prototype of a successful professional woman. An unconscious wish to borrow some of my supposedly magical powers came to the fore during the course of treatment in all of them. They also expected that because I was a woman they need not fear attack or ridicule from me as they would from a male therapist. Furthermore, while all were intellectually competent women and even highly gifted and ambitious for professional achievement, they experienced considerable conflict between their low esteem of their intellectual capacity and their actual excellent intellectual achievements.

The cluster of symptoms that appeared in these women, bewildering at first because of the intensity and chaotic character of the regressive trends, became dynamically meaningful in the analytic work only after it had recurred many times as a predictable and fairly regular pattern. The symptoms reflect aspects of all three of the major anxieties: fear of object loss, fear of loss of bodily integrity, and fear of being found out in relation to the genital imperfection they felt they had suffered. Symptoms reflecting fear of object loss included the sense of emotional distance and intense loneliness and depressed moods which appeared quite suddenly and were often so severe that the patients had to interrupt studying in order to establish contact with a female friend or a family member. Other symptoms relating to the fear of object loss were bulimia either during or interrupting studying, followed by remorse and guilt, excessive dietary restrictions, and often a retreat to sleep, which would then be followed by frantic bouts of overactivity. One patient described her experience as entering an unknown territory, a terrifying thought in itself; if she left one area of material she had once mastered and was now familiar with, she would forget this as soon as she began to study the next set of facts. These symptoms reflected anxiety about separation which apparently began during her very early years.

Another set of symptoms represent underlying anxiety over total bodily integrity. Concern over skin, hair, or body contour imperfections became the focus of constant self-inspection, and led to consultation with friends and physicians when these hypochondriacal concerns reached intense proportions. Impulsive clothes-buying and experimentation with cosmetics and new hair styles at such times inevitably ended in disappointment as their concerns about their bodily intactness were not allayed.

The examinations also revived old fears of anal loss in these women: one patient actually expressed this as a feeling that having to study was like being toilet-trained. Having to deliver the answers at a specific time and in a specific manner made her want to refuse to study, or even to refuse to take the examination at all—since this was like pleasing her mother when she had performed as a good girl in regard to her excretory functions. Her dream material repeatedly reflected the unconscious equation of the examination as a sadomasochistic anal attack by her mother.

Finally, concerns over *intellectual* imperfections appeared to represent feelings of genital inadequacy and imperfection for these women. Several patients complained that they would know nothing at all unless they had memorized every detail; haunted by the fear of not being letter perfect, they thought they would fail the examination completely if even one question remained unanswered. As these feelings of intellectual imperfection were explored during treatment, they were most often found to be connected with shame and embarrassment, reactions my patients expected to experience if their failures in performance actually materialized. These affects were frequently associated with memories of childhood urinary and fecal incontinence. Recall of the excretory experiences often evoked fragments of sadomasochistic fantasies which ordinarily did not play a dominant role in the conscious fantasy lives of these patients. It was all the more impressive, therefore, to observe the invasion of the capacity for concentration when these fantasies emerged. Not only was their intellectual functioning inhibited, but their usual capacity for enjoying sexual relations was also disturbed. In some instances the fear that the fantasies would emerge unexpectedly and would overwhelm them led several women to avoid masturbation as well as intercourse.

Many sexual exploratory "doctor" games of early childhood were also recalled during these periods of anxiety over the anticipated examination, along with the fear of being revealed as being without "that something," the absence of which they felt accounted for their stupidity and their intellectual "phoniness." The fear of losing control and bursting into tears during the examination further confirmed the sense of genital imperfection connected with their urinary functioning. Finally, symptoms of menstrual irregularities, pregnancy fantasies, and two episodes of pseudocyesis in one of the patients pointed to the underlying hope that their genital imperfection might be assuaged by acquiring a baby as a phallic substitute.

When these women regressed temporarily to relationships with female friends with whom they felt protected from male competition, transference manifestations would assume a preoedipal character. In contrast to the more modulated and mixed type of transference that usually prevailed during other phases of treatment, when examinations were in the offing, loneliness, primitive rage states, and acute depressive episodes with suicidal ideation occurred with surprising frequency, along with intense ambivalent feelings toward the analyst. These preoedipal reflections, both within and outside of the transference, would begin to subside remarkably rapidly as the impact of the examination faded.

The symptom complex I have been describing is relevant to the problems outlined by Applegarth (1976) in women suffering from work inhibitions in the course of an already established career. Those women expressed the idea that one is "born to do something" rather than progress from stage to stage. Rage reactions in the face of difficulties, a feeling of phoniness, and the conviction that they are missing a central feature characterize them, and they react to their achievements with a painful feeling of being fraudulent and having stolen their success. Applegarth describes their persistent magical beliefs and their attribution of a masculine character to intellectual achievement. She notes that in their problems around aggression, the preoedipal nature of their pathology became evident in that there was a conflict about surpassing the mother whom they considered weak and stupid and "only a woman." Enduring success is impossible since it leads them to feeling too powerful and sadistic, and they fear the reaction of others to their competitiveness. Applegarth concludes that problems of self-esteem seem to be different in women than in men; she links these problems with the area of penis envy. Applegarth emphasizes that women's conviction of their inferiority is extremely firmly held and difficult to modify.

Psychodynamic Features of this Syndrome

The option of choosing a career, particularly one that involves competition with men, poses a new type of challenge for the young woman. It often occurs at a time in life when commitment to a heterosexual relationship may be under consideration for the first time, a situation that revives anxiety related to oedipal wishes or may arise at a later time when presented with opportunities for acquiring a profession. Intellectual competition with men has then to be reconciled with the feminine role in the love relationship, further complicating the oedipal conflict anxiety.

Choosing a career also tends to revive preoedipal anxieties for those women whose identification with the mother of early childhood must be partially given up, if the mother had not been a career woman herself. This poses a different problem for women than for men, since most boys negotiate a partial disidentification with the archaic mother during the latter part of their second year and part of the third year (Roiphe and Galenson, 1973) as a necessary prerequisite for establishing a stable sense of male identity. Since the career woman's partial disidentification with the archaic mother occurs during adulthood, in contrast with the boy's much earlier disidentification, unresolved preoedipal issues may be revived in the career woman at a time when such shifts in identification are more disruptive to the already stabilized personality of the mature woman. Conflicts relating to the sense of sexual identity, which were only partially resolved at an earlier period, may once again be revived as competition with men on an intellectual level reaches a point of special intensity in connection with career-connected intellectual examinations. Anxieties relating to the genital examinations of early childhood, self-examination in particular, once again escape from their earlier repression.

The early genitality that was the subject of our research project involving 65 infants studied during their second year of life (Galenson, 1974; Galenson and Roiphe, 1971, 1976; Roiphe and Galenson, 1981) constitutes an early genital phase which occurs normally and regularly sometime between 16 and 19 months of age and is characterized by behavior indicating underlying genital arousal. It is free of oedipal resonance but is connected with ongoing consolidation of self- and object representations. All the girls in our research study developed symptoms that appeared to constitute preoedipal castration reactions. Although these reactions varied in severity, they affected the girls' subsequent development in both an enhancing and inhibiting direction. We noted regressive behavior characterized by reemergence of the recently allayed fear of object loss and of general bodily damage, as well as the new sense of genital impairment. From that time on, penis envy and genital concerns remain intimately linked with the two more primitive anxieties.

Most of the girls we studied also showed many advances in functioning under the impact of the preoedipal castration reaction. Many developed a new and special type of attachment to dolls and other inanimate objects, using them in a remarkable burgeoning in their fantasy life and the symbolic function. The girls began to use crayons and other writing material months earlier than most of the boys in attempts at graphic representation. They made additional advances in the area of symbolic functioning which are important aspects of the developing capacity for the symbolic representation of secondary-process thinking. These advances may serve as early defenses against the anxiety connected with the genital emergence and discovery of the genital difference.

In those girls who had experienced a relatively successful maternal relationship during their first year of life, the preoedipal castration reactions led to a new erotic attachment to the father and a relative increase in hostile ambivalence toward the mother. Where there had been difficulty in the relationship with the mother or important bodily traumata during the first year, hostile dependence on the mother mounted, and the erotic shift to the father did not occur during the period following the girl's discovery of the sexual difference. The character of the later oedipal constellation was influenced in due course, the milder castration reaction facilitating the girl's turn to the father as primary love object and enhancing her inner fantasy life and emergent symbolic functioning. The more profound castration reactions set the stage for a predominantly negative oedipal constellation, with constriction in developing fantasy and secondary-process thinking.

Of particular significance for the special type of anxiety in women described earlier was the richer intellectual life that followed the preoedipal castration reactions. This seemed to serve both defensive purposes and as an early form of sublimation in dealing with the three major anxieties of the early genital phase. However, precisely this development of the intellectual function in girls, with its ultimate expression in language (and its urinary-phallic resemblance), may render these intellectual functions more prone to invasion by conflict in adult life, especially when competition with men becomes an important intellectual problem. These women tend to continue to perceive the intellectual function as phallic in nature, since this function had been connected with their earliest discovery of the genital anatomical differences. This early source of conflict is readily reactivated by any circumstances that resemble the earlier constellation.

In summary, I have described a special type of anxiety in women with which the sense of genital imperfection and fears of object loss and body damage are inevitably intertwined. The three anxieties are a normal developmental feature in girls at the end of their second year and are revived by intellectual competition with men, particularly when examinations leading to success in a career are involved. These examinations also revive the early fears experienced in connection with the very young girl's genital self-examination leading to the discovery of the genital anatomical differences during the latter months of the second year. Analytic interpretations based on this dynamic understanding have succeeded in modifying examination anxiety in the women I have treated to a considerable degree, as these patients begin to anticipate their reactions and to recognize these patterns. The women I have described did not suffer from confusion in their sense of sexual identity, although they often experienced deep disappointment and rage in connection with their female identification and its vicissitudes.

References

Applegarth, A. (1976), Some observations on work inhibitions in women. *J. Amer. Psychoanal. Assn.*, 24:251–268.

Galenson, E. (1974), Emergence of genital awareness during the second year of life. In: *Sex Differences in Behavior*, ed. R. C. Friedman, R. M. Riehart & R. L. Vande Wiele. New York: Wiley, pp. 223–231.

————— Roiphe, H. (1971), Impact of early sexual discovery on mood, defensive organization and symbolization. *The Psychoanalytic Study of the Child*, 26:195–216. New York: Quadrangle.

————— ————— (1976), Some suggested revisions concerning early female development. *J. Amer. Psychoanal. Assn.*, 24(Suppl.):29–58.

Roiphe, H. & Galenson, E. (1973), Object loss and early sexual development. *Psychoanal. Q.*, 42:73–90.

————— ————— (1981), *The Infantile Origins of Sexual Identity*. New York: International Universities Press.

16

AMBITION: NORMAL AND PATHOLOGICAL ASPECTS

ADRIENNE APPLEGARTH, M.D.

Considering its importance, it is remarkable how few are the references to ambition in the psychoanalytic literature. In his article on "Character and Anal Erotism," Freud (1908) connects the character trait of ambitiousness to urethral erotism, but develops nothing further about the psychology of ambition. Scattered mentions of it appear in case material, and Jacobson (1964) touches on the subject in connection with the development of the ego ideal, to which I shall return presently. But attention has not been focused on ambition as a function in general, and certainly not as it appears in female development. Yet patients speak about many specific ambitions, and we have abundant opportunities to see how they handle ambitiousness as a function. We tend to pay more attention to the outcomes of the ambition—careers or life courses selected, fates of drives and sublimations—yet ambition is the guiding star for these courses of action.

DEVELOPMENT OF AMBITION

A few moments of thought reveal that the development and operation of ambition are a complicated matter. What first strikes us is that ambition and impulse have a good deal in common and yet essential differences. What are some of these? To begin with, both ambition and impulse contain the quest for drive gratification. This may be expressed in both with variable degrees of directness, and this component may have different levels of access to consciousness. Aggression can be readily identified in various ambitions as we hear about the drive to win, to triumph over old enemies. On the libidinal side, exhibitionism is amply expressed, as are abundant fantasies of winning love

241

and sexual fulfillment. These drives are intertwined with and express a variety of narcissistic wishes as well. We would look to the drive component to help understand a large part, but not all, of the urgency of both ambition and impulse. And yet, consideration of either of these in terms of drive alone would seem most unsatisfactory in that it would fail to do justice to what are clearly more complex functions, even in the case of impulse.

Obviously, important ego functions enter into the picture here. There is a striking difference between ambition and impulse in the long-term visualization and planning involved in ambition, although short-range planning is also involved in carrying out impulsive acts. Long-range planning requires taking into account all the aspects of outer and inner reality, which includes the use of the vital internal representations of self, object, and physical world that have been built up in the course of development. So the fate of ambition is inextricably entwined with the quality of these representations and the ego's ability to employ them freely in planning. Here, neurosis as well as more severe disturbances can strike deeply at the ability of an individual to use accurate evaluations of these realities in order to do the planning ahead that ambition requires. The representation of the outer world contains the possibilities of what human beings can do that the individual has been presented with in one way or another. Obviously, a very restricted environment provides a limited repertoire of these, but in our culture it is rare to find a patient who has not had ample opportunities to be exposed to quite a full range of human activities. On the other hand, what is remarkable is the number of people who have been unable to register these possibilities and make use of them because of mobilization of the ego's defenses. The self-representations provide an assessment of the talents and capabilities that may make ambitions seem realizable or impossible. But there is a whole spectrum of self-representations, ranging from the unconscious to the conscious and from the most wishful to quite realistic. And similarly, the object representations provide memories and predictions about possible responses to ambitions which have a range similar to the self-representations. So all of these are used to judge the possibility of one's being able to do in reality those possible activities that have presented themselves as attractive.

The ability to maintain efforts toward a goal also depends on other ego functions. Ability to tolerate the frustrations, disappointments, and depressions which inevitably attend such efforts is an essential attribute that allows us to sustain ambition until fulfillment arrives. An optimistic view toward the outcome would seem likely to contribute to the ability to tolerate the difficulties along the way. This optimism must itself depend heavily on representations of past experiences of successful persistence. In these areas of ego function, I am sure no one would have any difficulty calling to mind various patients who are either pathologically pessimistic or optimistic because of the activities of defenses as well as unconscious fantasies.

Ego identifications also play a vital role in helping lay down the mechanisms for problem-solving in general, which would also include the inclination and ability to persist. Here I would be referring to all the ways in which parents and other important figures show children how they approach and accomplish all life's tasks, including the emotional ones, much of the time outside the parents' awareness. All of these faculties contribute to an individual ability to be ambitious, since they are a foundation for a sense of possibility.

Clearly, the superego has a leading role in ambition. It provides the judgment as to what one may or may not aspire to as well as on what means may or may not be used in that aspiration. The ego ideal part of the superego also points to what seems desirable, necessary, enticing, and promising as a goal of ambition. Permission to fulfill all sorts of instinctual and omnipotent wishes may be provided here. What I am stressing here is the normal function of the superego in setting and assessing goals as well as actions. In this regard, both Schafer (1960) and Lederer (1964) emphasize the guiding, loving and protective functions of the superego. The formulation is of course familiar that the contents of the superego represent identifications with the superegos of the parents. It seems to me, however, that too often it is stressed that these identifications are with the same-sex parent. This follows Freud's (1923) outline of the resolution of the Oedipus complex, where the superego is formed through identifications with the parental figures, mainly the same-sex parent. Freud's account deals almost exclusively with the development of the superego in boys; his few remarks about this development in girls make clear his view that the superego is less well developed in women. Thus, for many years, the superego seemed to be almost synonymous with a paternal possession. But in spite of theory, it is clear, when we listen to patients, that their superegos contain large and important identifications with maternal superegos, including the ego ideals, which are so important in showing the way to achievement via aspirations and ambitions. Freud (1923) recognized the important role of the ego ideal when he characterized it as representing the last refuge of early infantile narcissism. Today, while recognizing the pathology that may be involved in this origin, we would also stress the useful, even essential aspects of these narcissistic currents. The origin of the superego contents and mode of function in identifications with the superegos of both parents also makes it easier to understand those personalities who seem to have such unintegrated superegos, where standards of conduct are at war with one another, not just with drive derivatives. The relations of ambition and achievement in the child to the ego ideal of

parents has been discussed by Goertzel and Goertzel (1962). In studying whatever could be learned about the upbringing and early lives of
men and women of eminence, they observed a strong correlation of
ambition and achievement in the individual who grew up with a mother
who had a strong, unremitting absorption in the child and all his or
her actions and an equally total belief in the wonderful future that lay
in store for the child. Often, in these families, the father was unsuccessful or an outright failure, or in any case, a disappointment to the mother,
so that her ambition and sense of possibility, which were disappointed
both in herself and her husband, came to be focused on the child.

DISTURBANCES OF AMBITION

These disturbances can be roughly characterized as too little, too much,
or of an inappropriate kind, and typically have complex roots in problems involving a number of functions supporting the exercise of ambition.

To begin with, it is possible to imagine a child who is raised
without the actual information that would point the way to various
ambitions, but this would be a most unusual environment. Our patients
often want to persuade us that such circumstances account for failures
of ambition, but we usually find something much more complex. For
example, a patient who was raised in a rather restricted subculture of
a major city wished urgently to impress on me how she had had no
opportunities to know of any way of living or thinking besides her
family environment. These assertions were possible for her to make
in spite of the fact that she read literature voraciously, and lived in the
rich, diverse atmosphere of the city. Clearly, there were important
reasons for her blindness. Her favorite resistance comment is, "It never
occurred to me." Conflicts arise over the function of having ambition
itself or over the content of the ambitions or over their mode of realization. Having ambitions may be so invested with aggressive, libidinal,
or narcissistic meaning that severe conflicts may prevent expression
of these in consciousness or in action. These conflicts may lead to a
blanket inhibition even of awareness of possibilities for achievement
of gratification.

Unconscious fantasies of object relationships may lead to ambitionlessness as, for example, a means to frustrate and thwart parents
who have been perceived as fulfilling themselves through the actions
of their children. Or a child may live up to parental fantasies that he
or she is worthless or defective and so has no future, or to put it
differently, may internalize such parental attitudes in his or her own
self-representations. Fantasies of parental envy may also lead to giving
up any ambition. There are limitless fantasies of the ways in which

old hopes for gratification and for avoidance of dangers may be worked out, and a sizeable number of them, of which those mentioned are an example, depend on retiring from the field of ambition and adopting an essentially passive stance toward life.

Certain problems with necessary ego mechanisms discussed above may also contribute to absent ambition. For whatever reasons developmentally, certain patients lack the ability to tolerate delay, frustration, unpleasant affect, including discouragement, which makes it possible to look to the future and plan in an effective way. Some patients with a narcissistic character disorder may present these features in vivid fashion. A self-representation of worthlessness or defectiveness undercuts the necessary optimism to do this. For these reasons, sicker patients may be so invaded and drained by conflicts that they are unable to look to the future and carry out ambitions.

There may be certain personalities in whom the ego ideal is one of absence of ambitions and an expectation of being done for or taken care of as a measure of self-worth. In other cases, an unconscious sense of guilt may dictate a life without achievement, as well as other gratifications, either generally or in specific ways.

There are also cases in which ambition is present to a remarkable degree. This may or may not be accompanied by actual accomplishment. If appropriate talents are present, such ambition will result in outstanding achievement. However, the ambition may be quite reasonable in its direction, but neurotic inhibitions may overtake the accomplishment of it. In practice, it may be difficult for some time, in a case of work inhibition, to distinguish an inhibition of ambition from a disturbance in the work function itself. In certain narcissistic characters, the ambition may be so grandiose that no achievements could possibly measure up or even come close. Such a person may then be unable to attempt to achieve but be tormented by ambition, envy, and rage. Or the ambition may, for various reasons, not be directed toward actual talents the person has, but rather toward ones not possessed; such an individual may persist in this inappropriate direction in a most remarkable way. This may arise out of a need to fulfill a parent's ambition, or perhaps to replace a dead child or other figure in a parent's life, or out of identification with a parent that replaces an unsatisfactory object relationship. These examples represent miscarriages of a process that is part of normal development. I am referring to the way in which both the self-representation and the ego ideal are gradually modified in more realistic directions in a manner very similar to the way the evaluation of the parents is gradually altered from the grandiose picture of childhood. If all goes well, and shocks and disappointments are not too severe, all these processes flow forward relatively smoothly.

SOME SPECIAL FEATURES OF AMBITION IN WOMEN

Any of these features of ambition, including its pathologies, can be seen in men and women, and many do not seem to be very different in one group or the other. But there are certain special aspects in women.

In all cultures, there seem to be economic and cultural constraints on ambition. In Western culture the constraints have been very great on women in the form of exclusions from many careers, a realistic factor that has been diminishing in recent times as far as the outside social structure is concerned. However, many inhibiting influences remain both outside and within families. Much attention has been paid lately to the ways in which individuals may reflect different expectations of girls and boys without their being aware of their expressing this at all. Reviews of textbooks, and children's stories provide objective evidence of this, evidence that is harder to come by in family histories. There has been strong pressure on girls to channel their ambition in the direction of marriage and motherhood, with the further injunction that their personal ambition should be realized only through the attainments of their husbands and children. All this joins together with the very strong drive and other satisfactions provided by these careers, with the result that marriage and parenthood become more of a career goal and the subject of ambition in themselves than they are in men. Women do not feel themselves in conflict with their fundamental identity as women when they aspire to or are devoting themselves to marriage and motherhood or to careers that are considered to be close to these goals, e.g., teaching, nursing. But all human activities seem to have a gender flavor, and most other careers have a masculine one. Men, too, suffer from this assignment of gender, as in the cases of male nurses, teachers, child care workers. But most careers seem masculine, and many women do not even respond to them as real possibilities in life. They may feel that they do not have the capabilities required, since they picture these as belonging to men. This reflects an idealization of men and their capacities, a true belief that men have a certain confidence, or certain kinds of brains, or a certain something that gives them a power and ability women lack. The constellation of penis envy with its conviction of inferiority can be seen here, as well as the influence of the idealization of the father by the mother. Some women are deeply caught up in and inhibited by these influences, while others are not inhibited in achievement, and in fact may be greatly stimulated by these challenges, although none can remain unaffected in various other ways.

For example, a woman patient in her forties, an accomplished scientist, recalls a conversation with her maternal grandmother when she was about four or five. The little girl had been playing with a white cloth which she put on her head to represent a nurse's cap. Her grandmother had recently been quite ill, and had been attended by both a doctor and a nurse. Her grandmother asked her what it was, and when the girl explained and said she wanted to be a nurse, her grandmother asked her why not a doctor. Already, this was unusual at that time—in most families that question would not have been asked—but the grandmother had been a suffragette and had worked for most of her life as a newspaper woman and writer of history. The girl replied, "Girls can't be doctors." Her grandmother answered that indeed they could, and she could be whatever she liked. This reply aroused skepticism, and, as the ultimate test, the girl said, "You mean I could be a mechanic if I wanted?" When her grandmother assured her that she could be a mechanic if she wished, it made a vivid impression on her and inspired considerable conviction. The child felt that a window had been opened on certain possibilities for her. As she recalled it, there was something about the specificity of the conversation that gave it realistic substance. It had a different effect than was produced by the sort of overblown assurances she had often heard, like, "You are so wonderful you can be anything," which she recognized as wishful hyperbole.

It is important in the story of the development of the patient's ambition that she was the youngest child and had several brothers. Moreover, both mother and grandmother had a worshipful attitude toward men in general and these brothers in particular, especially the eldest. So the little girl very much wanted to be a boy. The frustration of that particular ambition seemed to have lent much energy to her ambitiousness in general, once it was focused. For a time, she thought of being a writer, but at age nine, in the fifth grade, she was introduced to science and related how she knew immediately she had found her calling. So at that point, her ambition, which had a great deal to do with frustrated narcissism and other instinctual currents, met a rich stream of talent and intense pleasure in function, and so a highly focused ambition was forged. She poured her interest into biology, studying it outside of school at every opportunity. In high school, she luckily landed in the class of a gifted teacher who offered her many opportunities for advanced study and supported her ambition to enter a research career.

The path was not smooth, however. The mother, whose ambition it had been to be a housewife and to have children, was alarmed and disapproving of her daughter's different choice. Also, an element of envy seemed to be present, as the grandmother approved of her granddaughter's choice, while the mother seemed always to have to seek her own mother's approval in vain. The patient recalls many other voices in the background: "Oh, you will forget all about this and get married and have children," or "It's unfeminine to be so intense and ambitious,'' or ''Boys don't like girls who excel. Don't act so intelligent. Let them win,'' or ''A woman is supposed to marry and have children. The husband should have the career. Your children will suffer.'' In her case, this opposition only solidified her determination, but at the cost of her feeling herself to be a freak. What balance of forces led her to press on instead of giving up was not entirely clear. She was often afraid about whether her capacities would support her ambitions, and she had many fantasies of high scholastic achievement. Gradually, these came true, as her intense involvement in her work bore fruit.

A feature that obviously played an important role in the outcome was the patient's intense pleasure in thought in general and in science in particular. She described many moments of ecstasy as she experienced the working of her thoughts, and it was possible to clarify various pregenital and genital derivatives in this pleasure. Her relations to her work is, I believe, an example of what Freud (1915) describes in his paper, ''The Unconscious.'' He calls attention to a particularly strong and free use of faculties when instinctual currents are free to be expressed in sublimations in a particularly direct way (p. 195). She did go on to a career of outstanding achievement and deep gratification in her work. Her ambition never extended to getting married and having children, a circumstance related to her low valuation of women and her wish to be a boy. She did marry, but had no children. When she began to teach in a university, the patient found to her surprise that she developed nurturing maternal feelings about the students. She had never had any ambition to teach any more than she had to be a mother, but, once awakened, the pleasure was very deep.

I have presented this case to illustrate a number of factors that enter into the development of ambition and its influence as an effective force. Not only did the patient have the stimuli to her ambition as described, but also she had ego and superego qualities that helped her realize these ambitions. She was optimistic and believed that hard work was a good thing and would lead to success. Her favorite childhood story was ''The Little Engine That Could''—not a surprise. She admired people who overcame obstacles and persisted to the end, and also people of courage. She had conflicts around her intense drive to compete and succeed in a way that felt to her ruthless. She had certain psychoneurotic symptoms around libidinal conflicts, but these did not invade her work.

As already mentioned, a woman may feel a conviction that entertaining ambition enters on forbidden ground, and that a price must be paid, perhaps loss of her femininity or worse. For example, a woman began analysis because of obsessive symptoms, but it became clear that she also suffered from anxiety and depression about her difficulty in becoming pregnant. Her history revealed that she had an older brother and a younger sister; the brother was a successful lawyer, while the sister worked as a paralegal. Even though she had done well in school, the patient had not entertained personal ambitions early, but rather felt that both she and her family expected that she would marry instead. Accordingly, she married a young man in law school. She worked while he attended school. Her work and her contact with him aroused her own ambitions to attend law school; in fact, her unused capacities attracted attention at work and she was encouraged to aspire further. She met opposition from her husband, who wanted a family and was not interested in her career, and from her father, who seemed pleased but raised various apparently practical objections. It was clear in the family also that boys and men were more valuable.

The patient's resolve hardened, and she divorced her husband and was accepted by an excellent law school, from which she was graduated with a fine record. Although her work performance has continued to be excellent, she has been extremely troubled by fears of envy and disapproval on the part of others. She married a successful lawyer, and when her own career was well on its way, they began to want to have children. However, she was now in her mid-thirties and problems arose. She became pregnant and miscarried and then found that she was unable to become pregnant again. These difficulties, which would be upsetting for any woman, were devastating to her. She became frightened and depressed and her obsessional symptoms appeared. She began years of efforts to become pregnant by all means, but these efforts had a driven, almost desperate quality, and when there were failures, she became despondent but also angry. In the course of the analysis, it became clear that she felt unconsciously that her difficulties in becoming pregnant were a punishment for various crimes. One of the principal crimes was that she had allowed her ambition free rein and had pursued a career against the inner and outer voices telling her she was departing from the proper female path and entering a forbidden, male one. Since she had turned her back on motherhood at an earlier time, she now was being denied this reward, and it served her right. So she both submitted to the judgment and protested against it. Ultimately, she was successful in her efforts to become pregnant, and she found both the pregnancy and the relationship with her daughter richly rewarding. However, she continued to have conflicts about the fact that now she had *both* ambitions fulfilled, more, it seemed, than was fair. So she continued to struggle with fears that these successful outcomes would lead to tragedy.

Another fantasied price women fear who are struggling with their ambition is being ostracized or being left alone. In these cases, the state of being alone seems to represent a punishment for forbidden activities or impulses. The punishment seems to be the humiliation involved in being branded as a bad person. An example of this is afforded by a woman who came into analysis in her early fifties, having raised her children before entering on her professional career. She was a person of great vigor and intelligence, but she had not focused these for a long time. In her profession, she was very excited by the work and was ambitious, but she had many conflicts over this. She felt she was unwomanly, far too strong and loud. A prominent fear was of being shunned and left alone, mainly by women friends. She also feared being punished by tragedy; unfortunately, she developed a serious medical illness. As one might expect, she readily responded to this circumstance by feeling that it came because of her ambition. She was often tempted to give it all up and be "good," which meant being essentially huddled in a corner doing modest tasks. The analytic work has helped free her ambition, but the reality of her illness has reinforced her neurotic fears to a degree that threatens her progress.

It seems to me that women have generally more conflicts between the career of parenthood and other careers than men seem to have, although this may be changing at present. Ambitions for the development of their outside careers flourish at the same time that, in their mid-thirties, women experience a strong drive to become pregnant as well as the ambition to be mothers. In a number of cases, the attempted solution I have observed is to resolve to do both—at least this seems like a reasonable idea during the pregnancy. They confidently plan to return to work very shortly after delivery. However, after delivery, many women experience such an intense entrancement with the child that they cannot bear the deprivation of returning to work, so that a conflict of another kind develops with their ambition. Also, these women have a conflict within their superego, in that they have simultaneously the value of high achievement and the value of nurturing and giving way to others as an ideal of womanliness and motherliness. They are then plagued by the feeling of not doing the right thing, as well as the problem of not having enough time to do it. We have all seen these examples of the troubled "supermom." These conflicts are not absent in men, but seem more intense in women.

I hope that, in all of these remarks, I have not appeared to come too close to either extreme position, that is, all the difficulties have their origins out there, or on the other hand, all the difficulties are internal and the outside matters not at all. The point is that outside impediments to women's ambition and achievement have diminished, but, in subtle ways, not as much as it might seem. Since they have diminished, internal difficulties show up in clear form in the course of therapy. Perhaps some of the most significant differences between men and women lie in the different contents of the superego and its ego ideal function. By this I am certainly not referring to any difference in strength and structure, as Freud had suggested, but only to differences in content, which because of its guiding function throughout life, exerts a profound influence on lifelong development.

REFERENCES

Freud, S. (1908), Character and anal erotism. *Standard Edition*, 9:167–175.
London: Hogarth Press, 1959.
———— (1915), The unconscious. *Standard Edition*, 14:159–215. London:
Hogarth Press, 1957.
———— (1923), The ego and the id. *Standard Edition*, 19. London: Hogarth
Press, 1961.
Goertzel, V. & Goertzel, M. (1962), *Cradles of Eminence*. Boston: Little,
Brown.
Jacobson, E. (1964), *The Self and the Object World*. New York: International
Universities Press.
Lederer, W. (1964), *Dragons, Delinquents, and Destiny. Psychological Issues*,
Monogr. 15. New York: International Universities Press.
Schafer, R. (1960), The loving and beloved superego in Freud's structural
theory. *The Psychoanalytic Study of the Child*, 15:163–188. New
York: International Universities Press.

17

ON THE SENSE OF BEING "INCOMPLETE": FRAGMENTS FROM THE ANALYSIS OF A NARCISSISTIC PERSONALITY DISORDER

CHARLES W. SOCARIDES, M.D.

In his ground-breaking *The Analysis of the Self*, Kohut (1971) notes that the psychopathology of the narcissistic personality is expressed in "colorful syndromes," among which are pathological features in the sexual sphere, illustrated by perverse fantasies and perversions, as well as in the social sphere by work inhibitions. These patients are vaguely depressed, drained of energy, lacking in zest, "with an associated drop in work capacity and creativity" (p. 23). Their self-esteem is vulnerable; they are sensitive to criticism and to any lack of interest in themselves, and seek praise from people experienced as superiors. They are forever in search of guidance and approval and, for a limited period on such occasions, may do well in work, be creative and successful, while any lack of understanding or interest in their lives, or a mild rebuff, leaves them feeling drained, depressed, enraged, and indecisive; all creativity and work capacity deteriorates.

In an earlier publication (Socarides, 1988) I described in detail the luxuriant perverse pathology of my patient, Willard, briefly touching on the manifestations of his self disorder as it affected work. The narcissistic pathology depicted in this patient was explainable from two theoretical frames of reference: self psychology (developmental deficiency hypothesis—Kohut) and conflict-induced pathology (Kernberg). Although the latter was increasingly important in later phases of the analysis, the former was strikingly evident and explanatory of much of the symptomatology from the outset. My major emphasis in this current report will be on the description of his severe work inhibition through the application of valuable theoretical concepts first proposed by Kohut and later elaborated by his followers.

This fifty-year-old man never actually worked more than a few days of his life. He complained desperately of needing someone or something to "complete" himself without which he could not function. His desperate efforts to achieve this through both conscious and unconscious means provided me with considerable insight into the nature of self pathology and a gradual understanding of his perplexing condition. I was greatly helped in this regard by the patient's superior intelligence and his keen ability to articulate complex thoughts and feelings, some of which are repeated verbatim in these pages. It is beyond my purpose to present the complex origins of his devastating clinical conditions except to comment briefly on some etiological factors.

There is general agreement that early interferences with development and maturation are causative factors for the later emergence of healthy or pathological narcissism (Panel, 1973). Applying separation-individuation theory, Mahler and Kaplan (1977) conclude: (1) the absence of mirroring by admiring adults, especially during the differentiating subphase and even during the symbiotic phase, produces imbalances in fueling, which result in distortion of healthy narcissism; (2) disturbances in the practicing subphase, when the triad of self-love, primitive valuation of accomplishments, and omnipotence is at its height, deprive the infant of both the internal source of narcissism derived from the autonomous ego sphere and the narcissistic enhancement afforded by the normal, active, aggressive spurt of practicing (p. 199); (3) by the end of the practicing subphase, splitting is commonly encountered along with confusion between paternal images and a lack of internalization of erotic and aggressive impulses. Too sudden a deflation of omnipotent grandeur during these stages leads to profound mood changes and production of ambivalently loved and hated objects "split off and externalized in favor of internally contained, undifferentiated, negative, recathected, self-representations" (p. 207). This leads to the production of an "omnipotent, grandiose ego ideal . . . not adjusted to reality" (p. 207) and the search for substitutes in the external world who will meet the needs of highly overcathected self-representational units; (4) during the rapprochement subphase, narcissism is, of course, specifically phase-vulnerable.

In the case of Willard, his rapprochement phase was filled with hate, rage, envy, and threats of abandonment. For example, the most significant early memory of his childhood, and one that produced inordinate envy and rage, and lifelong hatred, was the birth of a brother, when he was two years and four months old:

> [This] literally put my life in tatters. I remember being horrible, angry, belligerent, and hostile to my brother, and my father feeling that this was ignoble, unworthy, and inappropriate. And I can remember his rejecting me for this. Oh how I hated my brother!

CLINICAL STUDY

Willard was a fifty-year-old, attractive, highly articulate, and intelligent man suffering from both a homosexual perversion and narcissistic personality disorder proper, in the middle or more severe range of narcissistic pathology (Kernberg, 1975). When first seen he was living with his severely ill father, on whom he had always been financially dependent. He entered treatment because he did not want to endanger a sizable inheritance at his father's death. Only later in treatment did it become apparent that this rather unusual aspect of his motivation for analysis was an expression of his basic core disturbance: a need for selfobjects to guide and control his behavior as well as to "complete" him. As a developmental deficiency, it could be seen to have had profound consequences for his total life performance, including the area of sexuality, and a complete inability to engage in useful or satisfactory work. He also experienced periods of depression, lethargy, exhaustion, and was engaged in intense homosexual activity, especially with young male prostitutes. One of his worst symptoms was that he had been "unable to complete actions" which he felt were normal for adult human beings; attempts to do so left him exhausted and depleted. He capsulized his position:

> There is a terrible negative force or energy in me which puts me in thrall. I am continually putting reality on hold, keeping reality not so far away, but just far enough so that I cannot be touched by it. I am a cipher with an incapacity to act at all.

Worldly demands or material requirements in life must be put on hold, must not impose upon his "tranquil integrity of being" as he attempts to achieve this integrity through living the way he does. He complains that society has not offered him "a place in the general social fabric," and it therefore cannot expect him to fulfill obligations such as engaging in work. He has remained forever indulged by parents and has "lived with grace and favor . . . as I'm someone who does not have his own position, his own place, his own life, his own anything, his own self."

Although dependent on others, if people do not satisfy his "ideal requirements," he simply "uses them" or otherwise disregards them as even having no particular validity because "their validity . . . whatever that validity is has nothing to do with me and my private, private world."

He disregards others unless they fulfill a function or, in a sense, complete him.

I'm looking for other people to fulfill me, whether as a sexual mate, or in any other way people normally take fulfillments as meaning for their lives. But I don't want to give anything because I don't want to have to relate to people. And it's easy for me to isolate this in respect to my sexual needs, which are so much greater than any single person I've ever met has been able to fulfill. . . . I am indifferent to most people unless they are very precise, conscientious, elegant, well-spoken representatives of a certain superior class which is, essentially, my own class.

This affords him comfort for the time being. Mingling, and speaking with the literati, the elite, the socially comfortable, discussing literature and art—and proceeding from one area of aesthetics to another without producing any contribution of his own, he ruefully confesses, has made him a "dilettante"—one with limited knowledge in many areas and expert in none. While recognizing that his own "limitations" may cause inconvenience, anguish, chagrin, or disappointment in others, his "philosophy" leads him to believe that he should find understanding in others. He idealizes his behavior by stating:

The minute someone sues me for money or becomes unpleasant about a debt, I consider that I don't have that debt anymore, because the relationship is smashed. Perhaps I don't have any superego that makes me think I really owe the money. I may not have a superego, but I have what I feel is a very correct and proper attitude toward people who have money, and even those whom I cannot repay.

EARLY HISTORY

The patient grew up in a wealthy household where the mother, a severely critical narcissistic and "aristocratic" woman, withdrew from the father, had a terrible sex life, chronically expressed superiority and disdain for worldly pursuits, and imparted this to her young son. The father was a hard-working merchant who could not tolerate his wife's coldness, drank at night, and argued constantly with her. During the patient's childhood the father amassed a considerable fortune which he doled out to his son at intervals, sustaining him without the absolute necessity for work.

As a child, Willard often pretended for several months to be sick, falsifying his temperature by putting his thermometer on top of the radiator in order to be allowed to stay in bed. Throughout early adolescence and early adulthood, he felt that his father resented all the ways in which he was "good."

My mother would gently tell me I'm too generous, trusting, and warm-hearted, while my father resented my erudition. Later my parents both resented my social life and everything that went with it. I have been a failure, in fact, in that I'm not a writer—which I wish to be. But for several months I've shown my nobility by the way I act, but I'm still far from the notion of princeliness that I wish for, and I resent that my father was not princely himself and was inferior to my mother.

His physical immaturity from puberty was a matter of great concern to his father who wondered about his sexuality. When he entered puberty he felt he had lost his "innocence," and that as his mother only liked "castrated men," he felt inferior as a man. He thought it demeaning to go to public school, did not have any friends, and was upset even when an acquaintance called, as he was above everyone. "I was horrified that my parents would think I had a friend."

It was his belief that his mother thought of work as a worldly pursuit, and that if one engaged in it, it was a "fall from grace."

In adolescence the patient engaged in an elaborate series of lies about himself, falsifying his academic record in order to be accepted at a prestigious prep school. At that time he described his mother, in his application, as a French aristocrat, making her a relative of Meurat, a "Princess Meurat," and himself as "a quarter Arabian." He did this, he explains, not entirely to aggrandize himself, but partly to explain why he appeared so "exotic" in the sense that he had "no virtue": "I was exotic in the sense of being alien—faraway, or foreign—in a sense being almost the enemy of society and the standard by which society lives." He began to behave with a singular disregard for the expectations and conventions of society and everyone, and he felt, somehow, that society represented both the mother and father against whom he was in revolt. Unable to do things for himself, he reacted with severe anxiety and a sense of being intimidated by anyone accomplishing something significant. Beginning in adolescence, he identified with prominent writers, was thrilled with their successes, and felt elated and overcome with emotion at great artistic performances at the theatre or opera. In identification with writers, playwrights, and great performers, he felt angry and deflated when in his opinion they "misused their talents."

He was capable of multiple identifications throughout his teens and early twenties, and he was never who he pretended to be. His only accomplishment was to become a prolific reader, especially in the literature of the theatre, and he presented himself as a social and literary critic, justifying this deceit by his belief that his real circumstances and accomplishments would lead many people to "misinterpret and misunderstand" him for "I am better represented by the lie than by the truth, for people have very strong misconceptions and tend to underestimate people." He was directed in this way, he believes, by both parents, being "assigned" the belief that he could never provide for himself and that he was "peculiar enough" and "unconventional enough" so that his parents could not turn their backs on him completely, even though at times his father concluded that he was "simply no good."

> So in many ways, my parents—putting aside this problem of how much I'm their creation, and how much I was acting out for them, and how much I fulfilled what they wanted, which I don't think is at issue here; it's vital and it's important, but it's not part of the immediate problem—given my state . . . reacted to me in ways that were always understandable to me. My mother really wanted to protect me; she didn't want me to be aggressive about my life. My worldly ambitions were always very different from my father's ambitions, and were threatening to him.

However, increasingly concerned over their son's inability to work and to make a life for himself, he remembers his mother once complaining:

> We have never lived like this, we have never lived with great eighteenth-century French furniture, we have never lived with a collection of pictures like the one you are putting together; we have never lived with a full-time manservant, and we have never lived with a fancy English car that you, somehow, have gotten hold of. . . .

On the Sense of Feeling Incomplete

Willard was comfortable in an environment of fine hotels, servants, and restaurants for they helped create a "perfect world" in which he felt safe. They provided him with emotional supplies and all but removed his sense of inadequacy for periods of time. When the "bombardment of reality" interfered with his "tranquil integrity of being," grandiose exhibitionistic demands came out of repression and collided with reality. On those occasions he suffered from regressive fragmentation and depletion depression. In states of narcissistic decompensation, even the thought of work was out of the question, he retreated to his bed, often defecated on the floor without cleaning up, and put clamps on his nipples during masturbation or homosexual relations to heighten his sense of self by direct stimulation of the erogenous zones. These actions made him feel alive and complete, and restored him to his former self.

In periods of threats to his narcissistic state of equilibrium, he frequently had self-state dreams (Kohut, 1971) of Italian Palazzi, of riding a huge horse on water, and so on. In states of decompensation his palace was in disrepair and decay; his effects were scattered, and his once-glamorous mother was now in great dishevelment. In a dream, he begged his mother to bequeath him some lamps, to which she replied in refusal, "But you'll never have a place for them; you have no place. It would be ridiculous to give them to you." His recollections of such dreams were often accompanied by overwhelming pain, feelings of deprivation, and abandonment. Such dreams not only reflected an early sense of hunger and abandonment, but represented all "good" and all "bad" split self- and object images, and pathological archaic grandiosity with its opposite: a deep sense of unworthiness. Regressive loss of self cohesion and splitting were interchangeable emotional states. In both, perverse sexual practices became pronounced and were punctuated by attacks of rage if he felt rejected by any sexual partner or by someone upon whom he depended for narcissistic enhancement and restoration. In response to the dream cited above, he states:

I never thought I could have put a roof over my head or food in my mouth. That's why my mother's remarks to me are not out of the blue. They're based on empirical observations. "You can't have that" means "you have never done it; you have never worked. Why would you suddenly be able to?"

His homosexual activities were part of a completion of himself. While sexual partners were needed for sensory stimulation, they served as objects to complete tasks he was incapable of doing for himself.

I want my partner to read about how a cadillac runs so I will know how, so that he can show me. And I want him to read the book about how the typewriter works so that he can tell me. And I want him to do practical things like that: drive me, take care of my mail. And I really want him to do things for me, not because I want him to serve, but because I am not complete yet myself, and so I really want him to perform actions which would complete me and which would bring me into reality: that is, complete my reality activities, which otherwise I could not do for myself.

When he lost his sexual selfobject, it was not loss of the object nor the loss of the object's love for which he grieved. He felt the anguish of the child, undernourished to the point of starvation, who has lost a selfobject response that kept him whole, complete, and free of fragmentation. For example, Willard, in narrating the event above to the analyst, was again immediately reduced to tears and sobbing in response to the analyst's empathic comment, "I believe it is some sort of ideal representation of myself in him, and that all the things he does for me are ways for me to *complete* myself, and to feel alive and in reality."

ON THE INCAPACITY TO WORK

Willard demonstrates disturbances in self function, as noted by Wolf (1995), and their severe consequences for the performance of work. He existed under the chronic threat of the fragmentation of the self. There was an imbalance between the constituents of the self due to a "hypertrophic overidealization of work," and there existed a "lack of energic vigor," a "weakened tension arc due to insufficient idealization of the poles of values and ideals of the self." For example, he reluctantly tried to be a stockbroker at the age of twenty-one. He attempted to be friendly with his clients but he "didn't really like their company," and as a result, felt he was being "false to the idea of friendship" (a hypertrophy, an overidealization of work itself). For a brief period he took a job as a typist, an act which it took him several months to get up enough "courage" to do.

> This ran against my "princely delusions." I have never been willing to work. I wasn't willing to work for it because I felt that there was no point—that it would just be "wheel-spinning," and that all my efforts would be for naught, and all that effort would be inevitably dashed. All my aspirations would find no fruition. My aspirations regarding becoming self-sufficient have all come to naught, real naught, zero, a cipher.

In contrast, he feels he has kept himself, through not working, "from failure, although a failure I seem to be." He carefully separates work from a "lack of attempt" at work:

> ... since I've assumed that failure was inevitable, and so I have lived accordingly. Just as I eat so well because my digestion is delicate and I can't handle, digestively, food that's not eaten under attractive circumstances, or that isn't itself of the best quality. Similarly, I don't expose my digestion or my life to that which I cannot handle in order to live. And so I avoid inevitable failure through inactivity.

In justification, he comments that throughout his life it has been important for him to discover "what really matters," and what really matters is to "interact with other human beings." Therefore, he presents himself as a glamorous, rich, and leisured man, and "acts for them" in a manner that they would like to be for themselves. In so doing, he says, "I find a definition of myself—that I really exist and that my actions have consequences." Grandiosely, he notes:

> I am the prince no matter in what hovel I am, and it has been of considerable satisfaction to me, when I was genuinely poor for such a long period of time, that I never appeared poor. I was never taken for poor. I had the image of myself as a prince who is in straightened circumstance much of the time—circumstances that I don't really understand and I don't really know how to cope with. But my princelihood is always evident. For that reason social success at the highest level is so accessible to me.

When pressed by his parents as to why he did not earn his own living, he replies:

> It is almost beyond my imagination. I say, 'But don't you know I don't have any energy, that I don't have a college degree, and it was agreed by everyone that I couldn't do anything, and I did try to work once for a period of time as an interior decorator, but being ashamed of that profession, I was unable to consider myself a businessman, and therefore I didn't make proper prices and all sorts of things.

He despises the attitude of prospering through work and considers it "very Midwestern"—the whole idea of being "one of the people." The job as a stockbroker was taken so that he:

> ... could get a loan at the bank, so that I could have normal credit as a way of making myself normal. I did not wish to be normal beyond what would be required of a lending institution or bank to hire me, but I wanted that normality.

Meanwhile, he conducts his life on the most "aristocratic levels" in order to become perfect and complete.

He recalls that he had taken the brokerage job at a point when the market was high and people were advertising for salesman, and he was told he did not need a college degree.

> So I suddenly saw, for the first time, one place where I could have a respectable position without the qualifications that I had always thought

were the *sine qua non* of that. I had no vocation to be a stockbroker, and no interest in it. I was one because it was the one thing that I could be where I could join the general society—and as a matter of fact, that was the most important thing about me, that I felt a part of the general society *for the first time,* if only for a short time. I had been a man without work and had asked my uncle for employment in the diamond business at one time, but he felt I was "too fine" to be in the business, and that I would never last because my sensibilities were too highly developed for it—that I was, in effect, overqualified.

DISCUSSION

The guiding principle of Willard's behavior revolved around the status of his self-cohesion: to protect it when it was threatened, to minister to it when it was damaged, and to recapture it when it was lost—in a sense, to avoid all threats and experiences of fragmentation. He complained that it was never imparted to him by anyone that through work he would be able to function as a self-sustaining being, nor that he would ever be able to support himself. He felt his actions would have no consequences, and since this was so, the analyst should and could prevent him from doing things that might end up in his getting into trouble financially.

Willard attempted to remedy severe defects in himself through the use of selfobjects and through perverse activities. Periods of narcissistic balance and compensation required empathic mergers with selfobjects and need-satisfying actions performed by such selfobjects (Ornstein, 1978). There was a pronounced interference with selfobject differentiation and integration in this patient, and a failure of internalizations crucial to the development and maturation so necessary to carry out any integrated personal functioning.

During the analysis he wished for a "collegial" relationship rather than a doctor-patient one. If he could not afford to pay on time, he felt the analyst should go on treating him, gratis, because the analyst should trust him, and if the money comes, the analyst will be paid. What was important to him was that we study his behavior, discuss his actions in the analytic sessions, and resolve the problems created by the "sources of my actions." The analyst must totally accept him, not for the money, but because of the collegiality he feels should be implicit in the psychoanalytic relationship. If and when the analyst is not "equipped" to handle the matter, it appears he will have to become "healthy" by himself. He asserts that he considers himself to be somewhat "like a genius" and that he should be treated as such. He compares himself to Aschenbach in *Death in Venice* (Mann, 1911), a man whom he feels he understands completely as a "failed genius" like himself, for Aschenbach is a distinguished man of letters, highly recognized, but who knows himself that he does not have genius. The perfection that Aschenbach searches for is to be found in the seduction of the young lad, Thaddeus. Loving Thaddeus and being loved by him would provide a completion of the self—an achievement of superiority and perfection he himself so fervently seeks in the pursuit of his own sexual partners.

He disavows the analyst's comment that perhaps part of his alienation from society may be due to his hostility to society, and that this may be at the root of some of his difficulties. Any such comments about his envy or rage evoke dangers or threats of fragmentation and are considered unempathic interpretations. They lead to a retort that he may be "casting pearls before swine."

The rage he feels toward the analyst is due to frustration of his needs for maintaining an absolute perfection of the self. It occurs when there is an interference to a merger with an idealized selfobject, and a loss of control over a mirroring selfobject (Terman, 1975). The necessity to exert absolute control over his archaic environment has left him alone—an alien from all other human beings. He desperately needs to coerce an affirmation of this sort from a recalcitrant world, and the analyst is part of this world. It is a necessity for the maintenance of his self-esteem, even for the cohesiveness of his self, a self that depends on the unconditional availability of approving/mirroring selfobjects or a merger/permitting idealized one (Kohut, 1977).

Willard's state of alienation is compounded by the ego's having "increasingly surrendered its reasoning capacity to the task of rationalizing the persistence of the limitlessness of the power of his grandiose self" (Kohut, 1977, p. 657). Therefore, he cannot acknowledge the inherent limitations of this power of the self, but "attributes its failures to the malevolence and corruption of the uncooperative archaic object" (Kohut, 1977, p. 657). It is then that Willard experiences narcissistic rage in a chronic form, which is then turned against the self as self-destructive depression, depletion anxiety, and psychosomatic symptoms.

What was strikingly apparent was that Willard did not recognize other individuals as a center of independent initiative with whom he happened to be at cross-purposes. He was like a child whose discomfort could not be prevented or dispelled. He held that his opponents were sadistic, all-powerful, and all-knowing, and that they had somehow brought about his discomfort *intentionally*. This attitude led to many difficulties in the progress of his therapy.

Finally, Willard, in rare moments of calm reflection, candor, and rationality, often preliminary to entering a state of impending narcissistic decompensation, was not completely devoid of understanding the consequences of his continuing in a state of "thralldom," from which there appeared to be no escape. Unless he could control the forces that completely obstructed his capacity to work and love, life would be faulted and, one after another, all doors to a true creative future would close, lock, and in time, disappear. Unable to work, to love or be loved, unable to be part of the community of normal human beings leads him to despair. He compares himself to the captain of the Flying Dutchman: ever restless, unfulfilled, wandering the seven seas in an endless search for a self—a lost and "cursed" man who tragically will never be fulfilled, can never act from and out of himself. As remedy for his condition, he treats life as a place for play—attending the opera, going to fine restaurants, taking one's time at lunch, making life "an adventure," doing both minor and exotic things. It is a "playing at life" whose function is to mitigate the deadness of his internal world through stimulating external experiences which, for the moment, help him overcome an inner inertia and apathy as well as provide a spurious self-esteem through the use of selfobjects that help him to "complete himself."

REFERENCES

Kernberg, O. F. (1975), *Borderline Conditions and Pathological Narcissism.* New York: Aronson.
Kohut, H. (1971), *The Analysis of the Self.* New York: International Universities Press.
——— (1977), *The Restoration of the Self.* New York: International Universities Press.
Mahler, M. & Kaplan, L. (1977), Developmental aspects in the assessment of narcissism and so-called borderline personalities. In: *The Selected Papers of Margaret S. Mahler,* Vol. 2. New York: Aronson, 1979, pp. 195–210.
Mann, T. (1911), *Death in Venice.* In: *Thomas Mann: Stories of Three Decades.* New York: Knopf, 1936, pp. 378–438.
Ornstein, P. H. (1978), Introduction. In: *The Search for the Self,* Vol. 1. New York: International Universities Press, pp. 1–106.
Panel (1973), Technique and prognosis in the treatment of narcissistic personality disorders. L. Schwartz, reporter. *J. Amer. Psychoanal. Assn.,* 21:617–632.
Socarides, C. W. (1988), *The Preoedipal Origin and Psychoanalytic Therapy of Sexual Perversions.* Madison, CT: International Universities Press.
Terman, D. (1975), Introduction. In: *Progress in Self Psychology,* Vol. 8, ed. A. Goldberg. Hillsdale, NJ: Analytic Press, 1992, pp. 1–51.
Wolf, E. S. (1995), A self psychological perspective at work and its inhibitions. This volume, pp. 99–114.

AUTHOR INDEX

Abelin, E. L., 40
Alter, R., 186
Applegarth, A., xiv, xxi, 143, 147, 237
Aristotle, 99–100
Arlow, J. A., 191, 218
Aurier, A., 51

Bail, B. W., xvii, 65*n*
Beckett, S., 76
Benedek, T., 106
Beratis, S., xx
Beres, D., 39*n*
Bergler, E., 209
Bergman, A., 40, 210, 211
Bergmann, M. V., xix–xx, 191*n*, 203
Bernard, C., 82
Berson, N., 164
Betcher, R. W., 40
Bion, W. R., 61, 62, 65–66, 76–77
Blum, H. P., xv–xvi, 25–26, 143*n*
Bly, R., 40
Boatman, B., 163
Börne, L., 90
Brickman, H. R., 40
Browning, D., 163
Buie, D. H., 38
Buxbaum, E., 226

Carlyle, T., 79, 152
Chasseguet-Smirgel, J., 40
Cohler, B., 100, 103, 108
Conrad, J., 134

Deri, S. K., 116
Dewald, P., 163
Donoghue, D., 187

Einstein, A., 63
Eliot, G., 47
Eliot, T. S., 187, 191

Elson, M., 106–107, 111
Emerson, R. W., 79
Epstein, J., xix
Erikson, E. H., xv, 21, 37, 39*n*, 81, 143, 144, 147, 148, 151–152, 156

Fast, I., 147
Federn, E., 84
Fenichel, O., 103–104, 189, 209
Ferenczi, S., 93–94, 162, 163, 174–175, 209
Finkelhor, D., 174
Fliess, W., 28, 85–86, 92
Flugel, J. C., 209
Frank, A., 173
Freud, A., 4, 20, 96, 101, 159
Freud, S., xiv, xvi, xvii–xviii, 19–22, 24, 27–30, 35, 37, 65, 79–97, 101–104, 111–112, 133, 143, 144, 200, 204, 216, 217, 221, 222, 226, 227, 241, 243, 248, 250
Furman, E., xv, 3–6, 9–14, 16
Furman, R. A., 3, 11

Gabbard, G. O., xx, 209–211, 214, 218
Galatzer-Levy, R., 100, 103, 108
Galenson, E., xx, 229, 238
Gedo, J. E., xix, 116, 140, 203
Gehrie, M., 140
Ginsburg, S. W., 147
Goertzel, M., 243–244
Goertzel, V., 243–244
Goethe, J. W. von, 184
Granatir, W. L., xiv
Greenacre, P., 24
Greenson, R. R., 20
Griffin, M., 163
Grigg, K. A., xiv
Gross, G. E., 192
Gruber, H., 87

Grubrich-Simitis, I., 95n

Harris, L., 187
Hartmann, H., 20, 38n, 221, 222, 226
Hemingway, E., 183, 188
Hendrick, I., xiv, 105
Hendricks, I., 143
Hendrik, I., 37
Herman-Gibbons, M., 164
Hoffer, W., 221, 222
Holder, A., 227
Holmes, D., xiv, xvi, 20–21, 143,
    144–145, 147
Hulbert, A., 188
Hulsker, J., 46, 47, 54

Ibsen, H., 148
Inman, L. D., xviii–xix, 115–116,
    117–120, 122–131

Jacobson, E., 222, 241
Jaques, E., xiv, 143, 152
Johnson, A. M., 163
Jones, E., 79–82, 85–91, 95, 96
Jung, C. G., 93, 94–95

Kaplan, D., 218
Kaplan, L., 254
Katan, A., 3, 165
Keiser, S., 159, 161
Kernberg, O. F., 175, 191, 253, 255
Kinston, W., 210–211, 216, 218
Klein, M., 61, 65, 116, 217
Kohut, H., 103, 106–107, 109–110, 111,
    155, 210, 253, 259, 263
Kramer, P., xiv
Kramer, S., xiv–xv, 163, 164, 169,
    212–213
Kramer, Y., 143, 147
Kris, E., 221
Kubie, L. S., xiv, 116

La Perriere, K., 221, 226
Lantos, B., xiv, 103, 104–105, 143
Laufer, M., 166
Le Gallienne, E., 148
Lederer, W., 243
Lerner, H. G., 147
Levine, H., xv

Levinson, D., 40, 108
Levinson, H., 40
Levinson, P., 213
Lewis, H. B., 218–219
Lewis, M., 213
Lichtenberg, 112
Liebert, R. S., 193
Litin, E., 163
Loewald, H., 23, 24, 196
Loewenstein, R. M., 221

Mahler, M. S., 40, 166–167, 210, 211,
    221, 226, 254
Mahony, P. J., xvii–xviii, 84, 92
Mann, T., 262–263
Margolis, M., 163
Markson, E. R., 37
Masson, J. M., 28
Mayman, M., 214–215, 216
McCarthy, T., 105
McDevitt, J. B., 166–167
McMurray, L., 213
Meers, D., 227
Meissner, W. W., xvi–xvii, 36, 37, 38,
    39n, 46, 56, 57
Menninger, K., xiv, 143
Michaels, L., 186, 187
Modell, A. H., 43–44, 214
Montaigne, M. de, 106
Myers, W. A., 216

Nagera, H., 222
Neubauer, P., 205
Novick, J., 203
Novick, K. K., 203
Nunberg, H., 84

Oates, J. C., 184
Olinick, S. L., xiv, xix, 184
Oremland, J., 192, 193
Ornstein, P. H., 262
Ovid, 79

Pearson, G. H. J., 226
Peller, L., 22–23
Pickvance, R., 51
Pine, F., 40, 210, 211
Podell, P., 213
Poland, W. S., xiv

Pollack, W. S., 40
Pontalis, J.-B., 116, 121

Ramzy, I., 141
Rangell, L., xiv
Reiner, A., xvii
Richards, A. K., 204
Rie, O., 92
Rizzuto, A.-M., 38
Roiphe, H., xx, 229, 238
Rose, G. J., 203
Rosen, V. H., 23
Rosenblatt, B., 191
Roth, H., xix, 186–189
Rothenberg, A., 116
Rubin, I. A., 192

Sachs, H., 84
Sachs, O., 176–177
Sandler, J., 25, 191, 197–198, 222, 227
Sashin, J. I., 38
Schafer, R., 243
Schwartz, L., 254
Shakespeare, W., 113
Shengold, L., 162–163, 173–174, 176
Silber, A., 163
Skolnikoff, A., 153
Socarides, C. W., xxi, 253
Solnit, A. J., 223, 226
Sophocles, 27
Stannard, M., 188
Stark, M., 147
Steele, B. F., 163–164, 165
Stein, S. A., 49, 50–51

Stekel, W., 95
Sterba, R., 96
Storr, A., 155
Strachey, 80

Terman, D., 263
Tolnay, C. de, 192–193
Trilling, D., 188
Trilling, L., xix, 188–189

Updike, J., 184

Vaillant, G. E., 40
van Gogh, T., 48
van Gogh, V., xvii, 41, 48, 51–53, 53, 54, 55
van Gogh, W., 48n
van Gogh-Bogner, J., 48n

Waelder, R., 22
Weiner, H., 213
Weinshel, E., 21, 23
Wharton, E., 184
White, R. W., 37
Winnicott, D. W., xvii, 23, 24, 43, 116, 152–153, 202–203, 222
Wittels, F., 83, 95
Wolf, E. S., xviii, 107, 260
Woodbury, M., 173
Woolf, V., 115, 117
Wurmser, L., 217, 218

Zetzel, E., 20
Zweig, A., 96

SUBJECT INDEX

Abandonment, fear of, 211, 254
Achievement, 109
Achieving self, 106
Activity-lust, 106
Adaptive behavior, work as, xvi
Adolescence
  ego identity in, 151–152
  work inhibitions in, 159–177
Agency, principle of, 38–39
Aggression
  body image and work inhibition related
    to, 221–227
  learning and, 13–14
  non-neutralized, xx
  stage fright and, 209–210
  as substitute for self, 75–76
  work and, 38
  of writing, 185–186, 187, 189
Aim inhibition, mechanisms of, xiii
Alienation, 152, 263
  of writer, 186–187
Alpha function, 77
Ambition
  conflicts over, 244
  development of, 241–244
  disturbances of, 244–245
  as forbidden, 248–250
  impulse and, 242
  normal and pathological aspects of, xxi
  special features in women, 246–250
Anal erotism, conflicts associated with,
  209
Anal loss fear, 231, 236
The Analysis of the Self (Kohut), 253
Analyst
  fantasy play of, 25–26
  role with incest victims, 176–177
Analytic pact, 20
Anger, taming of, 13–14
Anorexia, 118–119

Anorgasmia, 165
Anxiety. *See also* Castration anxiety;
  Separation anxiety
  examination, 229–240
  performance, 209. *See also* Stage fright
  three major types, 229–230
Artist. *See also* Creativity
  hostility toward creative products of,
    192–193
  suffering of, 187–188
  women as, 115–131
Artistic work, demands of, 47–58
"As if" fantasy, 24–27
Autonomy, 44
  achievement of, 203

Beta elements, 77
Bisexual wishes, 202, 203
Bodily integrity, anxiety over, 236
Body image, xx, 221–227
Body-ego integration, 12
Bulimia-anorexia, 200–201

Caleb My Son (Inman), 119
Call It Sleep (Roth), xix, 186–187
Castration anxiety, 31
  adult clinical syndrome in women,
    230–234
  clinical picture in women, 235–237
  preoedipal in girls, xx, 230, 235–240
  psychodynamics of in women,
    238–240
  school work inhibition and, 223–227
  stage fright and, 209
"Character and Anal Erotism" (Freud),
  241
Children
  activity of, 104–105
  first work of, 9–11
  sexual abuse of, 163. *See also* Incest

work inhibitions seen in, 159–177
work of, xiv–xv, 3–17
Christianity, work concept of, 100
Civilization and Its Discontents (Freud),
      96, 144
Clinical study, narcissistic personality
      disorder, 255–262
Cocaine, Freud's use of, 84–86
Communication, in analytic process, 25
Competence, 37
Competition, 183
   fear of, 237
Compulsive rituals, 231
Conflict, internal, 120–130
Consciousness
   as hunger of mind and self, 61–63
   work of, 64–65
Container and contained theory, 62
"Contributions to the Knowledge of the
      Effect of Cocaine" (Freud), 85
Core conflictual issues, xv
"Craving for and Fear of Cocaine"
      (Freud), 85
Creativity. *See also* Artist; Writers
   ambivalence about, 122
   emotional conflicts of, 116
   of Freud, xvii–xviii, 87–88
   impairment of, 193–194
   inhibition of, 192–206. *See also*
      Writer's block
   internal objects in, 191–206
   as object relatedness, 192
   psychic energy for, 62
   self-affirmation through, 184
   suffering and, 187–188
   work capacity and, 152–155
   work inhibition and, xviii–xix,
      191–206
   work obsession and, 111

da Vinci, Leonardo, as ego ideal, 83–84
Daydreams, study of, 27
Death in Venice (Mann), 262–263
Development
   capacity for work and, xv, 3–17
   crises of, 37
Developmental line, 4, 20, 159
Differentiation process, 221
Dilettantism, 256

Doolittle case, 204
Dreams
   Freud on, 27–28
   interpretation of, 65–75
   regression in, 28–29
   self-state, 259
   writing problems in, 120–130
Drives
   fusion of, 9, 14
   role of, 11–14
Duty, 104

Effectance, 37
Efficacy selfobject experience, 106
Ego
   in ambition, 242–243
   function of, 147–148, 242–243
   reality, 221
   work and in male identity, 143–156
The Ego and the Id (Freud), 96
Ego energy, 37
Ego ideal, 243–244
Ego identification, 243
Ego identity, 144
   consolidation of, 151–152
   work identity and, 147
Emotional development, incest and,
      165–170
Empathic merger, 262
Endgame (Beckett), 76
An Enemy of the People (Ibsen), 148–149
Envy, 183
Erotism
   ambition and, 241
   conflicts associated with, 209
Ethnic identification, 186–187
Examination anxiety, 229–240
Exhibitionism, 241–242
   stage fright and, 214–216

Failure, shame and, xx
False self
   abandoning of, 45
   parental expectations and, 43–44
   work and, xvii, 41–45
Family secrets, 160–161
Fantasy
   aggressive, 227
   of analyst, 25–26

enactment of, 21–22
imagination in, 23
masturbation, 195, 204
murderous, 195–196, 197–198
of object relationships, 244–245
sadomasochistic, 202, 203
self-fecundation, 84
of sexual fulfillment, 241–242
Father, castrating image of, 227
Forbidden pleasures, indulgence in,
    211–213
Fort-Da play, 22
Fragmentation, 107
Freud, Sigmund
    addictions of, 84–87
    anxiety of, 88–89
    courage of, 89–97
    creativity of, 87–88
    energy of, 81–82
    Jung and, 93–96
    work of, 79–97
    work theory of, xvii–xviii
    writing of, 92–97
Frustration tolerance, 11
"Fusion, Integration, and Feeling Good"
    (Furman), 9

Games, rules of, 22
Gender assignment, 246–248
Genital inadequacy
    anxiety over in women, xx, 231, 236
    stage fright and, 214–216
Genital self-examination, in women,
    229–240
Germ phobia, 194–196
Goal direction, motivation for, xvi–xvii
"Good enough" mentoring, 108
"Good enough mother," 222
Good-enough mother-infant unit, 6
Greek society, work in, 99–100

Hanna Perkins Therapeutic School,
    Mother-Toddler Group, 3–17
Health, relationship to work and play,
    29–30
Hemingway, Ernest, work avoidance of,
    183–184
High on a Hill (Inman), 119
Homosexuality, in narcissistic personality

disorder, 259–260
Hyperesthesia, 164–165

Idealization, nondevelopment of, 110
Ideals, living up to, 140–141
Identification, 14–17
    in ambition, 243
    mechanisms of, xiii
    with mother, 15–16
    multiple, 257–258
    with teacher, 16–17
Identity
    work, xv, 145–150
    in working men, 143–156
Imagination
    creative, 24
    role of, 23
Impulsiveness, 242
Incest
    emotional development interference
        and, 165–170
    later emergence of in treatment of
        adults, 170–173
    learning problems and, 162–164,
        173–176
    maternal, 163, 164, 165–170
    need for denial of, 173–174
    by parent, 163–177
    performance and, 212–213
    somatic memories of, xv, 162–164
Incestuous parent, defenses against, 173
Incompleteness, sense of, xxi, 253–264
Industry, stage of, 151
Infant
    first work of, 61–63
    mental dilemma of, 66
    nature of work and, xvii
Inhibition. See Work inhibitions;
    Writer's block
Instinctual drives, 36–38
Integrative function, growth of, 8–9
Intellectual performance
    anxiety over in women, 234, 235–237
    mental health and, 103
    perception as phallic, 239
Intelligence, superior, 161–162
Internal objects
    conflicts related to, 195–196, 197–198
    creative work and, 191–206

resistance to, 200–201
International Psycho-analytical
    Association, 91
The Interpretation of Dreams (Freud), 84
Intrapsychic conflict, xix–xx
Irma dream, 86

Judaism, work concept of, 100
Jung, C. G., writings of, 93–95

Knowing, conflicts of, xiv–xv
Knowledge, tree of, 35

Latency
    play in, 21
    work during, 20
Learning
    alliance, 31
    attitude toward, 12
    phallic impulses and, 12–13
    problems of, xiv–xv
    somatic memories and, 164–165
    in toddler period, 15–16
    work and, 7–8
    as work of children, 159
Learning problems
    emotional causes of, 159–164
    incest and, 165–176
Leisure, xix, 100
    as absence of work, 111–112
    self-esteem and, 140–141
    as sinful, 102–103
    value of, 133–141
Leisure class, 135–141
Libidinal dialogue, 191
Libido, sublimation of, 101–102
Long-range planning, 242
Loss, writing out of, 184

Masculine identity, work-related, xv,
    39–41, 143–156
Mastery, 5–6, 151–152
    instinct of, 105
    work and, 8–9
Masturbation fantasy, 195, 204
Maternal object, 82–83
Maternal sexual abuse, 163–164,
    165–170
Maturation, early interferences in, 254

Maturity, 21
"Me do" phase, 10
    focus of, 14–15
Meaning, of work, 39–41
Memory
    disturbances in, 205
    somatic, xv, 162–165
Mental dilemma, 66
Mental growth, xvii
Mental health, 103
Mentors, 108
Michelangelo, belongings of, 192–193
Mirroring
    absence of, 254
    lack of, 263
Moses and Monotheism (Freud), 96–97
Mother. *See also* Maternal object
    ambivalent identification with, 73–74
    archaic, partial disidentification with,
        238
    balancing gratification and deprivation
        by, 221–222
    "good enough," 222
    hostile dependence on, 239
    participation in activities, 15–16
    unconscious state of, 64–65, 77–78
Mother-child relationship
    drive balance in, 13
    overstimulating, frustrating, 226
    in personality development, 14–17
    self-care progress and, 10–11
    transitional space in, 203
    unresolved ambivalence in, 16
Mother-child symbiosis
    disturbance in and shame, 210–211
    interference in, 254
    unresolved, 163–164
Mother-infant collaboration, 64–65

Narcissism
    primary, 221
    secondary, 106
Narcissistic fantasy, 84
Narcissistic injury, writer's block and,
    185
Narcissistic personality disorder, xxi
    analysis of, 253–264
Nature, as female, 82–84
Neurosis, learning problems and,

161–162
Neurotic Distortion of the Creative Process (Kubie), xiv, 116
Neutralization, 9
  mechanisms of, xiii
Nicotine dependency, Freud's, 86–87

Object loss, fear of, 235–236
Object relationships
  creativity and, 191–206
  maternal incest and, 175
  memory and perception disturbances and, 205
  unconscious fantasies of, 244–245
Object representations, in ambition, 242
Object-coercive doubting, 164, 175–176
Oedipal conflict
  defective self-image and, 224–225
  resolution of, 243
Oedipus Rex (Sophocles), 27
Olivier, Laurence, stage fright of, 211
Overeating, 199–201

Pain, Freud's reliance on, 86–87
Parental expectations
  burden of, 41–42, 55–56
  false, 109
  false self based on, 43–44
Parental object, 191–206
Parental seduction, 163
Parents
  conflicted physical separation from, 175–176
  conflict-laden attachment to, 201–202
  incest by, 163–177
  overstimulating, 31–32
  projections of, xvii
  symbolic murder of, 195–196, 197–198
  unconscious of, 76
Partial deprivation, 221–222
Paternal mental representation, castrating, 227
Perceptual input, 221
Performance anxiety, 233, 234. *See also* Stage fright
Personality, motivations of, 40
Phallic sexual impulses
  learning and, 12–13

premature, 12
Physical stimulation, 84–86
Pieta Rodanini (Michelangelo), 192–193
Play
  complex, socialized, 22–23
  forbidden, 32
  function of, 21–22
  as opposite of work, 112
  in psychoanalytic process, 23–27
  solitary, 22
  spontaneous, 22
  symbols in, 5
  work and, 4–7
Playful work, xv–xvi
  psychoanalysis and, 19–33
Pleasure drive, 102–103
Preoedipal conflicts, in school failure, 225–226
Primal punishment, 35
Primal repression, 173
Primal scene, stage fright and, 217–218
Problem-solving, imagination in, 23
Projective identification, 65
Psychic energy, 37, 62
Psychic organizer, 106
Psychoanalysis
  aims of, 80
  imagination in, 23–24
  to overcome writer's block, 120–130
  as playful work, xvi, 19–33
  work metaphors of, 19
The Psychoanalytic Theory of Neurosis (Fenichel), 189
Psychology (Jung), 94–95
Purposeful activity, 105

Quantum psychoanalysis, 63

Rapprochement phase
  disruption in, 254
  separation anxiety and, 210–211
Reality, 5–6
  incest and interference with, 174–175
  work and, 20
Reality ego, 221
Rebelliousness, of writers, 187–188
"Recommendations to Physicians Practicing Psychoanalysis" (Freud), 101

Reconstruction, 25–26
Regression
    with castration anxiety in women, 237
    in dream, 28–29
    somatic memories of maternal incest
        during, 170
    in transference experience, 24
Regression-progression, 23
Relationships, 14–17
Repression, of incestuous memories,
    173–175
Retirement, 134–135
    self-esteem and, 140–141
Rewards, inner, 8
"Riding on a Horse" dream (Freud),
    27–29
Ritualized behavior, 195–196, 231
A Room of One's Own (Woolf), 115

Satisfaction, 6
School phobia, 161–162
School work inhibition, 223–227
Self
    achieving, 106
    creating sense of, 62–63
    disorders of, 107
    false, 41–45
    fragility of, 108
    fragmentation of, xviii
    mental representation of, 222–223
    as process of interactions, 63–64
    sex and aggression as substitutes for,
        75–76
    unity of, 64
    work capacity and, xvi–xvii, 35–58,
        107–111
Self psychology, work inhibitions and,
    xviii, 99–113
Self-as-agent, 58
Self-care
    as child's first work, 9–11
    mother-child relationship and, 15
Self-cohesion, lack of, 253–264
Self-differentiation, 11
Self-enhancing selfobject experience, 108
Self-esteem
    achieving self and, 106
    with castration anxiety in women, 235
    childhood incest and, 171

    genius and, 111
    incest and, 175
    leisure and, 140–141
    mastery and, 151–152
    reaffirmation of, 196–197
    regulation of, 148–149
    work and, 35–36
    work identity and, 145–150
    of writers, 184
Self-fecundation fantasy, 84
Self-image, oedipal conflict and, 224–225
Selflessness, failure of, 213–214
Selfobject
    empathic merger with, 262
    idealized, 110
    inadequate differentiation of, 175
Selfobject representations, 222–223
Self-realization, 58
Self-regard, 20–21
Self-state dreams, 259
Sensorimotor intelligence, 37
Separation anxiety, 231
    stage fright and, 210–211
Separation-individuation process,
    221–223
    inadequately resolved, 226
Sex, as substitute for self, 75–76
Sex roles, changing, 40
Sexual performance
    equated with stage performance,
        215–216
    inhibited, 236
Sexual selfobject, loss of, 259–260
Sexuality
    inhibition of, 103–104, 236
    of writing, 187–188, 189
Shame
    at genital inadequacy, 214–216
    incest and, 212
    in indulging in forbidden pleasures,
        211–213
    over writer's block, 183
    of seeing primal scene, 217–218
    separation anxiety and, 210–211
    in stage fright, xx, 209–219
    with success, 213–214
    as universal early affective state,
        218–219
Skill development, 6–7

Society
  meaning of work in, 39–41
  work inhibitions and, 100–113
Solitude (Storr), 155
Somatic memory
  definition of, 163
  of incest, xv, 162–164
  learning and, 164–165
Soul murder, 163
Splitting, 65
Stage fright, xx
  aggressive impulses and, 209–210
  continuum of, 209
  dread of success and, 213–214
  exhibitionism and genital inadequacy
    in, 214–216
  as indulgence in forbidden pleasures,
    211–213
  primal scene and, 217–218
  separation anxiety and, 210–211
  shame in, 209–219
Studies on Hysteria (Freud), 86
Sublimation, 84, 101–102
  mechanisms of, xiii
Success
  crashing after, 115, 118–119
  dread of, 213–214
  flight from, 115
Suffering, of writer, 187–188
Superego, in ambition, 243–244
Survival, work of, 61–62
Symbolic actions, 195–196
Symbolization
  freedom for, 129
  importance of, 116–117
  in play, 5
  tolerance of, xix
  unconscious prohibitions against,
    130–131

Teacher-pupil relationship, 16–17
Therapeutic alliance
  as communication bridge, 193–194
  with creative patient, xix–xx
Thought
  capacity for, 62
  without thinker, 76–77
Toddler period, learning in, 15–16
Toilet mastery, 11–12

Totem and Taboo (Freud), 84, 95
Transference
  "as if" nature of, 24
  reliving incestuous phenomena in, 165
Transference imago, xix
  writer's, 184–185, 188–189
Transitional space, 203
Trust, 116
  autonomy and, 205–206
  of incest victims, 176

Unconscious
  lack of awareness of, 77–78
  of mother, 64–65
  of parents, 76, 77–78
"The Unconscious" (Freud), 248
Unemployment, 153–154
"The Unrememberable and the
    Unforgettable" (Frank), 173
Urethral erotism, ambition and, 241

Van Gogh, Vincent
  artistic crisis of, 54–55
  artistic vocation of, 50–53
  childhood of, 46–47
  early life of, 47–49
  life work of, xvii
  psychosis of, 52–53
  religious mission of, 49–50
  work of, 45–55
Verbal bridges, 27

Women
  ambition in, xxi, 246–250
  confined roles of, 115–131
  creative, xix–xx
  genital anxiety in, xx
  genital self-examination and
    examination anxiety in,
    229–240
  superego development in, 243
  work inhibitions in, xiv
  work of, 40–41
Words, play on, 27
Work
  of artist, 45–55
  attitudes toward, 6, 144–145
  biblical roots of, 133
  capacity to enjoy, 3–17

characteristics of, 4–7
of children, 3–17
clinical examples of, 65–75
of consciousness, 64–65
dealing with reality, 5–6
defining self by, 134–135
definition of, xiv, 19, 99, 105
developmental aspects of capacity for,
    xv
dichotomization of function of, 20–21
difficulty of, 4–5
essential nature of, 61–78
false self and, 41–45
Freudian theory of, xvii–xviii, 79–97
idealization of, 141
inability to perform, xiii, 115
incapacity for, 260–262
of infant, 61–63
inner pressure for, 112–113
intrapsychic meanings of, 154–155
learning and, 7–8
male identity and, 143–156
masochistic submission to, 203
mastery and, 8–9
meaning of, xvii, 39–41, 144–146
mental health and, 103
obsession with, 110–111
play skills in, 6–7
playful, xv–xvi, 19–33
as primal punishment, 35
principle of, xvi–xvii, 36–39, 105
psychoanalytic theories of, xiii–xiv
reality and, 20
relationships and identifications in,
    14–17
as repository for conflict
    displacement, 147
roots of concepts of, 99–100
self and, xvi–xvii, 35–58

of self-care, 9–11
social and psychological dimensions
    of, 20
tasks of, 133–134
as wicked word, 43–44
Work capacity
creativity and, 152–155
disturbances of, 103–104
origins and development of, 150–152
self and, 107–111
Work ethic, 141
Work identity, xv
definition of, 147
negative, 149–150
self-esteem and, 145–150
Work inhibition
aggression and, 221–227
body image in, 221–227
in children and adolescents, 159–177
creativity and, 191–206
defective body image and, xx
disturbance in, 108–111
protective value of, xix
self psychological perspective on,
    99–113
Work product, loss of connection with,
    152–153
Working alliance, 20
Working through, 26–27
Writers. See also Creativity; Writer's
    block
women as, 115–131
Writer's block
developmental and psychodynamic
    origins of, 183–190
origins of, xix
overcoming, 115–131
Writing, history of problems with,
    117–120